SIGRID UNDSET

SIGRID UNDSET

A Study in Christian Realism

by

A. H. WINSNES

Translated
by
P. G. FOOTE

SHEED AND WARD
LONDON AND NEW YORK

FIRST PUBLISHED 1953
BY SHEED AND WARD LTD.
110/111 FLEET STREET
LONDON, E.C.4
AND
SHEED AND WARD, INC.
840 BROADWAY
NEW YORK, 3

PRINTED IN GREAT BRITAIN
BY PURNELL AND SONS, LTD.
PAULTON (SOMERSET) AND LONDON

Foreword

THIS biography of Sigrid Undset was completed a couple of months before her death on June 10th 1949, and is now published without alteration.

While I was working on the book, I had several conversations with her, both about its general plan and on some particular points. "I am delighted that you should want to give me a place in the Christian Renaissance movement" she wrote in a letter dated January 18th 1948. She gave an obliging answer to every question put to her,—most willingly when it was a matter of factual information. She left it to me to find out what she had "meant" in her books. She did me the great service of reading the finished manuscript. In a letter of April 4th 1949, she wrote: "It is difficult to express oneself about a book which has been written about oneself, but I can say that at least I have no objections to make against your interpretation—in the main it is certainly correct."

The interest which Sigrid Undset showed in my work was naturally both an encouragement and an inspiration.

I am further very grateful to all who have helped me in various ways. Amongst others I may mention here Miss Eugenia Kielland and Mrs. Signe Undset Thomas, Sigrid Undset's sister; their work in revision of the manuscript has been of the greatest value.

A. H. WINSNES.

Contents

		Page
	FOREWORD	vii
Chapter	INTRODUCTION	I
I.	CHILDHOOD AND YOUTH	10
II.	DREAMS OF HAPPINESS	36
III.	ITALY: *JENNY*	49
IV.	TAKING STOCK	57
V.	DISCOVERING CHRISTIANITY	76
VI.	WRITING ABOUT THE MIDDLE AGES	92
VII.	BETWEEN THE WARS: THE BATTLE FOR CHRISTIAN CIVILISATION	153
VIII.	NEW NOVELS OF CONTEMPORARY LIFE: *MADAME DOROTHEA*	175
IX.	THE STRUGGLE AGAINST NAZISM: WAR AND EXILE	215
X.	RETURN TO THE FUTURE	246
	APPENDIX—TRANSLATIONS OF SIGRID UNDSET'S WORKS IN ENGLISH	251
	INDEX OF NAMES	253

Illustrations

Facing page

Anna Charlotte Undset (*née* Gyth), 1893 . . 14

Ingvald Undset, *circa* 1885 14

Sigrid Undset, at the age of 1 18

Sigrid Undset, aged 16 30

Sigrid Undset: painting by A. C. Svarstad, Rome 1911 (Rasmus Meyer Collection, Bergen) 58

Sigrid Undset in the late 1930's 164

Acknowledgment

The passage from *True and Untrue and other Folk Tales*, copyright 1945 by Alfred A. Knopf, Inc., is reprinted by kind permission of the publishers.

Introduction

SIGRID UNDSET's writing takes its place as one of the truly remarkable phenomena in the literature of the twentieth century. She is, wrote a Swedish critic in 1927, the year before she received the Nobel prize, one of the very few contemporary authors of whom one may well use the adjective "great". That is no exaggeration. In scarcely any of her contemporaries do we find human life treated with comparable breadth of vision and depth of insight. In her thought and imagination, subjects from the present and from distant times are touched by the same convincing assurance and creative power. On her stage she presents characters from the Middle Ages who are as much alive as any of her creations from the present. "I am one who has lived two thousand years in this land" was her remark on a recent ceremonial occasion, with a playful reference to the famous reply of the Government minister, Skogstad, in Gunnar Heiberg's play *I Shall Defend My Country* (*Jeg vil verge mit land*). Sigrid Undset has no relish for the pathetic style, least of all when speaking of herself, but here there was no reserve. Two thousand years—why, it was self-evident! She is in fact not only contemporary with her own time but also with the past, with history. In 1909, two years after her first book *Mrs Marta Oulie* (*Fru Marta Oulie*), a story of married life in an Oslo setting of the most palpable everyday reality, she published *The Story of Viga-Ljot and Vigdis* (*Fortællingen om Viga-Ljot og Vigdis*), a historical novel set in the period at the end of the tenth century. Both books were magnificently alive. An interviewer asked her how it was that she had come to write about characters from such remote times. "One can only write novels about one's own contemporary world" was her answer.

I

Writing about the present and writing about the past do not belong to two distinct periods in her activity as an author, the one a closed chapter followed by the other. There are close links between them all the time. The past is not far away when she writes of the present, nor the present when she writes of the past. Already before her great medieval novels had seen the light of day, in 1919, she was writing to Nini Roll Anker: "I think the reason why I understand our own time so well, or see it so clearly, is because ever since I was a child I have had some kind of living memories from an earlier age to compare with it." In 1905 or thereabouts she had ready the first draft of *Olav Audunsson in Hestviken,* twenty years before the novel was published in its present form.

When Sigrid Undset had published her first book, she received, as a gift from her Danish mother, an edition of *Birds of Passage (Trækfuglene)* by Steen Steensen Blicher. This exhortation was inscribed in it: "May you as an author always look up to Blicher as your model, be as incorruptibly honest as he, fearlessly seeing life as it is and truthfully reporting what you see." And she has written in this way about the present and the past. Could anyone write more truthfully, more realistically?

She does not experiment with new forms of literary expression, with a technique better fitted to grasp concrete realities, in the manner of a Virginia Woolf or a James Joyce. In this respect at least, she is old-fashioned. She carries on the tradition of the great realistic writers of the nineteenth century, Balzac, Dickens, Tolstoy, the style which began in Norway with Camilla Collett and achieved its triumph in Kristian Elster the elder, Alexander Kielland, Jonas Lie and Amalie Skram.

But she is bolder in her description of reality than were most of her great predecessors. The picture she gives of humanity, the passions, hate and love, betrayal and loyalty, the idyllic and the tragic, of the whole of life from the move-

2

ment of the embryo in the womb to the withering of the body and death, from the smell of blood which a human child draws in as it comes into the world up to the highest forms of conscious existence—all this is presented by her without a trace of romantic idealisation or artificiality. Few writers have seen deeper into the unpleasantness of life, into mankind's destitution and wretchedness. We should not close our eyes, she said in a talk to other Catholic writers in America during the last war, to "what a shocking business human life is." But she does not close her eyes to what is most shocking of all: man's own guilty responsibility for his wretchedness. Here too she is without fear; indeed it is in this that her special daring, the boldness she has in greater measure than most of us, is displayed.

Experience of a longing to be nothing more than what we call Nature, without responsibility and without obligation, can come to all of us, she wrote in 1910. "Perhaps we dream that we should live a better and easier life, if our thoughts were to remain at rest, and the hard laws we have imposed on ourselves could be evaded. But then our life would not be human life. And thank the God of us human beings that it is impossible—Nature is not our teacher and neither are the animals."

A notable feature of the cultural life of the twentieth century is the opposition which has made itself felt towards the naturalistic or mechanical deterministic view of humanity, which, from the middle of the last century to the beginning of this, dominated scholarship, philosophy and many branches of literature. Attention is once more paid to man's unique position in the universe. Members of the human species are regarded not only as products of Nature but also as beings with the power to choose and to act in relation to a divine spiritual power behind the visible and material world. The *Hinterweltler*, so despised by Nietzsche, once again come into prominence. The reaction makes itself evident in many ways. In philosophy it takes the form of a liberation from the principal modes of thought which were hostile to metaphysics (metaphysics here implying the recognition of a supernatural reality). The new movement is suggested by names like Bergson, Croce and Whitehead, by the French and German phenomonologists and existentialists, and by neo-Thomists like Maritain and Gilson. Natural science can no longer be used as an arsenal in support of a materialistic world-picture. Characteristic is the tendency amongst biologists, physicists and astronomers to interpret certain natural phenomena as signs of a divine idea in the universe, marks of a reasonable plan or purpose. In history and the social sciences more attention is paid to the organic connection between culture and religion, and to the enormous importance of the religious idea. Arnold Toynbee's great work, *A Study of History*, is conditioned not only by the conception of "the creative spirit of man", but has moreover Augustine's *De Civitate Dei* as its deepest source of inspiration.

But all this is by the way. That which needs special emphasis is the new realism in twentieth-century literature. We are not concerned with the wave of primitivism which poured over Europe in the period after the first World War, perhaps more violently than ever before,—the outlook representative of the phalanx of "life-worshippers", the true anti-intellectuals, who saw creative and rejuvenating power only in the "blood", in the impulses and instincts. Nor are we concerned with that group of writers who have not unreasonably been given the name of Post-Naturalists, those who find in Marx and Freud assurance of the soul's imprisonment within the confines of naturalism. Here we speak rather of a series of writers who, independently or because of the influence of Bergson or Freud or both, have had their attention directed to deeper layers of the mind than could be grasped by the "hard-boiled" school of psychologists. It is their intention to capture not only

4

the physical but also the spiritual. Typical amongst them are authors like Virginia Woolf, James Joyce, Aldous Huxley, Rainer Maria Rilke, Franz Kafka, Marcel Proust, Sigurd Christiansen, Tarjei Vesaas, Harry Martinson, and Aksel Sandemose.

At first glance, the robust realism of Sigrid Undset may seem to stand far removed from the writing of this group. It would be difficult to conceive a greater disparity, as far as the means of artistic presentation are concerned, than that between James Joyce and Franz Kafka on the one side and Sigrid Undset on the other, or, to choose a Norwegian author, between Sigurd Christiansen and Sigrid Undset. With Christiansen one finds an intense concentration on the inner mental processes of a single character, and little attention is paid to the outer world. Sigrid Undset probes no less deeply into the inner life, but her work shows too that breadth of background description which is typical of the realistic novel, and the sharpest possible insight into the conditions imposed on the characters by their social position and mileu. There are however points of contact, for example in the essential part which memory, the great mysterious factor in our mental life, plays in the writing of these authors. And further, not all of these "Neo-Realists" lose themselves in the subconscious world or in the sub-human; they are brought face to face with what is specifically human: the spiritual in man. The religious factor, the craving for eternity, asserts itself. To take a single example amongst many we may name Franz Kafka, one of the great religious writers of our time.

In her outlook, however, Sigrid Undset's closest connection with present-day literature and the whole contemporary world of ideas is not to be found in the movement here briefly described. It lies rather on a broader plane, is less purely literary and closer to the common stuff of humanity; it is to be sought in that Christian-inspired movement which has expressed itself in many ways in twentieth-century thought, and which in literature has made itself so firmly felt that it has rightly been called a Christian Renaissance.

A Christian Renaissance in the twentieth century? It sounds paradoxical. The opposition which Christianity has faced perpetually since its foundation,—more than any other of the great world-religions,—has never appeared more aggressive than in this period, the century of Communism, Fascism and Nazism. The fight waged against the Church by Voltaire, in the eighteenth century, for example, was not prompted by any ideological hostility to the Christian ethical values. Jesus of Nazareth is the Master, because in His eyes all men are equal, are the words in the *Dictionnaire Philosophique*[1]. The paganism of the twentieth century, on the other hand, sees in the Christian religion the decisive, indeed the essential, obstacle to the realisation of its programme for human society. It attacks the entire Christian faith: and not without cause, for it seeks also to destroy the Christian ethic.

This intensified struggle against Christianity is certainly one of the reasons for the Christian re-awakening of our time. The repudiation of Christianity, which had been formerly a part of the enthusiastic and optimistic faith in "progress" and which was largely a product of intellectual debating-circles, entered a new phase when great nations began to put this idea of the abolition of the Christian faith into practice. With reference to his visit to Soviet Russia, André Gide writes, "Ignorance and denial of the Gospel and of all that has followed from it cannot but lead to the impoverishment of humanity and culture." But the Christian movement in modern literature is not the outcome of panic. It is important to recollect that its roots go deeper than the first World War and the explosions which opened the floodgates to the modern paganism. To writers and thinkers in many countries it had long been clear what the repudiation of Christianity and the general secularisation

[1] Alfred NOYES, *Voltaire*, London 1936, p. 638.

6

Introduction

of humanity would entail. In an article called *War and Literature* Sigrid Undset writes, with reference to this, "It happens that a writer seems to see in advance the gloom through which we must pass—'the dark places'—and seeks to find a way out."

The Christian writing and thought of the twentieth century possess a markedly realistic, sometimes almost anti-romantic, character. They have nothing in common with that "retreat from the world" which was at times the chief feature of the so-called literary conversions of the late nineteenth century. Admittedly, no one would think of classifying as mere superficial products of their age the Jacob's wrestle of August Strindberg, Léon Bloy's burning witness, the profound Catholic faith of Johannes Jørgensen, or Arne Garborg's restless search for some God to believe in. But these do not possess that intimate contact with reality which characterises the twentieth-century group of Christian writers and thinkers. There is an upsurge of healthiness in this group, a deep love for the normal and eternally human and for ordinary common sense. The lyric poetry of Paul Claudel is a hymn to the sensible concrete world, God's creation, and is sustained by the Psalmist's theme: the heavens show forth the glory of God. The religious poetry of Olav Aukrust, revealing Christian influence as it does, yet shows the divine acknowledgment side by side with the richest sensuousness. G. K. Chesterton's apology for the Christian religion sparkles with wit, humour and down-to-earth humanity. T. S. Eliot binds poetry to the realities of contemporary social life in a way which not only means a revolution in verse-technique, but also—and this is the important point—unveils the everlasting banality of a God-forsaken world: The Waste Land. But there is no *Weltschmerz*. The created holds within itself a message from the Creator: "We praise Thee, O God, for Thy glory displayed in all the creatures of the earth." In their vital concern with contemporary problems, the new Christian thinkers,

7

with Bergson as one of their forerunners and with Maritain, Gilson, Scheler, Berdiaev and others numbered amongst them, are raising the central question of all philosophy. *Philosophia perennis*, the doctrine that mankind belongs essentially to a supernatural world of the spirit, scarcely occupies the weakest bastion in twentieth-century thought. Modern society is analysed and criticised, but the criticism is animated by a living consciousness of the tradition behind it. Past and future are bound together, thanks to "the Christian road we have discovered" (Charles Péguy). And it is no less important that man does not take for granted the conviction that, when there is something wrong, the fault lies outside himself. Someone, writes Sigrid Undset, had to be led to the thought "that there is nothing wrong with the world other than the will of man" (in a private letter, dated January 18th 1948). The novels of François Mauriac, Georges Bernanos, Graham Greene, Evelyn Waugh and Sigrid Undset herself, to mention a few amongst many, give some of the most penetrating psychological studies of our time, often agonising in their merciless unveiling. They show us perhaps the least popular picture of mankind, man as "the architect of his own misfortune", to quote Sigrid Undset again. Paul Valéry writes that the Christian religion demands self-examination; it "sets the human mind to the most subtle of problems, the most important and the most fruitful." It is scarcely an exaggeration to say that psychological realism begins in earnest with the *Confessions* of Saint Augustine.

Sigrid Undset is the Christian realist *par excellence*. More than any other writer she gathers together the threads of the European realist tradition. Her writing has grown organically out of the powerful presentation of everyday reality which we meet in the nineteenth-century novel and which is the essence of literary realism. But the preconditions go further back in time, to Shakespeare and his contemporaries and to Chaucer. "One thinks of Dickens when one reads Chaucer," she writes, ". . . they are closely related, both were realists who described the actuality they found before them—and it was a better actuality than we can find." And her roots go back to the Icelandic family-sagas. She once described the reading of *Njáls Saga* as a turning-point in her life. It was precisely the intense realism of the saga which gripped her. But gradually the Christian point of view becomes decisive for her presentation of life, the attitude which gives to the ordinary average man a completely new significance, placing on him an emphasis quite unknown in non-Christian thinking. The realism of Christianity is indomitable, she writes. Even as a school-girl she had been impressed by the realism of the stories in the Bible. It was by virtue of her Christian outlook that she learnt to see all human relationships not in isolation and abstraction but collectively, to see her characters not only in relation to the commonplace, to the age or society in which they lived, but also as creatures in relation to the Creator, and then to treat this motive, as she herself says, "as a fact just as realistic as any erotic impulse or longing for earthly happiness,"

CHAPTER I

Childhood and Youth

SIGRID UNDSET was born in Kalundborg in Vest-Sjælland on May 20th 1882. In her veins flowed Norwegian, Danish and Scottish blood, and through the extensive branches of her family she was related to such noble characters as Petter Dass, Tordenskjold, Johan Herman Wëssel and Johan Falkberget.

Her father, the famous archæologist Ingvald Undset, came of a backwoods family in Sollia in Østerdal. They had the reputation of being "tough and headstrong folk". One member of the family, Sigrid Undset's grandfather, married a daughter from the farm Undset in Øvre Rendal; he died young and she returned to Undset. Halvor Undset, their son, did not take up farming but went to the training school for non-commissioned officers in Trondheim; he became a colour-sergeant and warden of the penal labour settlement at Vollan.

Halvor Undset was a very religious man, perhaps somewhat sectarian, but in essentials completely at one with the Church. As a small girl, Sigrid Undset was impressed by the deep sincerity of her grandfather's faith in God's will and his surrender to it. In her volume of childhood reminiscences, *Eleven Years*, she says that it almost terrified her. "It was somehow frightening that a man could *love* God as grandfather did." Both he and his wife would doubtless have preferred that their gifted son, Ingvald, who matriculated with distinction from the Cathedral School in Trondheim in 1871, should have chosen to study theology at the University rather than classical and Scandinavian philology. But when the interests and talents of their son pointed in another direction, they resigned themselves to it. They were delighted to hear of his progress and proud of the name he won for himself, not least abroad, as an archæologist. Sigrid Undset remembered once seeing her grandfather sit and look through the folio which contained all the letters from the foreign academies which had elected his distinguished son a member. "Grandfather nodded his head a little over each one. Good Trøndelag folk as they were, the old people certainly had that ineradicable feeling about 'foreign parts'. One could foster as deep a suspicion as one wished about everything in 'the great world' outside,— all the same, praise and fame from abroad were nearly the greatest a Norwegian could achieve" (*Eleven Years*).

Even as a boy Ingvald Undset reacted against much he saw in the clerical and lay "shepherds" who were for ever visiting his home in Vollan. Later, when he thought back on the various sides of their character, he could say, "The Catholics were content with a single Pope, and he was only infallible when he spoke *ex cathedra*, but the Christian circles of friends here in the north gladly accepted popes by the dozen, and they were infallible no matter whether they spoke in the chapel or over a well-spread dinner-table, standing in the pulpit or in their galoshes" (*Eleven Years*).

Ingvald Undset won his international reputation with the epoch-making work, *The Beginnings of the Iron Age in Northern Europe* (1881). He had however been an active archæologist since boyhood. He was one of those happy souls, writes the archæologist and historian Henrik H. Mathiesen, "who, when the hour comes, are never for a moment in doubt as to what work they will dedicate themselves to." Ingvald Undset and Henrik Mathiesen were constant friends from their school-days. They were thrown together from the start, for both of them had their heads full of Snorri, P. A. Munch and Trondheim Cathedral. The two boys played at "research" in the cathedral until they knew every nook and cranny, the partly covered passages in the walls and the inscriptions on the floors. Later in life they often worked in cooperation and in the summer of 1888 they went on a research trip together. Sigrid Undset heard them talk afterwards of the "great journey", as they called it. They began amongst the cathedral ruins at Hamar, went on up to the church at Ringsaker, and so on over to Toten and Valdres, passing from one runic stone to the next. In 1890, a couple of years before his death, Ingvald Undset wrote a small popular study, *The First Beginnings of the Oslo Valley*. The ordinary person, he says there, rarely thinks of how things looked here thousands of years ago, before the first human being set foot in this area: but it is different with the archæologist, "who in his thoughts and investigations has accustomed himself to seeking far back to the first beginnings".

Ingvald Undset was not anti-religious. He may perhaps be characterised most accurately as an agnostic with an impulse towards religious faith and with a deep respect for Christianity. It may be that it was especially from his way of talking about religion that Sigrid Undset as a child got the impression that there was something true in all religious conceptions,—as if, down through the ages, people had been able to grasp more and more of something they really knew but found difficult to express. His book of travels, *From Akershus to the Acropolis*, gives us an interesting glimpse into the world of his thoughts. The section, "Perspectives of World History", has an individual, personal flavour, and reads now like a foreshadowing of the imaginative writing which his then unborn daughter was to create. There we find this: "Slowly we return homeward, our thoughts busy with what was perhaps the most interesting and significant period in all history, the time when the ancient world sank into the dust and Christianity rose up to become a world-power. We go under the arch of Constantine and pass by the Coliseum, the mightiest remnant of antiquity in this

Rome so full of ruins; and herein many a martyr bled for the new faith, which had its source in the carpenter's son from Nazareth and which the ancient world found itself compelled to fight with fire and sword. But the new doctrine was victorious; on the ruins of the world-empire of ancient Rome there was built through its agency a new world-domination, different in character from the first, but more lasting and stronger, still stronger today than most believe. Even for the stoutest unbeliever, Christianity in its external activity and power must still remain the most significant factor in the development of the world. You may have visited Rome, entirely occupied with an interest in the ancient world and its remains, but if you have any real sense of the development of the human race as a whole, you will soon come to look with no less interest on the remains of the second Rome which lie deposited on those of the first, remains of the world-capital of the ancient Church and papal dominion."

Ingvald Undset's gifted daughter grew more and more fascinated by her father's work, and already before she could talk properly, babbled of "thick-necked" and "shaft-hole" axes, and played with the little terracotta horse from Troy which Schliemann had given to her father. It was his dream that she should become a scholar when she grew up, and continue his own work. That dream was not fulfilled in precisely the way he had imagined, but in different form and in richer measure than he could ever have suspected. She was in her twelfth year when he died in 1893.

Ingvald Undset met his wife-to-be, Anna Charlotte Gyth, when he was a student in Copenhagen in the 1870's. Her father, a chancery councillor in Kalundborg, came of one of the Scottish families who had settled in North Norway in the seventeenth century. The Danish branch of the family had come from Norway to Copenhagen with Sigrid Undset's great-great-grandfather, Anders Broch Gyth, who had tried his luck in the capital of the "twin kingdoms". He was present at the execution of Struensee and in letters home to Hellesviken in Helgeland described the impression made on him by this catastrophe. Luck was not with him; he could never afford to make the journey back to Norway, and his descendants were Danish. His grandson, the father of Sigrid Undset's mother, became a prominent man in Kalundborg; he had a considerable legal practice and estate agency, was prosperous, and greatly respected for his upright character and willingness to lend a helping hand. The Imperial-style house of the chancery councillor still stands, with its clean peaceful lines and the tall linden trees casting their shadows over the white façade and high stone steps. His wife, a daughter of Dean Vilhelm Adolf Worsøe, died when Charlotte Gyth, Sigrid Undset's mother, was a little girl. Signe Dorthea Worsøe, an elder sister of his dead wife, came to keep house for the widower and the six motherless children. She made a "cruel distinction" between the children, preferring the prettiest and most lively and cheerful at the expense of the others. Charlotte was her favourite and she spoiled her beyond all reason.

Charlotte Gyth was an intelligent, self-willed and capricious little creature, who admired her husband, took a lively interest in his work and accompanied him on his travels abroad. "She had the kind of intelligence which makes it easy for a person to learn anything he or she wants to learn, and it pleased her to work with a young enamoured husband and to have the opportunity of travelling and seeing so much" (*Eleven Years*). She never came to feel at home in Norway. People thought the small-town lady, who was made so much of, somewhat superior. For her part, she was inclined to look down on conditions in the provincial capital. She was temperamental, with decided preferences and antipathies. If she did not care for someone, she took no trouble to hide the fact. Mrs Mathilde Hassel, who was then Mathilde Klaveness, got to know

ANNA CHARLOTTE UNDSET (*née* GYTH), 1893

INGVALD UNDSET, *circa* 1885

Charlotte Gyth when she came, newly engaged, to Oslo
and lived in I. M. Nielsen's boarding-house. Mrs Hassel
was not only charmed by her person and impressed by her
accomplishments (amongst them was Charlotte's excellent
command of French), but also realised what a woman of
distinction and value she was. "Anna Charlotte had something unusual about her." Nils Collett Vogt, who met
Mrs Undset when she was considerably older, was capti-
vated by her brilliant and witty conversation. She preserved an air of *la grande dame*, even in the days of poverty
and adversity. She had something of an eighteenth-century
quality and it was indeed that period which represented
her ideal. There she belonged in her opinions, ideas and
literary interests. "To regard the world with the sanity
of a rationalist and everything human with a benign
scepticism,—that was the ideal which for Anine [the name
given her in *Eleven Years*] was easier to possess than prac-
tise." As far as religious and political matters were concerned, she was neither radical nor conservative. She grew
furious with people who wanted to preserve everything
which mere custom and convention had made sacrosanct.
But she reacted just as fiercely at the sentimentality which
she found in the "cock-crowing of a new dawn" of the
radicals. Later in life she became a Catholic. She was
punctilious in performing readily and completely all her
religious duties. She read Thomas Aquinas with enthusiasm.
She thought that in him she discovered for the first time what
true humanism is. She kept her sense of humour to the end.
It is a wonderful thing to pray to Our Lord, she said; it's
like telephoning—often there is no reply.

Charlotte Undset found it difficult to take to strangers,
but she loved her children and home all the more intensely;
her mother-love was strong and passionate. When she was
left on her own after her husband's death, with three small
daughters and a meagre widow's pension for her only
assistance, her will grew like steel. The Undsets' home

continued to be a little life-giving workshop of humanity and culture. The widow Mrs Wegener in *Spring* (*Vaaren*) bears some resemblance to Sigrid Undset's mother. Of Mrs Wegener the book says that she fostered the minds and thoughts of her children, poured out from her own abundance, from the poetry that filled her, a transcendant richness and splendour, which her children sucked greedily in.

When in 1880 Ingvald Undset had to turn back because of illness from his Mediterranean travels, the newly-married couple settled down in Kalundborg, living in one wing of the house of Charlotte's father. Here Sigrid Undset spent the first two years of her life. She had some recollection of that time—it was something "like a perpetual basking on warm earth in the sun" (*Eleven Years*). In 1884 the family returned to Norway. At first they lived in a house set in a large enclosure in the neighbourhood of Vestre Aker church. Then they moved to Number Ten in the idyllic Lyder Sagens Street, also in a district "on the border between town and country, on the one side Vestre Aker which was still farming-land, on the other Oslo which, great city though it was, still extended no further", as Sigrid Undset writes in *The Falling Source* (*Strømmen tyner*). She continues: "We could feel the year's cycle as an ebb and flow of the forces of growth. To us Nature did not mean *places* to which we made excursions, but a huge body which we could see arching itself in the light of dawn; in the noon heat it breathed and stared at us, with a tangible exterior and an interior of unplumbed mystic depth; it could be touched and felt like an animal, but remained enigmatic. And in the evening, the world turned over on its side, dozed off into the darkness of the night, and heaved out strange sounds as it dreamed."

The years in Lyder Sagens Street were happy ones, though the early stage of her father's sickness cast a slight shadow over existence there. But with the healthy instinct of a child for making the best of things, she kept all the disquieting signs at a distance. It was indeed a "golden childhood". Then came sudden reversal. Her father's advancing illness made it necessary for him to find a home nearer the University Museum. The family moved into the crowded town, to Number Five, Keysers Street. The new apartment was gloomy, and the tragic course of her father's disease became more and more apparent. Stifling impressions and feelings of disgust were forced on the child's mind. Now and then she could fairly revel in her melancholy. Nevertheless, in the dark cellars and court-yards there were strange and exciting places to play in, and there were glimpses to be had of a world outside the walls of home, a world which had seemed quite irrelevant when they were living in Lyder Sagens Street. She was enchanted by the whole area round the old cathedral school, Trinity Church, Saint Olav's Church and Hammersborg. "That was the true Oslo," she writes in her fascinating description of this part of the town in *Eleven Years*: "—in some ways a melancholy part, but homely and nowhere uninteresting." But it did seem dull to her when they moved to Observatory Street on the western side of the town, where in her opinion people were not free from snobbishness. The children talked of things which she had been taught to regard as foolish subjects for discussion— whether, for example, it was more elegant to go to Miss Conradi's school or to Miss Bonnevie's. She was happy when, after her father's death, the family moved to Steens Street, with the slopes and rocks of Blaasen near at hand; from it a few minutes' scamper would bring her to her beloved old Lyder Sagens Street.

Even though she lived in several parts of the town, each one with its own characteristic features, she never had a feeling of not belonging. Her home was always the place to which she could return for refuge with absolute confidence; it seemed to have a fluidity which embraced her wherever she went. And it was, she says, the same with the other children she knew.

There was little sentimentality in the way she was brought up. She paid no real heed if her mother gave her an occasional smack in order to get her out of some bad habit or to improve her manners. Her mother's temper was accepted just like the weather: it was a nuisance when it was bad, otherwise there was nothing more to be said about it. But she once got a beating from her father—she had told lies about her younger sister—and then she had to think seriously of what she had done.

There was in her upbringing nothing beyond what was conventionally religious. On Christmas Eve the Christmas Gospel was read aloud, and her mother taught her to say the evening prayer:

> *Now our eyes are closing,*
> *Heavenly Father, on high disposing,*
> *Protect me through this night;*
> *From danger, sin and sorrow*
> *Thine angel guard us till tomorrow,*
> *Who watched us in the light.*
> *Amen for Jesus' sake.*

"Our eyes" in the first line she could never understand as her own, but those of God who sat up in the clouds and saw everything. The evening prayer came to play a part in all her ideas of what religion meant. She had grown used to saying it with her mother, but without understanding what she said. One evening their mother was out and the girls lay alone and frightened in the dark nursery. The nursemaid came in. "Now say your prayers nicely and then you needn't be afraid of anything" she said and went out again. It seemed to the child almost unsafe to say the prayer by herself, but she set her mind to it. In *Eleven Years* Sigrid Undset remarks on this in a way which hints at something fundamental in her religious sensibility. She said the

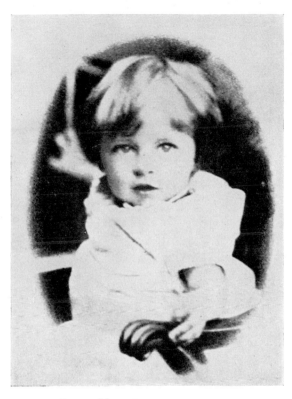

SIGRID UNDSET AT THE AGE OF 1

evening prayer, she writes, with a feeling that she was
embarking on a hazardous adventure, like going somewhere she had never been before. Somehow or other she
felt as if she had become much bigger after she had dared
to say the prayer by herself. "Alone with the Alone" are
the words in which an English mystic describes his religious
experience.

She interpreted the weather signals hoisted on Sankthanshaugen as signals or messages from God, indicating
His pleasure or displeasure with mankind. "When she
saw that only the triangle had been hoisted, then the sunshine and the clear blue sky became, as it were, the benevo-
lence of God Himself spread out over the earth and trees
and all men: now He was pleased with everything at once.
But the square was a symbol which seemed to show that He
had drawn the clouds between Himself and the world; He
was in a bad humour and had turned away, and the child
was despondent when she saw it. The square hoisted above
the triangle appeared worst of all, for it meant that something had happened at that moment to anger God, and the
signal showed that it might be some time before He was
amenable again. But it was wonderful when the triangle
was seen above the square—it was as if the whole world
had been told 'All is forgiven'; God was friends with us
again and now there would only be sunshine and good
temper,—until the next time something cropped up"
(*Eleven Years*). A psychologist who maintains that the
religious attitude is secondary or derivative will perhaps see
in this a typical instance of a childish projection of the
fear of *pater familias*.

The strong simple natural images in Ingemann's morning and evening hymns, which their mother sang for the
children, filled her childish mind with reverent wonder,
but most of the hymns she had later to sing in service at
school occasioned in her a positive aversion. They seemed
sentimental and self-centred, and did not make her think

"of God as One behind the cycle of day and night and the seasons. So long as He stayed *there*, she could think of Him respectfully and reverently, and with gratitude too for the light and the wind and everything that tasted or smelt good. But she had absolutely no desire for Him to be too much concerned with her behaviour and thoughts" (*Eleven Years*).

She reacted instinctively and firmly against any attempt to spoonfeed her with a cosy and comfortable religion. She felt that God was just the opposite of everything of that kind. A sense of the holy lay at the centre of the child's germinating and half-conscious religious life.

It was a pure accident that she went to church while still a child. One Sunday—she must have been nine or ten—the maid had told her she ought to go to church: "You who have only to cross the road and you're there! But there's no one in this house who ever dreams of going to God's house on a Sunday. I'm amazed that you're not ashamed of yourself, I am." It had its effect on the little girl. She went into Trinity Church. The organ-music and the hymn-singing made an impression on her, but it was completely destroyed when the priest went up into the pulpit. "She could make nothing of what he said, even though in fact he repeated words and whole sentences over and over again. And then he spoke in such a strange way, now his voice would rise as high as could be and then sink right down again; and sometimes he put such a peculiar emphasis on the words. She sat there feeling embarrassed: it was as if he was making an exhibition of himself" (*Eleven Years*).

Once at home again, she was reluctant to say she had been to church. But when they were at dinner, she thought she must announce, "I've been to Trinity Church." "You went to church?" said her mother; "why, that was an odd thing to do—what made you think of it?" "Well, I had never been before." "Oh yes" said her mother reflectively. "But you didn't have a hymnbook, did you?—If you think

of going again, you must take a hymnbook with you"
(*Eleven Years*). She tried going to church once more, but
only once.

The Undset family had no great circle of acquaintances
in Oslo, but Ingvald Undset's friends and colleagues were
frequent visitors, amongst them Sophus Bugge, Ernst Sars,
Ludvig Daae and S. Laache, the specialist in internal
disorders, Ingvald Undset's doctor and certainly his closest
friend. Naturally they discussed politics, the Right and
Left, the Supreme Court, Bjørnson and Sverdrup and the
tax on books. Sigrid Undset did not find these "feasts of
talk" so interesting, but she listened spell-bound when
the conversation got round to archæological and historical
subjects, ancient trade-routes, runic inscriptions, the age of
the Eddic poems, the riddles of the Golden Horn of Gallehus
and the Røk stone. A book by Japetus Steenstrup gave rise
to a whole evening's discussion on the runic alphabet in
the Black Sea region.

When her father grew weaker and was confined to his
wheel-chair, Sigrid read aloud to him. At first she was a
little hesitant, but she was gripped by what she read, even
if it was only half understood. When she fancied she had
really grasped something, she pressed blithely on—even
when it was a verse in Old Norse. Sometimes she was vain
enough to think how clever she was; at other times she
forgot everything except that the poetry was so splendid
that it made her shiver with delight:

Drag þú mér af hendi	*Draw from my arm*
hring enn rauða,	*the ring so red,*
fær þú enni ungu	*carry it back*
Ingibjǫrgu.	*to Ingibjörg.*
Sá mun henni	*It will be to her*
hugfastr tregi,	*a deep-set grief,*
er ek eigi kem	*when I return not*
til Uppsala.	*to Uppsala.*

The last piece she read for him, on the day before he died, was *Hávarðar Saga Ísfirðings*. In some parts she expected that he would ask her to read it in the Old Icelandic, but when he said nothing she realised that he must be very tired. Next day when her mother came out of the sick-room, she saw at once on her face what had happened. Their mother took the children into the little room for them to see: their father lay dead in his bed.

Sigrid Undset was set in the midst of living traditions. We loved these traditions so dearly, she says in *The Failing Source (Strømmen tyner)*, because deep down we knew from what a noble source they sprang, a source moreover which might perhaps soon dry up. "If we did not believe directly in fairies, goblins and trolls—we believed in ghosts as a matter of course, but then we had not been so injured by our powers of observation as to become materialists—we at least believed in the living mother of all such." The tales of Asbjørnson and Moe and Elling Holst's picture-book were in this way not to be classed with other children's books, with Bernt Lie and Dikken Zwilgmeyer.

Both her father and mother used to tell stories, for the most part tales which they made up as they went along. But on the ground-floor of the villa in Lyder Sagens Street, beneath the home of the Undsets, there lived an old lady, Anna Winter-Hjelm, born in Germany and the wife of Winter-Hjelm the organist. In *Eleven Years* she is called Mrs Wilster. There were ten children in the Winter-Hjelms' home, and each one of them had friends, boys and girls, who were for ever running in and out. Mrs Winter-Hjelm sat there with her darning-basket or sewing-machine, or else preparing vegetables; she was never without children round her. In the summer she took them for country walks. The fairy-tale tradition was deeply alive in her, and she told tales which could scare the little ones out of their wits or make them shriek with laughter. And the nursemaid, Caroline Thorvaldsen, who came of families in Smaalenene and Drøbak, told fairy-tales from the eastern part of the country, and drew on an overwhelming richness of fantasy. Sigrid Undset writes of her, "At storytelling she was a past-master above all others." But didn't "Moster"[1] in Kalundborg outdo her?—for she must have been an unsurpassed teller of tales. There was nothing placed in the way of the satisfaction of this hunger for stories. It was not accepted as a pedagogic principle that the child's mental life should be rendered barren. Mrs Winter-Hjelm, Caroline Thorvaldsen and "Moster" were able to sow their seeds unhindered in the childish mind of Norway's greatest woman storyteller.

She loved to be the narrator herself. Those who knew her best could not help becoming aware of her visionary fantasy and inventive power. At night, when the three sisters had gone to bed, Sigrid, the eldest, began to tell stories which stretched themselves out from one evening to the next; the characters were usually the same, but they were continually having new fantastic experiences. At an early age she showed an amazing ability to give characters to her purely imaginary creations, and she amused herself also by drawing them and pasting them onto match-boxes to create in this way a complete puppet-theatre (*Aftenposten*, May 14th 1928).

Their mother exercised control over the children's reading. She could not stand children's books full of sentimental moralising. Sigrid Undset was certainly not allowed to sit about and linger over "such rubbish"—"Out and play!" But her mother had no objection to the juicy humour of "Daddy" Holberg and Johan Herman Wessel. The children knew *Peder Paars* almost by heart. As time went on, Sigrid Undset became familiar with Holberg's world and characters, so that they too became homely and dear

[1] Signe Dorothea Worsøe.

to her, as Hans Andersen, Asbjørnson and the ballads (the Danish especially at first) already were.

The summer holidays yielded intense experiences which left bright clear pictures in her memory. The summer months spent at Kalundborg, in Østerdal or Trøndelag, Drøbak or Hvitsten, where the family often rented a house for the holidays, seemed times detached from all other time. She could recall sensations and moods which were inextricably bound up one with another. Her grandfather's old gardens in Kalundborg were enchanting. "One came into an air which was a surfeit of scents—bitter-sweet from the box-hedges, cool and pure from the phlox, and the rank sweaty smell from elder and ivy. . . . Then there were spiders of every shape and size, fat blue-bottles that flashed as they skimmed out of the shade into the sunshine, and the terrifying earwigs. . . . But the gloom under the old trees and the mystical insects only made the gardens more fascinating in my eyes" (*Christmas in Kalundborg and District* 1946; *Jul i Kalundborg og omegn* 1946). She remembered the fairy-tale evenings in Kalundborg best from the summer of 1887, when she was just five years old; they stayed there longer than usual because there had been an outbreak of diphtheria in Lyder Sagens Street. She and her sisters had a bedroom overlooking the square. Even on a summer evening, the magnificent great linden trees outside made the room dark early. "Moster came in, quickly and quietly, small and nimble as a mouse,—the tiny trains with which she always had her dresses made rendered the likeness even more striking. She settled herself in the seat by the window, lifted her knitting high under her nose in the gloom, and peered over her spectacles at the two of us in bed: 'Now, my little snails, what shall we have for a story tonight?'" One of her stories, Søll-Klara, has been given by Sigrid Undset in *The Failing Source* as she herself used to tell it to Norwegian children.

And then the summers north of the Dovre mountains!

Her father always thought of himself as a native of Trøndelag, and she too was always overcome by a deep and joyful
sense of recognition when the journey eventually brought
her down the long valleys to Trondheimsfjord. Best of all
she remembered the summer of 1891, the last summer she
spent there with her father. She sat at the carriage-window
opposite him as the train came down through the Gaul
valley. She knew all the names from history, Lunde, Rimul,
Gimsar, Mcdalhus, and her father told her where the farms
lay. She absorbed the whole landscape, the dark-green
fields, the white washing spread outside a farm with big
outhouses, the farmhouse itself long and brightly painted.
"New-laundered clothes spread out on a green field seemed
to be her earliest and tenderest impression of Trøndelag"
are her words. But never before had she realised how lovely
the summer can be in Norway.

It was in her grandfather's library at Vollan that she came
upon a copy of *Njáls Saga* in Sommerfelt's translation. It
went completely to her head. She would wake up in the
morning, dress and sit at breakfast, sick with impatience
to lay her hands on the book again and get outside to a place
where she could continue her reading. Both in *Eleven Years*
and later in a little essay in English, *A Book That Was a
Turning-Point in My Life*, she has described in detail this
first encounter with the Icelandic family-saga. She would
lie out in the green bleaching-field and read. Now and
then she was forced to put the book away from her to give
her time to absorb what she had read, or to give her a
chance to cool her burning face down in the grass. Everything lived so vividly before her eyes that it almost hurt:
Skarpheðin especially, reckless and unstable, with his pale
sallow-brown face, his dark eyes and beard. She could not
understand what was the matter with him. Whenever
the others had brought about a reconciliation and everything seemed to be going well, Skarpheðin, white-faced and
behaving like a madman, came and destroyed it all. But

she had, she says, a sort of premonition of how women could come to link their destinies with those of gifted misfits or neurotics.

Another such summer, one that was to remain indelibly imprinted on her memory, she experienced in Drøbak—in whose neighbourhood we are to imagine the situation of Olav Audunsson's farm, Hestviken. It was the year after her father's death, so that she was twelve or thirteen. The painter, Theodor Kittelsen, lived nearby, and at that time she was fully determined to be an artist when she grew up; she drew incessantly, both at home and at school. She was particularly enthusiastic about Chr. Krohg and Weren-skiold, but this summer in Drøbak they both had to give place to Kittelsen. She was in and out of his house all the time, where she found every wall covered with paintings and sketches. She discovered there in living form the whole world of all the whimsical and wonderful creatures she had heard tell of in legend and fairy-tale. Kittelsen looked at her drawings and was convinced that she had talent; he advised her to study painting when she had finished at school. One summer in Hvitsten there was the flame of a little childish romance. In *Eleven Years* his name is Olaf. "As I remember it," she writes, "there seemed to be sunshine every single day that summer."

Sigrid Undset was given her first lessons at home by her mother, but when she had reached third-form standard she was sent to Ragna Nielsen's school. Her father was a Liberal and had no misgivings about letting her go to the radical Liberal school. Sigrid Undset was struck by Ragna Nielsen's beauty—and she was always so handsomely dressed, in dark-coloured or light grey gowns, with a broad white bib which made the dress look like a kind of uniform. She inspired respect in the highest degree. Sigrid found it exciting to attend this radical school, although, it was true, Olaf, her friend from Hvitsten, had talked scornfully of boys and girls going to the same school. He had also left her with the suspicion that the Conservatives were not as black as they were painted: he said that all sailors were conservative. And on the seventeenth of May[1] it was certainly a fine thing to go in the children's procession, with the single flag everywhere, and sing Bjørnson's national songs.

All the same she felt some dissatisfaction with the school. Think for yourselves, said the teachers, but if she did and came to a conclusion other than that properly prescribed as radical, she was always wrong. At home she had learnt that the world of learning was always in motion, but at school the teachers were so "remarkably certain of the letter of the law" when it came to the final results of scholarship. As for God, she got the impression that they believed He was a great almighty Liberal, who stood by co-education and the single flag. She is without doubt essentially correct when she says that, already as a thirteen-year-old, she had seen through the radicalism of the 'eighties. Something central in her comprehension of life had dawned on her: she saw that the more people freed themselves from religious dogmas, the easier it was for them to bind themselves to political doctrines.

Sigrid Undset had few friends as a girl. She attached herself to only one of her schoolfellows, Emma Münster, and then not until her last year at school. Emma Münster, who afterwards became a doctor, would seem to be the only woman friend Sigrid Undset ever had who was completely in tune with her. The two schoolgirls had common ground in their passion for botany, and they roamed the countryside round Oslo collecting flowers. These trips laid the foundations of Sigrid Undset's quite remarkable botanical knowledge, and this hobby probably gave her more pleasure than any other. About three-quarters of every letter she

---

[1] Norway's Independence Day, the anniversary of the ratification of an independent constitution by the National Assembly at Eidsvole in 1814.

wrote to her sister Signe from her exile in America dealt with the plant-life she found there.

Religious instruction was one of the things she found least dull at school. Naturally there was a good deal in the Old Testament that aroused no response. "One must be completely grown up to perceive anything of the power which lies in the story of Job, or to be gripped by the light and dark, the idyllic and tragic, in the story of David." But she felt that the biblical stories dealt with men who were truly alive. "It was not disguised that, although King David was both hero and poet, he was capable of mean actions, or that the reckless Samson was considerably braver than wise, or that the prophets could sulk and whine in their self-pity" (*On Abraham's Sacrifice; Omkring Abrahams offer*).

Preparation for confirmation impelled her finally away from Lutheran Christianity. She has spoken of it not only in the autobiographical fragment contained in the book *They Sought the Ancient Paths* (*De søkte de gamle stier,* 1936), but also in the description of Rose Wegener's confirmation in *Spring* (1914). What first caused her revolt against Lutheranism was its treatment of the seventh commandment. Even as a schoolgirl she had recoiled from what Luther wrote about virginity, and she was now strengthened in her opposition. She got the impression that, yes, chastity was to be recommended, but at the same time it was unfortunate, almost ridiculous, if a woman became an old maid. Chastity came to be regarded as something negative, not as a positive virtue, implying perhaps a development of spiritual possibilities with a higher aim than simply that of being a useful asset in the marriage market. In this contact with the world of religion she received in effect no impression of the exalted and saintly. God was nearest to being a comfortable family god from Homansbyen.

After Ingvald Undset's death, the financial circumstances of the family were extremely trying. But rich as the traditions within the home were, poverty could yet help to increase their perception of the non-material values of life. She was embarrassed, she says in *Eleven Years*, when her mother went into a shop and kept on asking how much everything cost until she found something cheap enough to buy,—or else went away without a purchase. But she was ashamed of being ashamed! She understood quite clearly "that the most joyless form of poverty is that where submission is made without protest to the opinion which considers it a shameful thing to be poor. She did not want to submit to such an assessment of life's values, but at the same time she felt that something inside her was yielding under the pressure of circumstance. She knew that, in a way, she too would have dearly liked to be invited to the 'fine rich houses', though she knew she would never enjoy herself in them, the people were so boring. And she was ashamed of herself because she had become the same as they" (*Eleven Years*). But in reality she had not become and was never to become the same.

When Sigrid Undset had taken her middle-school leaving examination, Ragna Nielsen offered her the chance to stay at school to study for matriculation. She thought however that she could not accept this generous offer of a free place with a clear conscience, now that she felt herself so remote from the ideas in which Ragna Nielsen believed so ardently. In any case she had no real desire to stay on at school: as was said before, she wanted to be a painter. From infancy she had received every impression so intensely, with such definition and such delight, that the discipline of fixing them in colour must have stirred the creative artistic impulse within her.

Nevertheless, she still had to earn her living, and she went to the Commercial College. At this time she came into contact with Dea Forsberg, a Swedish girl of the same age, through a correspondence arranged by *Urd* and the Swedish young people's paper, *Kamraten*. She introduced herself to her in a letter which contained the following humorous self-portrait: "In character I am fanciful and vain, believing once that I had a good head and considered talented at school, but now proving I am nothing of the kind at the Commercial College I attend. At first it was intended that I should become a student, but I had no wish for that, and consequently I was put here, where they are busy in accomplishing my speedy decease."

Her certificate from the Commercial College was not superlatively good, but with the help of some good friends she found an office post with Chr. Wisbech, an agent for A.E.G. Sigrid Undset worked in an office for ten years and three months, an important part of her life and essential in her development as a writer. Office-work was not exactly to her taste. She liked none of the work she had to do, she used to say, except housework; and she often said how terrible she thought it was to be confined behind a desk. To have to be on the spot, for example, as soon as she was rung for! But she proved an excellent secretary, almost indispensable, not least because of her phenomenal powers of memory. She carried everything in her head down to the last detail. She never lost her imperturbable tranquillity. One of her colleagues relates that, if an attack of nerves had disorganised the rest of the office, Sigrid Undset would still remain at her work, calm and immovable. One mid-morning break she sat and chuckled over something she was reading. It was a piece she had written herself, a description of actual events, amongst them the arrival of the King in 1905. She read it to the others. It was written with such "warmth and humour", say her colleagues, "that we could not help interrupting: 'Good Heavens! Why don't you write instead of sitting in an office?'"

She had begun to feel seriously that she wanted to write. It was clear to her that her real powers as an artist lay in that medium. In many ways a completely novel world

SIGRID UNDSET, AGED 16

had been opened up to her by her office-work and the many new connections it brought, first and foremost with business people (a new kind of person in her experience since at home she had never come into contact with such), and the office-girls who lived in boarding-houses and digs. She became curious to know what they all "looked like on the inside". She had an exact comprehension of everything that conveyed an external impression to her senses; even as a girl of fourteen she had known that she possessed this ability in a far higher degree than her acquaintances of the same age—it seemed to her that they never really knew what they had *seen*. This assurance in dealing with the outward gave her courage to rely on her own observation, even when there was small possibility of checking it, and gave her more confidence in her own opinions. "Previously, I had always been afraid that my opinion was wrong when it differed from that of a whole mass of other people" (*Urd*, Christmas Number 1912).

Until she began to work in the office, she had always felt fundamentally rootless in Oslo, but now she felt truly at home in the city. "It was after I had settled down in the office and had come to feel myself on equal terms with the people I met there, that I realised that I was at home in my own town. I had roots everywhere in this earth which I had trodden all the while I was growing up, roots in all the suburban streets where I had lived as a child and played in the open spaces, in gloomy Keysers Street and in Pilestræde where I spent some wretched years, in Vestre Aker where I wandered when I was small, and in towards Frognersæteraasen and Vetakollen and up through Nordmark, penetrating further and further as I grew older, in the blue anemones' season, in the burning summer sun, in November's pouring rain, over the hard snow of winter and the slushy snow of spring."

It was in these years that she made the town a part of her consciousness to a degree unparalleled by any other

Norwegian writer. She came to love Oslo, to get the feel of the city and to delight in it. Shortly after writing her first story with an Oslo setting, she said to an interviewer, "And then, as you know often happens, every individual feature of the beloved one becomes 'one more delight', apprehended with sharpened senses and treasured in the heart. For me, Oslo is the most beautiful town in the world, its people the most delightful, their speech, in its every nuance from Homansbyen to Ekeberg, the most joyous means of expression for human thought" (*Urd*, May 28th 1910).

In the summer holidays she continued to visit the family in Kalundborg. On one of her visits, in 1907, her beloved aunt made strenuous but vain efforts to persuade her to marry a young and handsome Methodist minister. Aunty Agnes was worried by Sigrid Undset's lack of faith and had this dream of seeing her safely on the right road, arm-in-arm with Pastor Røddinge. Sigrid Undset has given a delightful account of this in the essay called *My Favourite Aunt*.

But her great holiday experiences at this time came on her trips to the mountains. She became as familiar with Gudbrandsdal and the mountains that surround it, particularly Rondane and Dovre, as she was with Trøndelag, Oslo and Nordmark. "I always took my summer holiday at the time when the tourist traffic in the mountains was more or less over," she says in *It's Haunted (Det spøker)*. In all her writing, from the youthful *The Happy Age (Den lykkelige Alder)* to *At Home in Værskei (Hjemme paa Værskei)*, written in America during the last war, her love for the mountains keeps breaking through, providing material for some of the finest descriptions of mountain scenery in Norwegian literature. Most Norwegians, it says in *The Wild Orchid (Gymnadenia)*, have almost a religious feeling for the mountains.

In more respects than one her time as an office-worker

was a period of learning and training. The enormous scholarship and high intellectual culture characteristic of her were given a solid foundation in these years. They were in fact her student days. She plunged deeper into literature and history, both Norwegian and foreign. She was not interested in the polemic literature of the 'eighties, "the preaching literature" as she called it; but she responded with admiration to Joans Lie and to Ibsen's *Wild Duck*. And she rejoiced inside herself when she found Bjørnson having a fling at the moralists, as at the end of *Det flager i byen og havnen*. She was taken by the children's verse in *En glad gut*, by Sigurd Slembe, and his magnificent poem to P. A. Munch. It was however her absorption of English literature which was of most significance. When she had finished Georg Brandes' book on Shakespeare, she determined to read everything that had been written in English,— and she went far towards this aim. She made not only Shakespeare her own, but all Elizabethan literature. Dickens became one of her favourite authors. She literally gorged herself on English lyric poetry, especially on Keats and Shelley. She presented a collected edition of Keats to her Swedish girl-friend, and furnished it with a long dedication in verse which, though extremely amateurish, is still extremely touching; for example:

Some evening when you sit alone and sad,
And feel how grief and longing break your heart,
When mind is dull, and ever in a mad
Eternal back-and-forth your thoughts must start
Like cagéd beasts,—perhaps then in this book,
—As I but late—you yet may find once more
Intoxication in this flowered talk,
Reposing on a far-off wooded shore.

Nevertheless, it was the Middle Ages which attracted her most of all, saga and ballad, the German minnesingers,

Chaucer and much more. She pried into rare and half-forgotten things. The librarian Aalheim had to stop and stare one day when he got a borrowing slip from a slim and beautiful eighteen-year-old, with long braided hair and big thoughtful eyes. The slip was from Sigrid Undset, and on it she designated herself Correspondence Clerk. She was asking for Unger's edition of *Heilagra Manna Sögur*: (*Stories and Legends of Holy Men and Women*). It had not been out on loan since it was published in 1877.

She had an ambitious programme of writing. First she wanted to write about people from the Middle Ages. Her own time, business people and office-girls, could wait. As early as 1902 she wrote to her Swedish friend that she was busy with a novel with a historical setting in the mid-thirteenth century: it was to be "well and truly timbered". A couple of years later, in 1904 or 1905, she had completed it. "And so I dressed myself up as finely as I could" she writes "—a big summer-hat trimmed with a mass of flowers, a light dress and silk stockings. Thus arrayed I went trembling with apprehension down to Gyldendal's, and took the manuscript in to Peter Nansen himself. The interview was short: 'Come back in a month,' he said. A month of anxious waiting. . . . But at last I stood once more in Peter Nansen's study. He gave me a friendly pat on my shoulder and said, 'Don't try your hand at any more historical novels. It's not your line. But you might, you know, try to write something modern. One can never tell!' Then I came home, my mind awhirl, and wrote *Mrs Marta Oulie* [*Fru Marta Oulie*]. That, I felt, should be modern enough."

We should probably be grateful for Peter Nansen's refusal, though the manuscript of this first draft of her medieval novel no longer exists—she burnt it twenty years later when the first volume of *Olav Audunsson* appeared. But she was in fact not ripe for the execution of this large-scale work on the themes of unfaithfulness and loyalty.

Mrs Marta Oulie was sent to the publishing house of Aschehoug. In the first instance this too was rejected. Their reader thought that people had had enough of such everyday stories of marriage and infidelity. Then the sensible Signe, her youngest sister, later the wife of Dr. Pantzerhjelm Thomas, had her brilliant idea: Why not send the book to Gunnar Heiberg? He was enthusiastic in his praise, and this authority on the Norwegian Parnassus promised to use his influence with Aschchoug. In the autumn of 1907, the booksellers had *Mrs Marta Oulie* on their counters. The opening words are promising, was someone's comment. They were, "I have been unfaithful to my husband."

CHAPTER II

Dreams of Happiness

THE first phase of Sigrid Undset's activity as an author spans a period of about ten years, beginning with *Mrs Marta Oulie* and ending with *The Wise Virgins* (*De kloge jomfruer*), which was published in 1918, two years before *Kristin Lavransdatter*.

Although the general impression given by her work in these ten years is one of unity, several stages in her development can be clearly distinguished. For the most part she writes novels and short stories on subjects drawn from her own contemporary world, but there are some exceptions: a little one-act play called *In the Grey Light of Dawn* (*I graalysningen*); a volume of poems under the title *Youth* (*Ungdom*); and with a setting in the Middle Ages, a period she never lets slip from her grasp, *The Story of Viga-Ljot and Vigdis* and *The Story of King Arthur and his Knights of the Round Table*. The mileu she normally describes is as commonplace as can be. Wealthy characters make an occasional appearance, but only in passing and for a fleeting moment. In *Tjodolf* and *Simonsen* we find ourselves near to a working-class background. Most of her characters belong, however, to the so-called "educated middle-class"; except in *Jenny*, they are not artists or men of letters and learning, not even men in official positions, but engineers, business people, office-girls, house-wives with much on their hands. There is nothing remarkable or eccentric about her characters. They are extremely commonplace people, very different from the problem-characters, often abnormal, of Hans E. Kinck or Knut Hamsun, to name the most prominent

36

novelists of the preceding generation. It was precisely her deep and piercing insight into the life of ordinary drudges which created the golden poetry to be found in this "grey" literature of real life from the Oslo of the pre-war period.

She is at her best in her description of childhood and innocent youth, especially in the description of young girls with their conflicting inner emotions, their self-preoccupation and their need for devotion to something outside themselves, their hopes, their dreams of happiness, longings which inevitably jar against common reality, the merciless touchstone of everyday life.

We find a typical expression of the attitude, which is both implicit and explicit in this writing, in the words of the young woman, Charlotte Hedels, in *The Happy Age* (*Den lykkelige Alder*). It is the young Sigrid Undset who is speaking here, the voice of her deep and all-embracing—one might say catholic—humanity. "I wanted to write about the town. You know,—all these half-lovely districts we respectable drudges live in. The wet dirty streets and the worn paving-stones, small apartments and small shops,—I should really love to write about the windows of such shops,—you know, shops selling chemists' sundries, and toy-shops with dolls and sewing-boxes and glass necklaces, where children stand outside in clusters and say 'Bags I that one'. Oh, when I now know how many tiny pathetic longings outside such shops have sprinkled their dew over every pennyworth of happiness bought in them . . . I could love and make use of all the worn-out little words which we all let fall so carelessly—words we use when we drop in on someone, words that go with some sign of love, words whispered in grief or in the surprise of some small joy. . . . I could write a book about you or about myself or about any of us office-worms. We carry on and find a job which allows us to live—we can't live *for* it."

She is careful with facts and logical; she experiments with her characters to find out what lies beneath, what standards they live by, what they are capable of and how much they can suffer.

She had no conscious contacts with religion when she wrote the earliest of these books. She says herself that she was nearest to being agnostic or atheist. On the other hand, no hostility can be detected towards the religious idea as such. If she had made such a rejection, it would have straightway formed a barrier between her and the total comprehension of reality, which was her goal; and in any case, it would have meant that she was dispensing in advance with one possible explanation of the human destinies and conflicts she describes.

Mrs Marta Oulie is written in the form of a diary, but it cannot be said to have a confessional character. An individual stamp is given to this remarkable first work of a young woman of twenty-five by the detached presentation, the cool objectivity, which nevertheless grips the reader. In the retrospective entries in this journal, almost in the same way as in the dialogue of a play by Ibsen, the curtains are drawn back to reveal the past and to enable us to follow step by step the belated self-realisation of the unfaithful wife.

Self-worship and egocentricity, narcissism decked out in the sexual-romantic guise of *grande passion*, are exposed in *Mrs Marta Oulie* in a manner completely new in Norwegian literature. Like Karen in Gunnar Heiberg's *Love's Tragedy* (*Kjærlighedens Tragedie*), Marta Oulie is a woman for whom love means everything; it is the ultimate and absolute spiritual experience. She has loved her husband, the handsome but rather dull Otto Oulie, and he has loved her in return. "Love—there was nothing else in life worth living for! I loved so fanatically that it seemed I could never dive deep enough into my passion. And day by day I felt how this love was making me beautiful and fresh and brilliant, how it gave me an unsuspected understanding of life and made me brave and gay and infinitely superior." Love stands alone, above house and home and children. It has no place in the sum of ordinary life; it cannot stand contact with the commonplace. But it demands its due. "It seems indeed that we have no soul outside the life of our bodies—it lives in us like the flame in something burning." When Otto Oulie no longer interests her, it is as if some insatiable natural instinct breaks loose and possesses her. As for being unfaithful, she had "really just drifted into it, almost innocently". All the same, in her diary she could confess: "I have committed a great sin." She had never cared about Otto beyond wanting him to think that she was delightful—"I had never tried to discover his true self and give it sympathy and love." As for her children, she thought it was enough if she saw to it that they were fed and clothed: and now, unashamed, she was with her lover two rooms away from where they lay sleeping! And her lover—"in reality I cared no more about him than I did about the mirror in my wardrobe". "I thought of nothing in the world except my own self." "Now I feel I have been blinder and understood less than anyone. I know no one whose life has fallen to pieces in the same way as mine. And it can only be due to something in myself."

She recalls a conversation with Otto. "I am not a Christian in that sense," he had said, "but I believe in God, you understand." "I don't believe in Him." The world was too unjust for that, she had added. "Don't you believe in an eternal life either?" asked Otto slowly. "No." There had been a time when she had felt the urgent impulse to kneel and give thanks for the wonderful love which filled her. But she knew no one towards whom she could direct her thanks. She realises that Otto "sees" deeper than she, despite her superior knowledge and intelligence. But can there be any consolation, she has to ask herself, in the thought that the day will come "when nothing in the life of one is hidden from another"? And this talk about a life of trials "by which God makes the obstinate bend—what a slave-driver for a god!" Human beings supposed to be created in God's image?—"I think it's childish to talk like that."

In her heart she rebels violently against this faith. But she cannot refrain from a secret wish that there were some-one above her, to whom she could confess. "I said once that I could commit murder and live on with my own conscience as witness and judge, punishment and reprieve. My God! —here I am wondering how I can confess to someone—and at night I lie awake and think about it." Perhaps confess to one of the children?—and meet horror and reproach. She puts the thought aside: Ugh! But she can understand "why criminals confess and why Catholic women sin in order to go to shrift". With her intellect, Marta Oulie can after all accept Christianity. It possesses an inner logic. "Seen from the inside, Christianity is consistent enough,—it's like standing in a lofty cathedral with stained-glass windows. Only I know all the time that the whole real world and the daylight are outside."

In the Grey Light of Dawn, a little one-act dramatic dialogue written in 1908, gives a picture of life in the same setting as in *Mrs Marta Oulie*. The motive is also related, although the rôles are reversed in that it is now the husband who is faith-less. Infatuated and irresponsible, he has left his wife, chil-dren and home. There was nothing glamorous about Lydia any longer, and there was no will in him to remain faithful. The life of a family destroyed, a new unhappy marriage, remorse and grief are the consequences.

This was modern enough! But she could not forget the Middle Ages. True, she does not return to *Olav Audunsson*, since she is not yet perfectly assured that she has a complete understanding of that period, the thirteenth century. But in dealing with early medieval times, as she said in an interview in *Urd* (October 3rd 1910), she felt herself on surer ground. She had written *The Story of Viga-Ljot and Vigdis* in 1909, where the action belongs to the end of the tenth century. Men are governed by the heathen attitude to life, above all by the revenge-ethic of the family-society. In the interview mentioned above, she says that it was the idea of the "avenging son" which attracted her. "It was fascinating to see the motive carried to the extreme."

The father of Vigdis has given up the old faith, and puts trust in his own "might and main". At bottom Vigdis feels the same, but she clings with determination to the old beliefs. The sacrificial grove with its altar has a powerful attraction for her. What she hears about the new faith seems too wonderful. "He can't be much help, your white Christ, since I hear He couldn't even free Himself, but was killed by His enemies in the land of the black men." She is baptised, but only because she has received such good assistance from King Olaf Tryggvason in her suit that she cannot doubt his faith is the true one. There is no real difference in the case of Ljot. He was baptised by a recluse, who healed an ugly and gangrenous wound in his leg. "He would take no other reward, so I let myself be baptised in order not to hurt his feelings." But Christianity has made some small impression on him. His wife, Leikny, gives birth to such a weakling of a son that people tell Ljot that he ought to expose him: "for he'll never grow up to be a man." To Ljot, however, it seems a dishonourable deed: "I am a Christian, and I shall never do such a thing."

But the mainspring of the whole action is the influence exercised on the minds of men and women alike by the duty of revenge, the ethical principle by which this family-society lives. Vigdis no longer has faith in the old gods, but she has no doubt in her mind that it is revenge, and revenge alone, which can redeem the dishonour and injury which Ljot, in violating her, has brought upon her. She bears a son, but puts him out in the woods to die. Everything seems to be closed about her. She has often thought it would be best if she wandered into the river; but she comes back to life when she learns that her son is not dead after all. "It was the perfect revenge—that Ljot's son should be Ljot's slayer." Thoughts of vengeance possess her—for she loves Ljot. Like Gudrun in *Laxdæla Saga*, she must at last confess

41

that she hated him so much simply because she loved him so passionately: "the worst of all was that of all men it was he I would most willingly have loved." Vigdis' son meets his father, but flinches from carrying out the deed of vengeance to which his mother has incited him. Ljot helps him by giving himself a mortal wound as they fight their duel. Perhaps he thought to atone for his crime: "I have long wished that my head should lie on her breast." A way out seems to open before "the avenging son". It dawns upon him that he may perhaps be able to help his mother,—who sits at home in poverty, cold and lonely and closed in on herself,—in some other way than by the fulfilment of the vengeance demanded by the old code. In *Laxdæla Saga* it says that Gudrun was the first woman in Iceland to learn the Psalter and to become "a nun and anchoress". Perhaps something of this kind lay open to Vigdis, but we only learn that she had Ljot buried beside the church she had built, and lived, alone and seeing no visitors, for ten years afterwards. Her grave was near the church dedicated to Saint Margaret in the valley which received the name of Margretadal (later Maridal).

For the time being Sigrid Undset wrote no more on historical themes—just this one ray of light piercing what was indeed an obscure medieval period, as if to reassure herself that the distance was not so immeasurably great between Vigdis and the young women she knew from her own age. "When one peels off the layer of ideas and conceptions that belong essentially to one's own time, one steps straight into the Middle Ages." (Interview in *Urd*, 1910).

The Happy Age is different in character from *Mrs Marta Oulie* which was in diary-form. Here Sigrid Undset reveals more of herself, tells more of her own childhood and youth as well as those of others, experiences both sweet and bitter. The childhood description in *A Dozen Handkerchiefs* (*Et dusin lommetørklær*) is full of a charming melancholy. It is a parallel in the short-story form to Olaf Bull's poem *Elvira*, with the same theme of a child's disappointment, the theme of "the little line of pain which is always eternally beautiful".

But first and foremost, *The Happy Age* is the most sensitive piece of writing about girlhood that has ever appeared in Norwegian,—at the same time it is nearest to reality. These young women have a certain coolness and reserve, but these lie only on the surface, and are no more than the shield which covers the warmth imprisoned within. Casual love-affairs are not much heeded in the milieu of lodging-houses and rented rooms in which they live. But these girls are so constituted that they cannot regard them so lightly, whether their attitude is natural in them or depends on the inheritance they have brought with them from their homes. As Sigrid Undset writes of one of them, there is something in them which makes any stain show up clearly not only to others but, above all, to themselves. They are not prudish, but they live with the dream of something worthy of complete surrender, something which will demand their faith utterly and absolutely. It is precisely this way that lie the adventure and the hazard, youth itself.

Edele Hammer in the short story *A Stranger (En fremmed)* is the first such personality we meet. Her mother is Swedish; her father, who had been a headmaster and is now dead, was a Norwegian from Østerdal. Edele grows up in Oslo but never comes to feel at home in the city. Now she lives in a boarding-house and lacks the ability to accustom herself to the fortuitous collection of people she meets there. She longs to escape from her loneliness and is grateful for friendship, even when she knows it springs from pity. Joys and pleasures cheaply bought have no attraction for her. The scandalous love-stories, which were meat and drink to the others, made her flesh creep with loathing. "I just go on and can never be rid of it, never stop thinking about it. How could any woman do such a thing?" But she is frightened too, frightened of what lies within her. "Can any one of us be certain how pure we wanted to be when we first joined

in the game?" Edele joins in the game: half willingly and
half unwillingly, she slips into an affair with the boyishly
attractive but superficial young engineer, Aagaard. She
realises that she has entered a world in which dark and blind
forces reach out to clutch her. She too has allowed herself
to be tempted "by the elfin gold which turns to withered
leaves when morning comes". She understands now that
what the "emancipated" call "the prejudices of the stupid
are in fact the judgments of the wise. The stupid say that a
girl should be chaste and they cannot say why. But those
who first said what the rest repeat after them—they knew
the reason". Because she feels intensely the depth of her fall,
it is possible for her to raise herself again when she meets Per
Dyrssen, a man who knows how to accept her whole love.
It is not elfin gold which he has to offer, but a "handful of
the real stars of heaven". She believes in him and would go
through fire and water to reach the stars he held out to her.
It was easy to win the elfin gold, but one does not gain for
nothing the real stars of heaven, with which he has it in his
power to endow her. She must achieve them for herself in his
company. She can make no demand for palpable proof that
he is in fact solvent in this respect. She must believe and give.
A love like this touches her religious feelings and seems to make
an appeal to her to regard marriage as a vocation. She will be
married in church. "Yes," says Per Dyrssen, "but that's only
a matter of form." "Not for me any longer," she answers.

The second short story, *The Happy Age*, gives the book its
title, and here we are introduced to a whole series of young
women of the period. In this story a great number of Sigrid
Undset's artistic qualities celebrate a combined triumph:
her accurate art of characterisation, her perfectly attuned
receptivity and reproduction of the Oslo speech, her powers
of description in showing to us the streets of the city and
Nordmark, and the precision with which she puts her finger
on the pulse of mood and emotion. The central figures are
Charlotte Hedels and Uni Hirsch, who both belong in the

same setting as Edele Hammer. The contrast between life's ample unfolding, which youth so fiercely craves, and the pinch of external conditions, makes itself more strongly felt here than in *A Stranger*. But here too is the longing for that which neither moth nor rust can corrupt.

Charlotte's character is the most interesting. It is only a sketch and the psychological motive which lies behind her attitude to life and her suicide is merely suggested. But she stands before us, clearly defined and alive. None of the modern young women described by Sigrid Undset feels so keenly as Charlotte the spiritual vacuum of her own time, its lack of any absolute standards, its inability to see things *sub specie æternitatis*, and the absence of any real desire for adventure. "We leave nothing to chance—there is no prospect of loss or of gain to keep our thoughts in suspense when we have left the office or shop or school. And we all of us want the same thing, no matter what different ways we choose to obtain it: to live one instant with our whole being turned inward—so that our eyes look not outwards into the fog and gaslight, but inwards to our own burning hearts." But Charlotte finds no object for her desire, nothing beyond herself. She understands this clearly; she says, "We are in love with ourselves." Uni asks, "Do you mean like the man in the story— you know, Narcissus, the one who loved his own reflection and drowned?" "Yes," says Charlotte quietly; "but don't you think there are a good many of us today who are just the same?"

Uni too is an example of youthful narcissism. Her dreams of becoming an actress only mask her self-infatuation. She is cured, however, thanks to Kristian Hjelde, the man to whom she is engaged. Like Otto Oulie and Per Dyrssen, he is the son of a farming family who is now in business, and he is of the same solid mould as they. Probably he comes from Østerdal: if a man in Sigrid Undset's novels of contemporary life has anything in him, then he usually has his origin there. His moral notions about faithfulness in love and marriage are old-fashioned. Even with regard to mere questions of conventional rules, he knows instinctively that they guard something which life requires should be guarded. Uni struggles against his protective and chivalrous love. Only when she has experienced failure as an actress does she first learn to appreciate him. She knows that she must sacrifice her self-centred dream of happiness, the false fairy-gold; she knows even that there is perhaps some longing within her which will never be satisfied in Kristian Hjelde's home. "But no one shall ever know of that." With this good intention the story ends. Whether Uni is equal to her task we learn later in the story called *Mrs Hjelde*.

Sigrid Undset also wrote verse in these early days. Three poems by her were published in *Samtiden* in 1908, and in 1910 she published the collection called *Youth*. There are echoes of folk-poetry in *Grief (Sorgen)* and *Folk-tune (Folketone)*, while the ballad *Eternal Love (Evig kjærlighet)* is a grimly humorous commentary in verse on her prose stories—themselves full of poetry—on the theme of love's fairy-gold:

> *Came a girl to Saint Peter, weeping sore,*
> *To look for her lover within Heaven's door.*
>
> *"I don't know him at all," said Saint Peter then,*
> *"Best go and seek him amongst the men."*
>
> *She sought him low, she sought him high,*
> *But her lover's face she could nowhere spy.*
>
> *So she wandered down to the gate of Hell,—*
> *It seemed familiar, she knew it well.*
>
> *Scarce had she knocked upon the door*
> *When her lover was standing there before.*

*   *   *

> *With loving arms she wreathed his head:*
> *"We've always been used to the warmth," she said.*

46

Most of her poems are expressions of a longing for something to worship. "Eternity, I saw your face tonight," is a line in one of them. One is reminded of Henry Vaughan's "I saw Eternity the other night", although at that time Sigrid Undset certainly had no acquaintance with the great English mystical poets of the seventeenth century. There is no mystic revelation in her poetry—only this longing for some divinity to adore. Her verse is only totally alive, however, when she is writing of the longing itself, the naked yearning of youth, as for example in *Steensgaten*. Here and there one finds an echo of Nils Collett Vogt, but the poem remains her own:

> *Sometimes I wander to and fro,*
> *Most on spring evenings bright and long,*
> *In parts we have left long since, I know,*
> *But parts where I lived when I was young.*
>
> *The same old houses, more worn-out*
> *With poverty and grey decay;*
> *Though now more buildings crowd about,*
> *For still the town has spread this way.*
>
> *But yet beyond stands Blaasen hill,*
> *With paths made by street-urchins' feet,*
> *With rubbish, paper-bags and peel—*
> *I walk there knowing all I meet.*
>
> *   *   *
>
> *There are the same old games and romps,*
> *The swarm of youngsters, big and small,*
> *Playing with dolls in the dog-rose clumps—*
> *Against the sky how wild they call!*
>
> *This street to me is very dear,*
> *For all its gloom and ugliness,—*
> *Desire was the lesson I learnt here,*
> *Desire for all I could not possess.*

These first books by Sigrid Undset appeared at about the same time as the new realistic poetry of Olaf Bull, Herman Wildenvey and Arnulf Øverland, and the new realistic prose of authors like Olav Duun, Johan Falkberget, Nini Roll Anker and Kristian Elster. There is an affinity between Sigrid Undset and these others. She has most in common with Olav Duun and Arnulf Øverland, sharing with the one a powerful attraction to the past and with the other characteristic feelings of loneliness and longing. But with the exception of Falkberget, she is alone in introducing a religious motive, slight though it is in its first manifestation. Her closest spiritual allies were outside Norway—men like Paul Claudel, Charles Péguy and G. K. Chesterton. At that time she could scarcely have known of their existence. Ten years were to pass before she took her place with them and the other great Christian authors of the twentieth century.

CHAPTER III

Italy: Jenny

AFTER *Mrs Marta Oulie* and *The Happy Age*, Sigrid Undset could feel confident enough in her ability as an author to give up her secretarial post with a good conscience. She received a travelling scholarship from the Government, and in 1909 set out on her first journey abroad. In Berlin she paid a visit to the old directors of the A.E.G. firm: she had written so many letters to them that she wanted to meet the people she had been in contact with. They were amiable old gentlemen; but otherwise she did not take to the Germans. It was true that they could be kind in their way, but she was struck by their arrogance, their boundless self-importance and their nationalism. "They lived in an atmosphere of self-importance," she wrote, "convinced that whatever they do is the only right and proper thing to be done." Theirs was the care of the whole world—in that they showed an admirable unanimity. She had intended a longer stay but could stand no more than eight weeks there. Via Bamberg, Rothenburg, Dinkelsbühl and Munich, she made her way to Rome. There she lived first in a boarding-house, but it was not long before she took a small flat in the Via Fratina. She kept away from the stream of Scandinavian and other tourists, and had more intimate contact with a smaller circle, which included amongst others Kitty Kamstrup and Helene Fagstad from Lillehammer. "A Roman tavern is almost cheerless without her [Kitty Kamstrup's] face, shining a glowing red, at the end of the table," are her words in a letter to Nini Roll Anker. Helene Fagstad provided some characteristics for the capricious

49

and fascinating Francesca in *Jenny*. In Rome Sigrid Undset also met the man she was later to marry, A. C. Svarstad the painter.

In the new surroundings and in the confidence of her own powers, her youth blossomed afresh. All who remember her from these years confirm the report of her beauty and of the good humour she created in her circle of close friends. She knew so much—in effect she knew the whole town, *Roma Æterna*, beforehand,—and she was such an entertaining story-teller. She would often fill evening after evening with tales and legends from the Middle Ages, and they never grew tired of listening to her. She employed her most delicate art in shocking people with her remarks, when she thought the occasion was appropriate. A rather patronising lady asked, "I hear that you are an authoress, Miss Undset. Tell me, in what genre do you write?" Sigrid Undset answered, in the most matter-of-fact tone, "In the immoral."

She wrote little "letters from abroad" for the newspaper *Aftenposten*. Amongst them is the enchanting *Children in Ara Cœli (Barna i Araceli)*, in which she tells of a visit to the church there on the feast of the Epiphany. Children, boys and girls of six or seven, were acting scenes from the sacred story, while admiring parents stood around, proud of the cleverness of their child actors; nearby people knelt in prayer, undisturbed by the performance. "Oh yes, there is no doubt that the Italians are very backward. Perhaps they don't even have anything called 'mother's-meetings'. I don't believe that Italian parents ever discuss how they are to win the trust of their children. For then the children in Ara Cœli would scarcely have come forward and acted their parts with such wonderful confidence. God knows, there is precious little pedagogy here. It was as if nothing had brushed the dew off these young souls."

In the summer of 1910 she went on to Paris. Her descriptive letters from there, *Père Lachaise and Belville* and *Out Over the Roof-Tops (Utover takene)*, are not so full of pleasure

at what she sees as are her Italian letters, but they sparkle
with life and startling observations. "Amongst other things,
this thought occurred to me: what are vegetarians to use for
boots?" But more serious problems also engage her attention, including for instance the rights of women. "Some
years ago we introduced a new marriage ceremony at home.
It was demanded by women's circles, who objected to the
command that a wife should be submissive to her husband.
So we disposed of the words of the Bible, 'Thy desire shall
be to thy husband, and he shall rule over thee'; and, as far
as I can see, of Saint Paul's words too, 'Wives, be submissive
to your husbands, even as Sara was submissive to Abraham
and called him Lord'.[1] But did not these ladies consider
that, if a woman goes to the altar, not wishing to hear such
words, then she must do so at her own risk? For these
selfsame words carry nature's own legal prescription for
marriage: that a woman shall marry the man whom she
can call her lord—and no one else."

In the autumn of 1910 she was back in Oslo, settling
down in her old home with her mother and two sisters, who
now lived in Eilert Sundt's Street. It was at this time that
Nini Roll Anker got to know her and became her friend;
they shared the same views on various questions to do with
the suffragette movement—on that movement's depreciation
of motherhood, for example. Nini Roll Anker used to visit
Sigrid Undset at her mother's house, and she received, as did
everyone else who came there—"the happy few"—the
impression of that remarkable atmosphere of ancient culture
which permeated the home. Even as a gifted and celebrated
author, Sigrid Undset was still able to limit her circle of
friends. Those who were especially near to her were Nils
Collett Vogt, Kristian and Ragnhild Elster, Peter and Anna
Egge, and the imaginative narrative-writer, Regine Normann. She admired Nils Collett Vogt's poetry; Egge and

---

[1] The reference seems to be to the First Epistle of St. Peter, iii. 1, 6.—
TRANSLATOR.

Elster portrayed character with a realism closely related to her own; and Regine Normann at least believed in ghosts. But first and foremost she liked them because of their genuine and honest humanity.

Nini Roll Anker gives a sketch of Sigrid Undset at this time of her life: "Everything about her stirred the imagination: the large eyes with that extraordinary glance which seemed as much turned inwards as outwards, but which still seized every detail of her surroundings with the precision betrayed so clearly in her books; the beautiful slender hands, which on a rare occasion, as the conversation took her, would move most expressively; the lazy voice without marked intonation and with the slightest trace of Danish pronunciation in single words. She was strikingly beautiful, slim as a boy, and with a suggestion of classical perfection about her head which she seldom moved. She took short steps when she walked, and there was something reminiscent of a sleepwalker in her whole movement. But from her whole physique one could sense the strength and power of endurance which stood her in such good stead later in life."

In 1911 she was working on *Jenny*. She stayed at the little boarding-house in Bundefjord in the summer and worked hard. "If only this wretched book will turn out well," she writes to Nini Roll Anker. "S. [Signe] says it is *dreadful*, but certainly good. It is certainly the first, I wish the second were true too."

Jenny, like *Mrs Marta Oulie*, is also a kind of *roman expérimental*. Its tone is quite different, however, since in *Jenny* the author experiments with the possibilities lying within herself, and in making them actual she identifies herself with their extension into reality. In consequence, the novel has the character of a confession. Jenny belongs with the young women in *The Happy Age*, related not so much to Edele Hammer and Uni, both of whom succeed at last in making a compromise between their dreams and reality, as to Charlotte Hedels, who could find no object for her consuming longing and took her own life.

It is Charlotte's story which is told in new and profounder
form in *Jenny*,—a love-story, sordid and unpleasant, but
with a brilliance lent to it by Italy, Rome and the Campagna,
by the life which blossoms in it, by the writer's joy in art and
nature, and by the dream which comes true. Helge Gram,
a young archaeologist, stands on the Pincio on his first
evening in Rome and watches the sun go down. "At last,
now at last, there was a sight richer than all his dreams.
Helge whispered out over his dream-city, whose streets his
foot had never trod, whose houses sheltered not a soul he
knew,—'Rome, Rome, eternal Rome.' And in his lonely
soul he grew shy and afraid because he was so touched to the
heart."

There is not only the sheen of Italy over *Jenny*; one also
finds occasionally a supernatural element. This is due to
Jenny herself, for the foundation on which her character is
built is her inherent religious nature. She is in fact intensely
religious, longing to serve someone she sets higher than herself. But she does not believe in God. If she has faith in
anything, it is in herself and her own strength. How far will
that carry her?—that is the theme of the book.

Jenny has grown beyond the self-engrossed narcissism
of youth; she is twenty-eight when we meet her. Her younger
years have been hard and wearing; like most of her acquaintances, she was flung into the struggle for existence
before she had grown up. Any youthful illusions have been
knocked out of her, but she remains unbroken; she has not
lost her joy in life or the courage to go on fighting. She has
seen that there are some people who have the power to
maintain their integrity. "And simply the fact that there
are some who will not let life degrade them is enough to make
one optimistic." The one irreparable hurt we can suffer
is always something we deserve: of that, at least, she has no
doubt. She has schooled her will to control her emotions and
impulses. If they should ever master her and destroy her
self-respect, she feels it would be best to shoot herself: this

c   53

reflection is her sheet-anchor. She has given up her post as an elementary-school mistress, but she can find no satisfaction in art or work—they do not lift her out of her loneliness. Beneath Jenny's moral barricade beats a trembling heart which longs for love, for a man she can respect and whose authority she can feel. She despises the temporary, casual liaisons "on which people embark, knowing full well that they will grow tired of one another." She will meet her lord unsullied, "renounce all the small cheap joys, reserve every power in expectation of the one great joy— which *perhaps*—perhaps will never come." Jenny's ideal of purity is no camouflaged dread of sex; it springs from her unconscious religious feelings. "Jenny Winge knelt down on a straw stool, her hands folded on the desk in front, her head tilted back a little." Helge Gram thought to himself that presumably Miss Winge trifled in some small way with Catholicism. But he knew little about Jenny or of the nature of that exactingness which impelled her to take her place amongst those who knelt. She describes it to herself: "Happy all the same not to be contented. They are happy, the people who have never simply said 'Thank you' and knuckled under to a life of poverty. But all the same, I have faith in my dreams,—I call nothing happiness if it's not the happiness I required. I still believe such happiness exists. If it does not exist for me, then it was I who failed, it was I who was a foolish virgin who could not watch and wait for the bridegroom. But the wise virgins shall meet him and go into his house and dance."

Jenny might have preserved her integrity in two ways. She could have waited until the man she must irresistibly love came to her, or she could have gone on waiting and waiting for the bridegroom who never came. Neither of these possibilities is realised. Her life's ideal founders completely. She is not as strong as she believed, and she experiences one defeat after another. On two occasions, she loses her way in love-affairs which prove utterly disappointing and humiliating. First, in her relations with Helge Gram, she is carried away on a surge of emotion, with which is mingled something of a protective and mothering feeling for the gauche young man; perhaps too there was some desire in her to make the experiment and to be like the rest for once. She feels it humiliating, as if she had thrown away a part of herself. Her relations with Helge's father cannot help her—they prove still more degrading. His love is complete and strong, but she has nothing to give in return. Here the scene is laid in Oslo, and there is a glaring contrast between the Italian setting and the oppressive and confined life in the home of Helge's parents in Welhaven's Street. But it is not the surroundings which break her; it is her own life-force which is destroyed. When she comes back to Rome and the artist, Gunnar Heggen, meets her with his love, she is finished, burnt out. She loves and admires him, but she is not the woman she wanted to be. She cannot accept his love and she knows of nowhere to turn for help. The mountain to be climbed was too high. She sees no other way out but death: she does not reflect on her action—it happens "with a sudden jerk".

What strikes us in Jenny's character is not, as it was said when the book first appeared, her "proud uprightness", which makes her take life into her own hands and kill herself when she has lost her self-respect. This uprightness is simply not there. In reality, there is nothing sublime about Jenny's suicide. She is merely one who gives up the struggle and lets herself sink. But her fate, her tragic attempt to break out of her isolation and to free herself from herself, is none the less gripping for that.

Jenny is one of the most distinctive women characters in Norwegian literature. It would not seem out of the way to compare her to Ibsen's Nora and Gunnar Heiberg's Karen. But how far removed she stands from them both! Unthinkable that Jenny, when *her* dream of the wonderful is shattered, could possibly be transformed into a champion of the suffragette movement and sally forth into society to bring about legal reform. If she had done so, it would at any rate only have been to reintroduce the old laws, which those who followed in Nora's footsteps had succeeded in repealing. But Jenny can blame no external circumstances —it is she who has proved inadequate. As for Karen, her self-worshipping eroticism has nothing in common with Jenny's dream of love. Jenny is no less exacting in her demands than Nora and Karen, but it is alway on herself in the first place that those demands are made. It is not simply that she is more intelligent than they—there is in her a spiritual ferment, a more highly developed consciousness, with which Nora and Karen are unacquainted.

Einar Skavlen could write with full justice: "*Jenny*, besides being of considerable importance as a literary work, reveals to us also a fermentation, in which thoughts and feelings undergo a slow process of change" (*Samtiden*, 1912).

CHAPTER IV

Taking Stock

JENNY occasioned a violent scandal in suffragette circles. The book was selected for discussion at a meeting of the Club for Women's Suffrage on February 19th 1912. They were seething with indignation, writes Nini Roll Anker. Tirades were poured out against the author of the book, against men, love and literature. Sigrid Undset was herself present. "I do not remember very much of this meeting" she wrote some years afterwards; "I thought it was so much the essence of comedy that I had enough to do watching and listening to the ladies. . . . I sat and waited for them to start beating one another about the head with their handbags, but unfortunately it never got so far." Fernanda Nissen, Regina Normann and Nini Roll Anker attempted to calm the storm, but with little success. The only one who preserved her tranquillity quite undisturbed was Sigrid Undset. She took no part in the discussion, and when the chairman asked her if she was offended and disappointed at the book's reception, she answered with her usual unfathomable glance, "No, on the contrary. I expected nothing else."

The scandal was partly due to the boldly realistic description in some of the scenes in the book. But the essential reason was that people did not like the characterisation of this woman as a being so much more closely dependent on her sexual nature than men. It was felt that the human value of womankind was thereby reduced, and that it told against women's equality with men.

Later that spring, Sigrid Undset again went abroad. The journey first took her to Belgium, where her marriage to A.C. Svarstad took place in the office of the consul in Antwerp. Svarstad was divorced and had three children from his first marriage. He was a brusque headstrong man with bad nerves. He had nevertheless a keen intelligence and possessed to the full the courage of his convictions. He had a sensitive artist's mind, being a painter with an extremely individual colour-sense and with the deepest respect for technical ability. His pictures of scenes from the industrial quarter on the east side of Oslo are well known— seen through his artist's eyes, evanescent qualities of loveliness have been immortalised, qualities not unlike those which Sigrid Undset has captured in her descriptions of poor grey surroundings in the city of her childhood and youth.

The newly-wed couple went from Antwerp to London, where they lived in Hammersmith. Svarstad painted, while Sigrid Undset worked at stories which later appeared in the collection called *Poor Fortunes (Fattige skjæbner)*. She enjoyed being in England—it was an old love. "I have always felt affection for England," she says. "London is enchanting. Except for Rome, I know no city I like so much," she writes to Nini Roll Anker just after her arrival. She absorbed herself in the English literature of the Renaissance period, in Webster, Massinger and Marlowe. Of Webster she writes, "It is enchanting to read something that makes you tuck your feet up under you in rapture—and for me at least it is a wonderfully fascinating thing that these burning, flaming outbursts, centuries old though they are, can enthrall us so absolutely and so miraculously,—wonderfully fascinating too that there is something in life which will never be different, whatever happens."

She does not however forget the affairs of the moment. She comes across Mrs. Charlotte Perkins Gilman's book, *Man-made World, or Our Androcentric Culture*, and sends an

Sigrid Undset: painting by A. C. Svarstad, Rome 1911
(*Rasmus Meyer Collection, Bergen*)

article on it to *Samtiden*. It was called *Some Reflections on the Suffragette Movement* and, though not particularly challenging, was heretical enough to give offence in orthodox circles.

In December 1912, the couple settled down in Rome and took an attic apartment in the Via Fratina, where they had first met three years before. Later that winter their first child was born. Care of the baby and of the home took time. She is somewhat regretful that she is "an unhandy housewife"—we follow her all this time through the letters she wrote to Nini Roll Anker—and she is moved "almost to tears of joy" when she is successful with some new recipe.

She works on an address she is to give in the Students' Union in Oslo. She tells Nini Roll Anker that it is to deal with the Fourth Commandment. "On the duty of parents to live their lives in a way which makes it possible for children to honour their father and mother. Confidence, warmth of affection, tenderness and the rest, may all be very well, but other people can provide them more effectively and more abundantly than parents. At home one must learn reverence, and to be able to honour one's father and mother is something for which no substitute is possible. I shall probably say something about love for one's country as well—not the love which boasts of being Norwegian or English (and Englishmen and Norwegians alike have been guilty in this respect)—but the love which *does* something and says, 'This I do in the sacred name of my country'. The fate of Scott and his companions has made a deeper impression on me than anything else at this time, excepting only the baby—it is, indeed, the only thing other than the baby which has struck really deep into my thoughts."

The child did not make proper progress. She had hoped that when spring and the warm weather came, the Italian sun would put everything right, but in the heat the baby fell ill. A children's doctor advised her to return to Norway at once, and there the baby's health gradually improved. Svarstad returned from Italy, and they rented a house out at Ski, half-an-hour's journey from Oslo, so that he could have his studio in the city.

Nini Roll Anker has given us a description of their home at Ski: "There was not much furniture, but every piece was beautiful and most of it was old. She has always rejected anything which approaches the luxurious, but her feeling for line and form is exceptionally sure and true; and from the time she made this first home at Ski, all her possessions have merged one by one into a harmonious whole, so that today [Mrs. Anker is thinking of Sigrid Undset's home in Lillehammer] her home shows one of Norway's most individual and lovely interiors."

Her second child came while they were living at Ski, and she also had Svarstad's three children from his former marriage to look after. They lived for some time with her in the new home, and when they were not staying there, they were always coming out for Sunday visits. She had some help with the housework, but she looked after the children and prepared the meals herself. Mrs Anker says that guests never had any impression of rush or bustle. "When she presided over the white table-cloth in the panelled living-room, sitting upright with her hair plaited over the back of her head in big bright braids, her movements calm as she dispensed food and drink to us guests, she had a tranquillity and dignity which always reminded me of the household mistresses of times long past."

She wrote continuously. In the summer of 1914 she produced her great novel *Spring (Vaaren)*, a story of domestic and married life, which, though not a book full of sunshine, is nevertheless written in praise and honour of the home. In the summer of 1915 she wrote *The Story of King Arthur and His Knights of the Round Table*. It was during the war and the book was inspired by her love for England.

In the summer of 1916, the family left Ski and moved into apartments on the first floor of a wooden house in East Aker, the last house in Trondhjemsvei towards Sinsen. It was detached and light here, and Sigrid Undset enjoyed her new surroundings. The step-children came to live with her again. They attended school, and every morning she was up to see them on their way; after dinner she sat with them while they did their homework. A great sorrow befell her here. Her third child, a little girl, began to show symptoms of the disease which was to overtake her. The little piece called *From the Jottings of a Crippled Woman* (*Julehelg*, 1912) stands as a remarkable witness of her self-projection into such a fate. Nini Roll Anker is undoubtedly right when she says that the years in Sinsen were the hardest in Sigrid Undset's life. But she had a strong constitution and imperishable strength of will. In 1917 she had finished *The Splinter from the Magic Mirror* (*Splinten av troldspeilet*); in 1918 *The Wise Virgins* (*De kloge jomfruer*) was ready.

In the New Year of 1919, a small party was held at the Svarstads' home. With a few others, there were present old Mrs Undset, Nini Roll Anker, Nils Collett Vogt and Johan Ellefsen, the young author of those two intelligent and deeply human novels, *Doktor Friis* and *Advokat Wagner*. "As we went down towards the tram," writes Mrs Anker, "I remember that Johan Ellefsen stopped and straightened his lanky form as if seeking inspiration, and he said: 'One of those stars is Sigrid Undset's—one day her genius will hang like that, shining over the North.'"

Sigrid Undset's writing in these years from 1912 to 1919, —talks, articles, short stories and novels,—has fundamentally the character of a critical appraisal of the period which had fostered her, more or less the period just preceding the first World War. She does not castigate. She makes things clear, presents facts and interprets them. Her criticism is levelled against the individualism which is egotistic and which refuses to acknowledge its obligations. This she exposes, no matter in what fine phrases it may be concealed; such statements, for example, as, "I have the right to do what I please with my own life". She is not yet a Christian, but she realises to the full that if individualism loses its footing in an ethical system based on the Christian evaluation of the human being, then the individual is cut adrift from the bonds of human society and will become the slave either of himself or of some external authority, which cannot comprehend that any single person is of intrinsic value.

From the start, her opposition to the suffragette movement depended on this basic consideration, this rejection of irresponsible individualism.

In the article, *Some Reflections on the Suffragette Movement,* which she submitted from England in 1912, she expresses the deepest respect for and gratitude towards the champions of women's rights at home and abroad, and begs us not to forget "how often these women have voluntarily undergone the bitterest martyrdom a woman can ever suffer—the martyrdom of ridicule". But she does not accept the common doctrine that man has tyrannised over woman through thousands of years. It is modern social developments which have made the rights of women such a burning issue. The industrial revolution squeezed out home industries and made the maintenance of numerous women in one household superfluous and unprofitable; and it was only then that it became imperative for women, who had no men to represent their interests in society, to see to it that some influence over the decisive factors in life lay in their hands. That marriage need no longer be a sort of charitable institution is the great good which the movement has brought about. But when women believe that, simply because they are women, they have some special capacity not given to men to establish peace on earth, for instance—then according to Sigrid Undset, they are living in a dream-world, like those people who believe that the workers' movement will create a universal brotherhood and make war impossible. In her view feminine "chatter about world peace and disarmament" can only be frivolous.

The real substance of her criticism does not lie, however, in this ironic attitude towards feminine dreams of world-reform. It finds its mark in something closely connected with the real advance which the movement has signified. What she regards as a danger, as a development completely off the rails, is the desire to make the unmarried self-sufficient woman the norm and ideal, and in that way reduce woman's standing in life's most fundamental aspect, undermining her position as wife and mother. For her, the essential problem concerning the rights of women in our time lies in the struggle *against* this development. Even if being a mother, she writes, means in itself no more than a physical fact— "this physical fact means that in human society a woman can become nothing better than a good mother, and nothing much worse than a bad one".

In March 1914 she gave her great address *The Fourth Commandment* in the Students' Union in Oslo. She begins with a reference to the fate of Scott of the Antarctic and his comrades—"that wonderfully beautiful tragedy played out down there in the Antarctic winter". It is impossible "to measure the immeasurable riches which these men, who now lie dead down there in the eternal winter, have bequeathed to the whole of humanity". The event illustrates and symbolises civilisation's first demand—that the individual should be willing to sacrifice his own life for the sake of another greater life. This demand is the first seed-leaf of civilisation and has found its universally applicable formula in the words of the Gospel, "And fear not them which kill the body".

The origin of civilisation lies not in the individual's consciousness of his rights, but of his duties. Civilisation means

plainly and simply civic awareness. To say that an individual
is cultured must imply that he recognises himself as having
even greater responsibilities. "The more highly cultured,
the less confined the obligation." A cultured individual
feels himself bound in duty towards "the inheritance which
has been left to all humanity by men whose names are, as
we say, immortal, and by every single anonymous individual
who has felt the urge to exert to the uttermost the capabilities
he owned; the inheritance bequeathed by scientists and
artists, soldiers and priests, nurses and explorers, doctors
and gardeners, schoolmistresses and nursemaids, carpenters
and weavers. The products of civilisation are diphtheria
serum and the story of Thermopylæ, motor-cars and aero-
planes and the work of forgotten mothers in bringing up
their children, the masterpieces of old craftsmen and the
Catholic legends of the saints."

The heritage of civilisation is toilsome to acquire, and it
is easily squandered. Knowledge and skill are not enough;
technical progress holds no guarantee that the cultural
inheritance will be preserved and enriched. Techniques are
tools which may be used as easily, indeed more easily, to
destroy than to build up and protect. A child must have
knowledge of certain facts so that it can find its bearings in
the world. But the civilised human being must above all
learn reverence and obedience. Without piety the heritage
of culture is forfeited. "Because civilised man must have
someone to honour and obey, civilisation everywhere has
created a God."

The most precious heirlooms of civilisation are moral
concepts: "The bright and ancient words, names of virtues
which are half-way to becoming ridiculous—these are the
words which people need to learn—strength, wisdom,
justice, truth, compassion, chastity, moderation, courage—
and all the other shining words." The man to whom these
words mean nothing relapses into barbarism. These virtues
are unalterable, even though their technical application

in social life may vary according to different circumstances of time and place.

Sigrid Undset speaks most nobly of loyalty and chastity. She takes Brutus in Shakespeare's *Julius Caesar* as an example to illustrate the nature and inner affinity of these virtues. When on the field of Philippi, Brutus sees that he has lost everything—the cause for which he fought, the friends who had fought beside him, the wife who had been one with him in heart and soul—he says:

> *Countrymen,*
> *My heart doth joy that yet, in all my life,*
> *I found no man but he was true to me.*

To this Sigrid Undset adds the following characteristic commentary: "These words, uttered as they are on the threshold of physical death, express the finest thought ever to enter a man's mind. They contain in themselves the very nature of chastity—the chastity which is nothing else but passion for intellectual beauty. Note that in the ancient pictorial language of the human family the symbols for chastity and for clarity of mind are most often identical—moonbeams, running water, shining steel, and the pearl in whose sheen all colours melt harmoniously together. Like every other virtue, chastity is in reality an intellectual concept and not a physical quality. It means love for everything immaculate and steadfast, aversion to everything which a man feels himself sullied in touching. Brutus feels such triumphant joy at the moment of death, when he knows he will experience no more of life, because he can now say for certain that disloyalty, which is for him the ugliest sin, has never come near him." She adds that, unfortunately, this is not something which happens in real life. But Shakespeare's Brutus is "the noblest figure in all literature".

The example which will show that it is possible to try to

live up to the standard represented by the cardinal virtues must come first of all from those who bear the gravest responsibilities in the family group—the parents in relation to their children. The family home and the national home, each is a nucleus of civilisation. If a home is laid waste or a country subjugated, then one of the workshops of civilisation is destroyed. For that reason, a civilised individual is willing to defend his home and his country, no matter the cost. "If I had a son who denied me and said he had no motherland, I could only answer, 'I know not the man, death has taken my son from me'—the second death of which Saint Francis speaks, damnation."

She sees clearly that religion and culture are indissolubly linked together, but her views are still to some extent conditioned by the half-rationalistic evolutionary doctrines common to the age. Man has created God in his own image. He is a concept, the common denominator of all that is good; He is a symbol, and not the origin and source of all virtue.

The modern idea of progress, which has no object outside the temporal world, is rejected as something which severs the innermost thread of life in man. The work of civilisation points towards a transcendental goal. There is significance in the words she appends to a quotation from Saint Francis of Assisi. He writes, "Blessed are they who are resigned to your most holy will so that the second death cannot hurt them;" and she adds, "To possess this prayer written in the heart is to possess culture."

The ethical and religious idealism in the *Fourth Commandment* has an important place in the spiritual history of the Norwegian people. The reaction of the eighteen-nineties against naturalism had made itself felt in Norway as in other European countries. Here, however, it was limited in the range of its effects. Where the movement went deeper and exerted an influence on the individual attitude, the result was most often a somewhat primitive mysticism and cults which worshipped impulse and instinct, vitality, youth, the life-force and the like.

Sigrid Undset certainly had Hamsun's famous talk, *Honour the Young* (*Ærer de unge*), in mind when she planned her own address. It was in 1907 that Hamsun had given his witty speech on "the Soul's" age of decline, in which he extolled Life (with a capital L), youth and vitality. The immortal longings, which were already apparent as an undercurrent in Sigrid Undset's earliest realistic writing, appear now clearly defined throughout her talk, though perhaps nowhere more characteristically than in the description of old age with which she closes. Despite physical collapse, age, in her eyes, can be possessed of superhuman value: "For the most part, the older we get, the uglier we get. Features grow blurred as new layers of fat or shrinking muscles play havoc with them, and the body loses its buoyancy and erectness. Only the noblest kind of beauty can suffer age, the beauty which belongs to the bone-formations themselves—the fine chiselling of the cranium and the harmonious composition of the skeleton; or, on the other hand, age can be withstood by the beauty which is completely incorporeal and shines out from a human personality. Most of us will not grow wiser with the years, neither wiser nor better. The wisdom of age and the goodness of age are rare. But whoever has encountered them knows that they are more profound than all other wisdom and goodness. They are the same qualities as those we have had to attribute to God. The beauty of age is the rarest beauty. But it is mightier, it grips and touches us more nearly, it is high above all other beauty in the world. To gain it for himself is the best that any man can do for his child."

The new elements in Sigrid Undset's writing in the years immediately following *Jenny* do not make themselves evident in any obvious or demonstrative fashion. The material in *Poor Fortunes* (1912), *Spring* (1914), *The Splinter*

of the Magic Mirror (1917) and *The Wise Virgins* (1918) is on
the whole the same as before—the reality of everyday life,
with characters drawn chiefly from the middle-classes in Oslo.
But to some extent, the attitude towards the material is
different. The tone of personal confession, which often
breaks through in her earliest writing, is now rarely heard,
and when heard is damped down and restrained. The
presentation of a story may now take on a retrospective
character. On the whole, her material now seems to have
been set at a greater distance. The intensity may be less,
but not the fervour of her mind, not the sympathy and
clearsightedness. There may be keen and clever satire,
as in the descriptions of poor souls like Selma Brøtter and
Miss Smith Tellefsen, but there is satire too of the tenderest
kind, where it trembles on the verge between tears and
laughter, as in the masterly short story *Simonsen*, where the
dissonances of life are resolved in a humour closely related
to that of Dickens.

A love-story forms the theme of her great novel, *Spring*,
as it does in other of her books. But the history of the
child-love of Torkild Christiansen and Rose Wegener, their
engagement and marriage, the collapse of that marriage
and its resurrection, is related from a clearly conscious
social point of view. *Spring* is essentially a social novel, and
the story of Torkild and Rose and the people around them
is used to throw light on a concrete social phenomenon—
the home. All the characters are seen in relation to the
homes from which they come, and they are explained,
tried and judged, according to their ability to shoulder
the responsibilities which the home, as the protocell of
the life of society and of all higher culture, thrusts upon
them.

The ideal of the home is most strongly alive in Torkild.
The home of his own childhood has not been a home at all,
not because economic conditions were unfavourable, but
because its essential fabric had been ruined. His parents

had lived "their own feverish lives" so forcefully that, where his father and mother were in the same house, there could never be a home. On one occasion, Torkild talks to his sister about the home from which they have come. She has decided on the line she will follow, and expresses her maxim for life thus: "It seems that the individual's most sacred right is to lead his own life." At bottom she admires her father, who had the courage to break away from the home—"courage to lead his own life after his own inclination—without reference to others". Torkild is not impressed, —"For there is no one who can live his own life without plunging into the lives of others." With Torkild's love for Rose has been merged his reverence for her home, which has made her what she is, and his longing to create with her the home which he has never had. His brother is his rival. His nature is coarser and more ruthless, but for him, too, Rose symbolises a dream of home. He says to her, "You come from a home—everything about you, even the smallest things, show that. Everywhere you went would become home, the man you loved would have his home in you."

The picture of the Danish-born widow, Mrs. Wegener, and of her efforts to hold the home together, despite straitened circumstances and her husband's death, is given reverently and without sentimentality, yet always with freshness and humour. Mrs Wegener's feeling for the family, her "soul's paganism", a religion which no rationalist free-thinker could ever master, is not to be uprooted. When Rose and Torkild decide that they will not be confirmed, because there were some things in which they could not believe, she answers, "Such airs!" She doesn't really believe in them either: "But that didn't make one a freethinker—by free-thinkers she meant people who expressed themselves with bad taste and in ill-bred loud voices and who tried to deny what was to her a fact: the immortality of life. She knew it, because her dear dead ones were just as near to her as the living; she felt them about her continually and received messages from them in many ways."

This home had been, from Torkild's boyhood days, a place of peace where he sought refuge from the eternal unpleasantness of his own "home". Instinctively and driven by an impulse of self-preservation, he would retire to this life-giving little oasis. The qualities he had with which to face life had been fostered and nurtured here.

Rose is a woman not unlike Jenny. She has the same idealistic nature, the same proud and militant virginity, the same feeling for chastity and loyalty, and that longing for a love which can take her wholly and completely and "tear her out of herself". She too fails to meet the man who can give her what she has dreamed of. She feels affection for Torkild, but "he was *not* the one she longed for". But she knows what she is doing when she joins fortunes with him, and she does not share the accommodating views on marriage of the period. It is a matter "of most desperate earnest".

The home which Torkild and Rose make together is at first neither one thing nor the other. It is on its way to ruin; but it survives. As they come to regard life as a problem they are setting out to solve together, so in the same degree they become closer to one another.

One is not carried away by the story of Torkild and Rose as by the tragedy of Jenny, but the book, although weaker in composition, is no less truthful and no less soundly based psychologically.

Closely related to *Spring* is *The Splinter of the Magic Mirror* (1917). It consists of two stories, one called *Mrs Hjelde*, the other *Harriet Waage*, though it is not by accident that the two are set side by side in the same volume. Each completes and illuminates the other, a fact suggested by the circumstance that Mrs Hjelde and Mrs Waage live in neighbouring apartments in the same house. Sigrid Undset is not a writer who makes much use of such external pointers.

The essential fact is that the two women, each in her own way and in quite sharp contrast to the other, are illustrations of the same case. Each of them has a splinter of the magic mirror in her eye—the mirror which, according to Hans Andersen, made people see everything crooked and distorted.

Mrs Hjelde's story tells how she removes the splinter and so discovers the reality in front of her. Her marriage with Kristian has gone badly not because they were not in love, or because of the vexations of everyday life, or because of the birth of their children—something which gave her an opportunity to develop her small talents as an actress—but simply because neither of them has become truly aware of the other. They have gone on in this way, each waiting to be discovered by the other. "Every nasty thing they had done to each other sprang from the fact that they had not *known*." Kristian has a splinter of the looking-glass too. Faithful as he is, his excellence has made him a little unimaginative. He shows little sensibility for what lives inside his wife's mind, for the small dreams which she has had to sacrifice of becoming an actress. On her side, she has never realised what security he has given her. But just when she is on the verge of slipping and yielding to the excitement and passion called forth in her by their friend, Vegard, something makes her draw back. She is restrained by loyalty to her husband, who has had such unquestioning faith in her and on it based his whole life. His trust appeals to all that is good and strong in her. His faith being absolute, it is for her to make the choice. She experiences "the coveted moment when someone has control over all the days of his or her life". Vegard tries to combat her belief. Uni talks, he says, "just as if we had free will". "However it may be," she answers, "we have a will. I have said that I wanted to live only for this home, but I couldn't do it—that only means that I would willingly have done it if it had been easier, but the price was something more than I was willing

71

to pay. As for our will—it is only a question of whether I command my will or my will commands me." She takes up the struggle, for in it she finds something "wonderful and alluring"—on the one hand, "repudiation of responsibility and rebellion" and on the other, "fulfilment of duty and obedience". She knows she must make a sacrifice in choosing the path of duty. She elects to be what she is,"an ordinary average human being". "And I can no more run away from my place than a soldier can in battle." Uni must sacrifice something, but what she gains is more precious. It may be happiness or unhappiness, but she has retrieved the substance of her life, and she can now accept the hours of happiness which life offers. "Happiness, she thought, happiness—how is it that I, at my age, can go on believing in happiness—or doubting it either? The happiness which Kristian and I once knew together; the happiness which is like a falling star—in the brief moment it glimmers, you must remember and wish for your heart's desire; in the brief moment when love's caresses are new and make the blood flutter, you must understand and take control of all your life. And happiness in the children is such a matter of course that you never think about it. Joy shines in your heart at every moment—at the funny things they say and the comical first steps they take. There is joy in their natural wisdom and the caresses they bring to you and every feeling you share with them; joy even in some fear which has passed over and in a sickness which has not proved dangerous after all. We don't think that all these thousands of tiny gleams are happiness; still, they are the things we live on. No one could live unless he was happy in-between-whiles. But we don't think about it when it's there. We really only take notice of ourselves when we are unhappy. As long as I have my children I know that I can go on living, and gladly too, no matter how everything else in life turns out for me."

Harriet Waage lives in more comfortable circumstances

than Mrs Hjelde. She is not acquainted with the nagging
of the petty worries of everyday life. But her position is all
the more difficult. Her husband, it is true, is in a position to
make the same demands regarding the inviolability of
marriage as Kristian Hjelde, but he has nothing of the same
warmth and strength. She has moreover, to some extent,
allowed herself to be thrust into this marriage. Her upbringing does not make it easier for her. She has learnt that
religion is something obsolete, of which progressive people
have rid themselves long since. Her father was an honest
free-thinker. It sounded so attractive—Nature is the great
God, and happiness is to bend before whatever Nature wills
for us. It suited Harriet admirably, for must not her pleasure
and whim be also Nature's will? Nature demanded its
rights and no power could resist that demand. The tempter
finds easy prey; there is no struggle in Harriet Waage's soul.
It is blissful, she feels, to let oneself be carried away—at
last! But in her life there remains neither joy nor sorrow.
She sees before her only the gaping jaws of emptiness. The
sensible woman doctor, Alice Falch—the counterpart of
Miss Bormann in *Mrs Hjelde*—tries to explain to her how
deluded they have all been—she and Harriet and the whole
age they live in. If one believed in God, she says, then one
would see everything, and above all the people one lived
with, in relation to Him, and not primarily in relation to
oneself. Amongst other things, one would know when something was sinful. "It must surely then have been better
to pay for a precious hour of happiness with a whole lifetime of penance and prayer than to go on fretting oneself
into grey hairs and bitterness." This woman doctor, who
must also be counted a psychologist, is pointing out the way
from the egocentric to the theocentric.

The three stories in *The Wise Virgins* deal with characters
from a more ordinary background. Here, as elsewhere, it
is the common stuff of humanity that Sigrid Undset wishes
to grasp, the instincts, needs and desires which may appear

differently under different circumstances, but which remain essentially the same. The lives of the servant-girl, Helene Johansen, the dressmaker Fanny Erdahl, Klara in the factory and Emma in the milk-shop, are different in their externals from the lives of Mrs Hjelde and Mrs Waage. Nevertheless, where something primary like the sexual life is concerned, they belong to the same human family. Some women feel their sex as an impulse to live for someone else; others feel it as something which gives them the right to live on someone else. But splinters of the magic mirror have not perhaps reached so many of those who live in the milieu described in *The Wise Virgins*. All three stories are variations on the same theme of mother and child. The development of the theme in *Tjodolf* is masterly. The story of Helene Johansen's love for a little child she has taken to herself but must give up again, is one of Sigrid Undset's loveliest pieces on the theme of mother-love. It is built up with an eye to the effect of contrast, but there is nothing schematic or artificial about it. The opposition between the frivolous Fanny Erdahl, the real mother of the child, and the steadfast Helene, has the same solid basis in living reality as the opposition between Harriet Waage and Uni Hjelde in *The Splinter of the Magic Mirror*, or between the homes of Torkild Kristiansen and Rose Wegener in *Spring*. *Tjodolf* is more than a deeply moving and pathetic story: it bears the stamp of greatness, because in a flash it gives us insight into a mother's love, the love which in the psychic organism of this one human being is the very thread of life.

Some critics spoke scornfully of the moral messages in *Spring*, *The Splinter of the Magic Mirror* and *The Wise Virgins*. But this is not moralising literature—a better name for it would be literature about moral values and moral heroism. Somewhere in her collection of essays, *A Woman's Point of View* (*Et kvindesynspunkt*, 1919), she says, "Ordinary people— that is, people who are neither specially gifted nor specially handicapped in any way—set free their innermost selves

74

first and foremost in family life; the normal human being, without particular attributes of good or evil, has always had a central shrine, the fireside of his home, and from there he has kindled all his altar-fires." It is fire from this central shrine which has kindled the flame in this writing of hers.

CHAPTER V

Discovering Christianity

ONE CAN never do more than form a very incomplete
picture of the factors which have decided an
individual's religious development. It is easy to succumb
to the temptation of making generalisations, which may
seem reasonable but which, on closer inspection, either
prove untenable or are so all-embracing that they tell us
nothing or almost nothing, of the case under examination.
For it is indeed the truth, as Sigrid Undset writes in *They
Sought the Ancient Paths*, that there are as many roads to
faith as there are human minds.

It may therefore seem rash to attempt to describe the road
which Sigrid Undset followed. On the other hand, she has
given us some guidance, directly in her autobiographical
fragments, essays, and contributions to current debate, but
chiefly indirectly, in her imaginative writing. It is possible
for us to catch some glimpses of the road.

On several occasions, Sigrid Undset has told us that in her
youth she did not believe in anything. In her childhood and
youth she had felt in spite of everything that she stood in
some very distant and indefinite relationship with the religion
she knew, but already when she was of an age for confirmation, it was clear to her that she did not believe in it. Afterwards, she says, she invented for herself a kind of "humanistic
private religion". As late as 1915, she writes to Nini Roll
Anker and says, "Mama frets a little now and then, because
she did not manage to bring us up in 'religion'" but she
adds, "I am grateful to her for nothing more than for the

healthy un-Christian atmosphere of our home." She had just read Regine Normann's *The Kingdom Coming* (*Riket som kommer*), and had been shocked by the picture there revealed of the prayer-meeting and revivalist Christianity of Norway.

In reality, Sigrid Undset was by then far on the road towards religion. In the same letter, she says that she had never nursed any ill-will towards Christianity—"for it was a fact that I scarcely knew what it was. I looked on the Church as an extremely picturesque ruin standing somewhere in the background". But now she has begun to see it from a closer angle. She has read a little, she says, of what the priests write. "I have also read a number of Catholic authors, both new and old—the Church of Rome has at any rate form; it does not irritate the intelligence as do these diverse Protestant sects. Once poured out of the form of the Roman Church, the whole of Christianity has the effect on me of an unsuccessful, burst omelette. . . . Well, that's something else we have to thank the Germans for. They are undeniably vastly superior when it comes to taking modern science and technique into the service of barbarity and torture—there is a genius in their war-material from Big Bertha down to their anthrax tablets—but in my opinion, *das Volk der Dichter und Denker* both write and think damned badly."

Three years later, in the important article, *Women and the World War* (*Kvinderne og Verdenskrigen*), we find not only a positive discussion of the Church and Christianity, but clear and explicit conclusions drawn from it. In spite of all the Church's failings and of all the shameful stains on her past, "the history of the Church is like a paradigm which illustrates the fate of the divine when it comes into human hands. It has been the bearer of those ideals which cannot die—the majority of men do not succeed in living in accordance with them, but they always rediscover after a time that they cannot live without them".

Torn from their context, these remarks might give the impression that there was in her development a radical split between before and after, a turning-point which meant a complete break with what had gone before; they might suggest that her nature was of the kind called by Høffding, following Francis Newman (Cardinal Newman's brother), "twice-born". But such is scarcely the case, although naturally she has passed through crises. There is, it seems, nothing in her religious evolution which answers to a sudden revelation of the divine mystery and of the truth of Christianity, such as appeared to Pascal, and nothing similar to the religious experience which overwhelmed the eighteen-year-old Paul Claudel in Notre Dame on Christmas Day, 1886,—an experience which has justly been called *un choc spirituel*, and which, from that day, made him see the world in a completely new light. In Sigrid Undset we find no such sudden *illuminatio*, no spiritual earthquake which throws down the existing structure and clears the ground for a new one. One has the impression that Christianity gradually revealed itself to Sigrid Undset, as a confirmation of what thought and experience had already taught her. It is in this that her discovery of Christianity consists—a discovery like that spoken of by G. K. Chesterton in *Orthodoxy*: "—my startling discovery that the whole thing had been discovered before. It had been discovered by Christianity." If one is to speak of conversion in the case of Sigrid Undset, then it can only be in reference to the decision of her will to accept as true what her intellect already recognized as true. Continuity is the characteristic of her religious evolution. She does not belong amongst the "twice-born", but amongst those personalities who have been led throughout their lives by the same fundamental feeling or general disposition.

She was not, as we have seen, brought up to be anti-religious. There is an obvious mental and organic connection between the emotional life and world-picture of the child on the one hand, and the ethical and religious motives in her pre-Christian writing on the other. A feeling for the "sacred" is always present, the sacred in that word's specifically religious significance, as it is described in Rudolf Otto's analysis, *Das Heilige*. The sacred is the numinous—the totally *other*, the elevated and inviolable which is an object of both fear and love. A sense of the sacred may be counted peculiar to mankind. Chesterton says that with the raising of an altar, man first distinguishes himself from the beast. As a child, Sigrid Undset felt the divine as something opposed to the security of the home, something set overpoweringly high. But, as she says in the account she gave in 1936 of her conversion, it was a long time before she had the courage to conceive of "a God who was the 'Absolute Other', yet at the same time a Person who could hold communion with me—whose ways were not my ways, whose will could be separated, unconditionally and definitely, from my will, but who could, nevertheless, lead me into His ways and bring my will into harmony with His own."

The strong and healthy well-spring in her mind of scepticism and criticism was a protection for her natural religious feeling. She had always had to smile at "cheerful and straightforward atheism". And to her it was a perfect comedy, when people summoned God, as it were, before their own tribunal, and thought that they were in no position to believe in Him when there was so much misery and injustice in the world, or because the world was not governed in accordance with their notion of how a God should govern. Most free-thinkers she met were at bottom angry with God; they suffered from theophobia. "I know that I was the same—most of the time" (*They Sought the Ancient Paths*).

But not for a moment was she inclined to fall down and worship the new gods of the age. As the years passed, she saw more and more clearly through the mythology which was being swallowed under the labels of Evolution, Progress, Science. Evolution is the "saving doctrine" of the nineteenth century, writes Vilhelm Grønbech. But what of human will? asks Sigrid Undset. "I know very well that most people, probably ninety-nine in every hundred, will say that evolution leads in that direction, and so forth. For me, however, the really burning question of this age is precisely this: how far is 'evolution' a mystical God Almighty, who sends us hither and thither? Or is it not perhaps our *will* which in the main decides the course evolution is to take? It seems to me at least that a certain element of mass-suggestion lies at the bottom of this modern conviction of evolution's arbitrary nature." The modern evolutionary mythology urged her on to a study of the doctrines of the transcendental and supernatural, which for nineteen centuries had stood as the foundations of Christianity. She comes to the conclusion that the doctrine of evolution makes at least as great "a demand on man's never-failing power to believe in something he knows nothing about", as does the story of the Creation. She absorbs herself in the study of Christian dogma, freed from any preconceived idea that its doctrines are no more than "fossilised and ossified" relics of the past. In those doctrines, in the way in which Christianity formulates its experience of a world of spiritual reality, she finds more reason than in the so-called scientific outlook. Perhaps it was the Christian metaphysics which had really been in operation all the time? Christianity was in no worse agreement with the knowledge of human nature gained from experience of life, from philosophy and literature. It taught, at any rate, that whether "evolution" led to Heaven or to Hell, it was the individual who was responsible for the way he chose to take (*A Woman's Point of View*).

It is in the light of this that her opposition to certain features of the suffragette movement, discussed above, should be viewed. It was precisely in this movement that she found telling evidence of the fate in store, when people surrendered themselves to the power of "evolution" or based their control of that power on a so-called "scientific outlook".

She wrote three great articles on this theme, *Women and the World War*, mentioned above, *Confusion of Ideas*, (*Begrepsforvirring*), occasioned by Katti Aiker Møller's pamphlet, *A Birth-Policy* for *Women* (*Kvindernes fødselspolitik*), and *Postscript* (*Efterskrift*). In 1919 she published the three together in the book called *A Woman's Point of View*, for the edification of "like-minded reactionaries". She had little faith that anyone else would bother with them—"evolution" went a different way!

Confusion of Ideas marks a high point in Sigrid Undset's polemic writing. "I usually write articles when I am angry," she once said. There is no doubt that she was in a particularly angry mood when she wrote this. But her feelings have not obscured her understanding. She is not merely slashing in her wit and scorn, but illuminatingly clear-headed, raising problems into clear and sharp relief and setting them in a perspective far plainer than that normally found in Norwegian intellectual debate.

She begins with a criticism of the various popular formulations of the "so-called scientific outlook", and indicates the confusion which arises when people do not understand how to distinguish between science on the one hand and an attitude to life on the other. It can be remarked that she has profited from the definition of science given her by her father: "Science—it meant that people experimented and conjectured and worked to find out whether this was perhaps a method by which to get to know something for certain. But after many men had worked on one thing for several generations, all the certainty gained was only a tiny crumb. And even in a matter where we now believe we have certain knowledge—why, one fine day somebody or other will make a discovery which puts the whole question in a different light, and we shall be obliged to start all over again from the beginning" (*Eleven Years*).

Thanks to the "half-learned and quarter-learned vagrants" of science, and sometimes to the uncritical thinking of honest scientists, people are accepting "the materialist outlook" in steadily growing measure. Fortunately, she writes, the working classes of society have gone a long way towards improving their economic condition; but unfortunately they have swallowed a good deal of the materialist evaluation of life which is common amongst the economically superior classes. "The pseudo-scientific jargon, the soulless materialism and the failing realisation of the distinction between spiritual, organic and mechanical phenomena, are now all served up by workers' papers throughout the world. Many an honest glove-maker in Europe now knows no more of the difference between a hand-shake, a hand and the glove that fits it, than does an upper-class clothes-hanger."

If anyone wishes to see how far the confusion of ideas and spiritual disorientation of our times may be carried, she says, he may read with profit Kitti Anker Møller's pamphlet, *A Birth-Policy for Women*. "It is far from dull." In this essay, when a family is spoken of, it seems to mean something after the style of an industrial concern, where a man engages a woman to bear and bring up his children. "The State" and "Society" are conceived as mystic beings to whom women are to hand over their children for a cash-payment, much as a woman who sews at home delivers children's trousers to the draper. Mrs Møller had recommended the wage-dispute of economics as a means of improving the lot of mothers. Women should go on strike. "We must try to get down to a level of ten births per thousand of the population." Then people will understand that the State must take the care of the young into its own hands—and "a new era for motherhood will dawn"!

Mrs Anker Møller is certainly idealistic, says Sigrid Undset, and there is no need to take "her particular brand of nonsense" seriously or be offended by it. "She will scarcely persuade any grown woman to follow her in her conception of women as so many 'birth-machines' and of children as so many 'goods'." Nevertheless, her chain of reasoning is symptomatic. It has its roots in the economic-materialistic approach to problems, and this is a "threat to the dignity of human life".

She maintains that, with social conditions as they are, it is often necessary for a mother to undertake duties and labours which may be beyond her strength "to a heart-breaking degree". What society can do to help her is good. But all the same, motherhood is not a job like others. Motherhood is *life*, it is sacred. Mothers are not helped if people close their eyes to the fact that nature has given women a different function from men in human propagation and different tasks in the life of a society. "If one considers the fundamentally different positions in which the two sexes stand with regard to the child whose quickening to life can only be brought about by both of them together, all talk about equality between men and women becomes utter nonsense." "Any woman who becomes a good mother is greater than most ministers of state, for she is indispensable in her work, whereas very many ministers can be replaced with advantage."

Christianity's high esteem and sacred regard for motherhood and its religious consecration of marriage helped perhaps more than anything else to open Sigrid Undset's eyes to the truth of the faith. In scarcely any other of her articles is her personal concern so strongly marked as in *Postscript*, where she collects her reflections on the position of women in society and presents them from a Christian point of view, taking as her motto the ballad lines,

> *How on the earth can the green grass grow,*
> *When a son can't find his mother true?*

There she writes that it may well be true that Christianity is not alone in having found it desirable to give marriage a religious consecration, and not alone in having called "the names of Father, Mother and Son holy". "But it is, however, certain that Christianity with its doctrines of the pure virgin, *Virgo Virginum*, as the door through which the Creator returned as the Saviour to His creation; of the gentle mother, *Mater Amabilis,* into whose hands God entrusted Himself as a true man-child, little and hungry and cold; of the sorrowful mother, *Mater Dolorosa*, who saw her innocent son tortured and killed; of the *Mater Misericordiæ*, who intercedes for the transgressors and for those who mourn, who had shelter under the cloak of her compassion for all who believed and prayed, even when belief and prayer sprang from man's most pitiable dread and cowardice—it is this Christianity which has given to women the most honourable position they have as yet been assigned."

The significance of the catastrophe which broke over European civilisation with the outbreak of the first World War was immediately clear to Sigrid Undset. The war and the following years confirmed her doubts concerning the ideas in which most people had believed: liberalism with its moral core scooped out, the suffragette movement, nationalism, socialism, pacifism. All this wishful thinking, she writes, could avail little, "for it refused to see human nature as it really is". Nini Roll Anker says that her letters from this period are stamped with dread and horror. And she did indeed feel horror. With her, however, the outcome could not be the collapse of her ideals. Precisely that moral heroism in which she had put her faith was now to stand the test. It was during the first World War that she discovered the Christian foundation for the faith which, in her address to the Students' Union, she had formulated in the words of the Gospel, "And fear not them which kill the body".

Naturally she was not blind to the fact that the war revolved round the interests of the Great Powers. But that did not exclude the fact that the war meant something more than a struggle for dominion and influence.

In her view, the general mode of thought had nowhere departed further from the Christian evaluation of mankind than in Germany. And are we not to admit the truth of her view? Hegel's deification of the State, Bismarck's power-politics, and the philosophy of power of Marx and Nietzsche had not failed to produce results. All of them, willingly or unwittingly, had prepared the soil for the cultivation of a cynical contempt for law, for the growth of the worship of brute force, for policies of violence and the totalitarian state.

In the article *Women and the World War*, written in June 1918 when German arms could still appear victorious, she writes that, unless it is stopped, German militarism will crush humanity. "It is therefore neither envy nor rancour, not even in the first place fear, which moves those who shudder to hear of Germany's advance. It is a matter of instinctively taking sides with the humanity which has its solid frame, its backbone, deep inside itself, and which presents only a soft and sensitive covering of flesh to the world as it struggles with the ugly claws of the giant crab."

In such a time of war, she says, we cannot avoid personifying the nations. We are forced to leave to one side the individual goodness and badness of the single Englishman, Frenchman and German. "We realise the souls of the nations as personalities." They become symbols.

It was no accident that in the first year of the war she gave us her masterly version of Malory's *Morte d'Arthur* in *Tales of King Arthur and the Knights of the Round Table*. In a different connection, she writes, "The central fact in the legends of King Arthur is that it was a Christian people who were being pressed back, foot by foot, fighting against the floods of Angles and Saxons from the North Sea coast of Germany." The chivalrous literature of Europe, which flourished at the same time as the Icelandic family-saga and which treated motives which were the common property of all the peoples gathered by the Church into a firm cultural unity, had long been familiar to her. As a child, she had been taken by a story in a Danish Christmas volume, *The Holy Graal* by Johannes Jørgensen. She knew the Old Norse redaction of the legendary Celtic material about King Arthur and his knights, the *Bretasögur*; but Malory's work came to take first place in her affections. It was one of her favourite books. In Rome she had told stories from it to her friends, and they had begged her to give them a book of King Arthur in Norwegian. Now was a fitting time to re-tell the stories of *Spes Britonum*, the hope of the Britons, as he is called in one ancient chronicle. He told of something indestructible in the English spirit, of something also in the fundamental stuff of humanity which never alters. "Manners and customs are always changing greatly as times pass and people's beliefs are altered and they think differently about many things. But the human heart alters not a whit through all the days."

She wrote the sensitive and penetrating article, *Three Sisters*, on Charlotte, Emily and Anne Brontë, women who were firm as rock in their faith in the immortal soul, which, she says, modern pedagogues and demagogues have tried to root out as a relic from a primitive stage, a result of the arrogant and excessive value man has set on himself. Her other writing from this time, *Postscript* for example, is also full of references to English literature, to Chaucer, Langland's *Piers Plowman*, Dickens and others. Everywhere she finds evidence of man's "incurable pride"—his faith in immortality.

Above all, it was France which during the first World War was for her the symbol of all the values "whose loss would seem greatest to us". France, she says in a review written in 1917 of Marika Stjernstedt's book *The Soul of France* (*Frankrikes sjæl*), has scattered her seed-corn through all the ages. "In the history of Europe, France has been like the fairy-godmother in our tales, and it will be a terrible thing if the fairy-godmother is vanquished." The Church's conception

of a Christian humanity has been advanced first and foremost by France. It has not come to fulfilment, but neither
has the French Revolution's conception of a republic under
the banner of liberty, equality, fraternity. And yet these
two ideas are immortal conceptions, to which sooner or
later men will return. The fateful event in Europe's history
was when the democratic and Christian ideals parted company. "The freedom we love has come to us with Christianity," wrote Erik Vullum. "Democracy," writes Sigrid
Undset, "is after all one of the ideals for which Christianity
has fought—and one which her retainers have occasionally
betrayed. When, towards the end of the eighteenth century,
the Church was in one of its sleepy moods, it put the idea of
democracy away, much as one puts a ring on the dressing-
table before going to bed. France, Rome's eldest daughter,
picked it up and wore it."

In *A Study of History*, Arnold Toynbee writes that in
"times of trouble" weaker spirits can feel that reality is
nothing but chaos. On others the situation can have the
opposite effect. Observation of the external confusion can
serve to sharpen one's perception of the eternal spiritual
unity, despite the disorganisation and disintegration.

This unity was revealed to Sigrid Undset during the first
World War. The war and its attendant disturbances did
more than confirm the justice of her own analysis of the age,
and the truth of her demonstration of its spiritual decadence.
She saw also what had been lacking; she knew that something had been lost which must be found again. She discovers Christianity not only as a subjective experience, but
also as an objective reality, a concrete historical fact. Its
unwearying tenacity of life did more than impress her—it
took possession of her. In spite of the most energetic attempts to destroy it, refute it, revile it, in spite of the most
desperate onslaughts upon it, still it stood immovable and
taught what it had always taught: that man is created in
God's image and called to be His servant in the world. For

Sigrid Undset

the whole of mankind, as for the individual, it is a matter of "obvious and vital importance whether a man believes that we have created God or God has created us". Whether it is the duties of everyday life or the great tasks sometimes set before us which are in question, it is equally important to remember the ancient phrase, *Soli Deo Gloria*—these are her concluding words in *A Woman's Point of View*.

It is significant of the distance between Sigrid Undset's thought and the general outlook amongst Norwegian intellectuals of the time that even Ronald Fangen, in his review of this article, declares that he is not in a position to appreciate "what Mrs Undset really means by her reference to the ancient phrase, *Soli Deo Gloria*".

Sigrid Undset was led to Christianity not by sentiment or emotion, not by "revival" or "experiences", but by her love for truth, the absolute truth. It is, in fact, as simple as that. For when everything has been said about external events, about psychological and social factors which may have affected her religious development, hindering it or helping it, giving it its particular colour and character— behind it all stands the indisputable fact: her unquenchable thirst for knowledge. The account given by Sigrid Undset herself of her conversion, in the concentrated passages of the little book, *They Sought the Ancient Paths*, is in agreement with all the knowledge a detached observer can have of the case. The question of absolute truth is never put aside. Her intellectual honesty made it impossible for her to reject Christianity before she knew what Christianity was. Study and reflection were driving forces. "That one truth should really exist, one and one only in which all other truth ends"— this she had in effect always believed; and if she had sometimes despaired of the possibility of ever finding absolute truth, then she must admit it was because of a secret hope that it *was* impossible, for she imagined that life would then perhaps lose its enchantment, even that then "there would be an end of our freedom".

"There are many who are content to sit on the church-steps and sun themselves," she once said. Her search for the absolute had brought her so far—to the church-steps. She had discovered the light and warmth which came from within the Church. She could not remain sitting there on the steps; she must discover from where the Church obtained its light and warmth—she knocked on the door and enquired. There could, of course, be no question of proof in the scientific sense of the word. It bore no relation, she says, to anything like a "chain of descent in botany"; but it had to do with a chain of descent of another kind, about which biology, if it rests content as a science and does not usurp the place of religion, cannot possibly give information. What she learnt of man's spiritual chain of descent convinced her—all the pieces fell into place. Mankind's solidarity lay in this— that we are all "inheritors together of an insolvent estate, after the bankruptcy of the Fall". There remained the question of harmonising her will with her understanding and its new achievement—for "in the end, it is with the will that man makes his choice and decides whether he will isolate himself in himself and the hell of egotism, or whether he will give himself into the power of God and so be freed from the shackles of self-worship, to face eternal possibilities".

For Sigrid Undset it was a matter of course to turn to the Catholic Church, the Church which from the first beginnings had carried the Gospel to mankind. Only there was to be found authentic knowledge of the faith's transmission: it was not to be had in all the other sects and congregations and individuals with their subjective experiences and their notions as to what Christianity originally was and what Jesus had really meant. "I had nothing else to do but go to a priest and ask to be instructed in all that the Catholic Church taught as true." Father Karl Kjelstrup gave her that instruction, and on November 24th 1924 she was received into the ancient Church of our forefathers. Only with great difficulty is it possible for a biographer to give an account of this last phase. The divine love met every-thing in her which reached out to grasp the truth. It is a mystery. She writes, "Only supernatural intervention can save us from ourselves."

At Easter-time in 1925 she was in Italy. In a "letter from abroad", published in the Christmas volume *The Bells Are Ringing (Kimer i klokker)*, she describes her participation in a service in the church on Monte Cassino. For once Sigrid Undset tells us directly of her own religious experience. "All these tens of thousands in the church, believers and doubters and unbelievers, the prayerful and the curious, good Catholics and bad Catholics—the first pope in his tomb and all the popes who are at rest around him, and the last pope who kneels in prayer, while around him now prayers rise up from this church like the flood-tide. The prayers spread themselves like an atmosphere over those who pray and those who do not pray, as does the cry that mounts up to all those who have gone before, innumerable myriads of dead Christians, begging that they too will pray with us. I cannot explain it properly: it is, I feel, as if the names of ideas which I have accepted purely with my intellect were suddenly illuminated by an object-lesson. The Christian congregation, the catholicity of the Church, the communion of the saints, the relative reality of time and space and, outside the eggshell, the absolute reality of eternity, the untold souls who have lived through the ages, each of them imprisoned in the ravelled net of his own self, from which no doctrine can set us free, only God, and He only by dying on a cross. One can recognise it as the only thing which makes sense in the end: one can understand it, but sometimes it seems as if one can *see* it. . . . Something of the kind I can see this evening also—the fleetingness of time and every event, the reality of eternity and of the spirit; but actually I see it bare of ceremony, as a sober truth—even so, it is no less overwhelming."

Her writing showed new and healthy buds. They un-folded in a strength and beauty unparalleled in her earlier work; and they grew to trees, which took their place amongst the proudest and most magnificent of all those which stand outlined against the luminous sky of Scandinavian literature.

CHAPTER VI

Writing About the Middle Ages

FROM the summer of 1919 until April 1940, the town of Lillehammer forms the background of Sigrid Undset's life. She does not give up travelling; she visits Italy, England, Scotland and the Orkneys, Iceland, and the neighbouring countries, Denmark, Sweden, Finland and Gotland. But her home is in Lillehammer and her roots strike deep in this idyllic little town. It is situated "out in the country", as people say, at the northern end of Lake Mjøsa, and covers the entrance to Gudbrandsdal, the valley of valleys, in extent, influence and tradition the richest in Norway. Saint Olav had passed through it on one of his journeys, the most memorable of them all, when nine hundred years ago he brought the light of Christianity to Norway. Throughout the centuries, pilgrims had tramped over the Dovre mountains on their way to Saint Olav's shrine in Christ Church at Nidaros. Their path at times lay near the track which the Dovre railway now cuts through valley and plain, glen and mountain, linking Lillehammer directly with the capital of ancient Norway and the city of the holy king. South of Lillehammer lies Hamar, with its old cathedral-ruins. "Bishop's Hamar" plays an important role in Sigrid Undset's novels about the medieval period—in *Olav Audunsson of Hestviken* especially, with its account of Bishop Torfinn's activities. In 1924 a Catholic church was built here, the chapel of Saint Torfinn.

At first sight, Lillehammer as a town seems worthy of no special notice. But it possesses atmosphere, a charm and temper peculiarly its own. It has always had a powerful

The Middle Ages

attraction for artists, especially for painters, but that has never entailed the loss of its special character. It is and remains itself, with its great stretches of woodland, its luxuriant countryside and the old farms nestling close within, the whole majestically crowned by the harmoniously rounded hills which recede far into the distance.

One institution owned by the town is indeed worthy of attention: Maihaugen, one of Norway's richest and loveliest national museums, where the genius of the keeper, Anders Sandvig, has succeeded in collecting a hoard of relics of the culture of the past. One of the most monumental of these museum-pieces consists of the farm-buildings from Bjørnstad. They are not from the Middle Ages—in all probability they were first built in the seventeenth century—but visiting them one is led involuntarily to think of the farm Jørundgaard in *Kristin Lavransdatter*. Sigrid Undset has provided the English edition of this novel with a sketch of Jørundgaard, which agrees in all essentials with the farm from Bjørnstad.

Sigrid Undset came to Lillehammer in July 1919; with her came the children, and she was pregnant with her third child. Svarstad had bought a house in Kampen in Oslo, and it was intended that, for the time being, husband and wife should live apart. Now and then Svarstad visited his family in Lillehammer. But the rift between him and his wife grew steadily deeper—divorce was the only possibility. When Sigrid Undset was received into the Catholic Church the marriage was *ipso facto* declared null. She continued to look after her step-children like a mother.

She bought a house in Lillehammer, an old one from a farm in Sør-Frøn which its previous owner had transplanted down into the town. It is beautifully situated where the road to Nordseter begins to mount the hill and turn towards Østerdal. Some years later, in 1924, she had another old house from Gudbrandsdal moved from Dalsegg, near Hundorp, down to Lillehammer. The steep slope below the house was turned into a garden, an untrained but well

93

tended country garden, with trees and magnificent flowers. Sigrid Undset's passionate love for flowers was something that had to find expression.

The name she gave to her new home was Bjerkebæk— "just to irritate my Danish family," she would say with a smile. Bjerkebæk is the well-known name for "a Norse Norwegian from Norway". There was to be no doubt as to where she belonged. She has given a charming description of life at Bjerkebæk in the book *Happy Times in Norway* which she wrote during her exile in America.

The new environment would seem to have been favourable for literary production. Her plans for a great novel in a medieval setting could now be realised, plans she had conceived in early youth and to which she had clung tenaciously. But that this idea actually grew to such rich and wonderful reality remains, nevertheless, one of the great miracles of art. The Finno-Swedish writer, Jarl Hemmer, says that it is in itself remarkable that a mighty epos dealing with the Middle Ages of a nation should see the light of day, but that it should be created just at this time is quite overwhelming. "What the nature of this woman may be, who in the midst of a thousand crying questions of her own time sits down in sovereign isolation and brings dead centuries from the grave, remains a riddle."

As we know, it was the Romantics who, some hundred and fifty years ago, really discovered the Middle Ages. Their enthusiasm for this period was due to a reaction against the rationalism of the Age of Enlightenment; often it ended in escape into a dream-world. The powerful pull backwards in time which the Middle Ages exercised on men's minds had however a profounder origin than the mere need to flee from the contemporary world's lack of imagination. It was also a matter of spiritual regeneration, an energetic attempt to grasp through the centuries, and re-knit, the threads of an organic cultural development. It was realised that the Middle Ages were not simply the dark ages or *medium ævum*, which, for the humanists of the Renaissance and later for the rationalists, cast as it were a shadow between them and the glories of classical antiquity or the sun of "enlightenment". Men began to understand the Middle Ages from the point of view of that period's own assumptions, in the light of the religious idea which, at the beginning of the medieval period, had been formulated in terms of historical philosophy by the genius of Augustine, and which, through the expansion of the Church, had created on a wholly spiritual basis a European universalism. The truth glimmered in men's minds that it was in the Middle Ages that the real European community was born. "Christendom, or Europe" wrote Novalis.

Scholarship has confirmed what the Romantic writers perceived. No historian speaks now of the Dark Ages. The twelfth and thirteenth centuries stand in the history of European culture as one of the great creative epochs.

It was long before medieval Scandinavia was given a place in relation to Christian Europe. This delay was connected with another element in the Romantic Movement —the racial romanticism of the Germans, which excluded the northern lands from Europe. We meet the tendency already in Herder, about 1770. Of Charlemagne, for example, he writes that he took away the German's home, and therewith shut virtue out. Monks and swarms of priests, with the sword in one hand, the cross in the other, brought in the idolatry of the Pope. . . . and "poisoned the marrow of the people". Christian humanity was still for Herder a significant supra-national factor; but his words are symptomatic of the anti-European trend in the "Nordic Myth", which from his time had Germany as its centre of dissemination and which reached its climax in National Socialism. By then, the mysticism of race-biology had completely ousted Christian humanity.

Scandinavians of the nationalist-romantic school were also generally inclined to regard the people of the northern countries as outside the common civilisation of Europe. And when Scandinavia, by its conversion to Christianity, became a part of that community, it was in their view a purely superficial adherence. Like the neo-pagans of modern times, they considered the conversion of the Scandinavian peoples either as a break with the pristine creative spirit of the race, which had been seen in its glory and greatness in the Viking Age, for example, or as nothing more than a mere external phenomenon, a movement which, in reality, had nothing to do with the mass of the people. In later periods of Norwegian history—the time from the loss of national independence and the Reformation down to the present day—the picture drawn of the Middle Ages in Norway has varied, its colour, feeling and character depending on the ideas of the age in which it was produced. In the sixteenth-century *Chronicle of Hamar*, there is a touching leave-taking addressed to the Norway of the past, woeful and melancholy, like a farewell for ever: "O God the Father in Heaven, if we do not meet before, then God grant we may meet in Heaven. . . . *Vale, vale, vale*." For the generations which saw the achievement of the Eidsvoll constitution, the picture of ancient Norway is coloured by the feelings aroused by the re-birth of the nation and the late eighteenth-century enthusiasm for liberty. There is no lack of boastful and swaggering tones in the praise accorded to the Norwegians of early times—"a folk of giant race". They are Vikings, warriors, stalwart brothers-in-arms. "To take his sweetheart's kiss with chin hewn in half—that was the Norseman's way," are the words of the poet-priest, Claus Frimann, in his *Song of the Birkebeiner*. But the essential factor in their enthusiasm for ancient Norway was their view of the land as the age-old home of national liberty, "la ressource de la liberté de l'Europe", as Montesquieu wrote. There was to be found a society based on law, not on the arbitrary measures of a despot. In swelling alexandrines Nordahl Brun extolled the liberty of the nation in *Einar*

Tambarskjelve. The chieftain from Trøndelag declares to the despot, "You know the law of Norway—it behoves you to obey." Henrik Wergeland dreams of Norway's resurrection in the splendour of the great age of the thirteenth century:

> *From the ruins they would raise*
> *Haakon's hall and Olaf's church.*
> *Ha! And what was Akershus?*
> *Was it not the Norseman's work?*

The fact that the nation was so absorbed in its past prepared the way for a truly historical and critical knowledge of the medieval period. The rhetorical declamation, the poems that pledged and the speeches that celebrated, gave way to pragmatic research. P. A. Munch, Rudolf Keyser, C. R. Unger, Chr. A. Lange, M. B. Landstad and others wove a pattern not easily unravelled. After their time, the Middle Ages became an integral part of the nationality-conscious mind of the people.

In the first decades of the twentieth century, interest in the medieval history of Norway was extraordinarily alive. Eminent scholars like Magnus Olsen, Haakon Shetelig, A. W. Brøgger, Halvdan Koht, Harry Fett, Edvard Bull, Knut Liestøl, Fredrik Paasche, Sigurður Nordal, Oluf Kolsrud and others, shed new light on the period. Their investigations are modern and realistic. In determining the relative value of their sources, they examine the problem of saga-transmission with critical eyes; and they apply the methods and results of modern economic and social history to their study of the Middle Ages. Their modern and realistic attitude is finally not least evident in their investigations into ancient Norse religion. The basic ideas in Sophus Bugge's *Studies in the Origin of the Norse Religious and Heroic Legends* (*Studier over de nordiske gude- og heltesagns oprindelse*) prove valuable and fruitful. Magnus Olsen writes, "The confined view of the Romantics had to give way to breadth

97

of vision and the sense of reality." In place of the Romantic interpretation of "Germanic mythology" as a beautiful "symbolic language", the direct offspring of a resplendent Germanic or "Arian" divine world, comes archaeology, with its sociological emphasis, to help the historian to appreciate "the place of religion in life, in man's struggle for his daily bread". Greater psychological insight creates a sympathy which can "feel itself into the 'holiness' with which everything is permeated". And from studies in literary history one learns to take into account the individuality of the author, his religious personality, in the mythological poems.

An essential feature of the new medieval scholarship is a clear-sighted awareness of Scandinavia's coherence with the general cultural evolution of Europe, the crucial junction between Christianity and paganism, the place of the Catholic Church in the life of the people, and the whole Christian contribution. The problems were not of course new. They had long occupied both foreign and Scandinavian scholars. The conclusion generally reached was that the impulses from Christianity and the Catholic Church had not gone deep. This was the view both of Konrad Maurer and A. D. Jørgensen and of ecclesiastical historians like Rudolf Keyser and Bishop A. Chr. Bang. They believed that, in general, the heathen conceptions lived on, clad in Christian dress perhaps, but still fundamentally pagan. Protestant prejudice and ignorance where the culture, doctrine and essential nature of the Catholic Church were concerned, had influenced this point of view. Another real influence was the Romantic tendency to regard the pagan period—and not least the Viking Age—as the time which saw the most marvellous flowering of the "heroic spirit of the North".

It is a leading thought in the work of the writer, Hans E. Kinck, that contact with Christianity spoilt and hindered the free intellectual and spiritual life of paganism. His short story, *Mot ballade*, written as a reply to the medieval novels of Sigrid Undset, has its roots in the primitivism of the Romantic school. When Kinck spoke of "that power we call the Middle Ages", he thought of the meeting between the Germanic peoples and Roman-Christian civilisation. In his eyes, the measure of "greatness" depended on the ability of the new nations to keep this foreign civilisation out of their own life. We find a reminiscence of this same romantic attitude in Edvard Bull's *Nation and Church in the Middle Ages (Folk og kirke i middelalderen)*. Bull thinks he can demonstrate that it was impossible for the Church to teach sturdy Norwegian farmers to accept the Christian doctrine of humility, much less that of sin and grace. "It would have been a task for other men than the priests of the eleventh, twelfth and thirteenth centuries, to teach self-sufficient and independent Norwegian farmers that they were sinful mortals, who before everything else had need of grace and redemption."

A completely new approach to the medieval Christian culture of Norway first appears in the study of the history of art and literature. The pioneers are Harry Fett and Fredrik Paasche. Here too, the local and confined must give way to the vision which embraces all Europe. In his books, *Sculpture in Norway Under the Sverre Dynasty (Billedhuggerkunsten i Norge under Sverre-ætten*, 1908) and *Painting in Medieval Norway (Norges malerkunst i middelalderen*, 1917), Harry Fett dealt for the first time with our old pictorial art as if it were art. He gives it a place in the art-history of Europe, sets it in relation to the leading schools of the West, and shows how the mighty impulse contained in the Gothic ideal was also responsible for the creation of a great age of culture in Norway.

For Fredrik Paasche, surveying the medieval literature of the Northern countries, the great problem was how far Christianity—i.e. the Catholic Church—had been a living force in the minds of the Norwegian people. Old Norse Christian literature had received surprisingly little attention.

Unger's editions of texts like the Bible translation, *Stjórn* (i.e. God's government or "steering"), the sermon-collection called *The Old Norwegian Homily Book*, and legendary compilations like *Maríu Saga* and *Heilagra Manna Sögur*, came long after almost all the Icelandic saga-literature had been published and translated many times. Scholars had taken small account of the rich material which here lay ready to hand. Fredrik Paasche demonstrated the Christian element in the scaldic poetry and the poetic power and personal authenticity in the great Christian poems of the medieval period. The Christian religious poetry takes its place beside the pictorial arts, church architecture and lawmaking (in which the Christian ideas of justice and humanity enter), as a telling witness of the position occupied by the Church in the minds of men. Not the Viking forays, but the creative and constructive will towards peace and order, the desire for the beautiful and the spiritual elevation of existence—aspirations liberated by Christianity—come into the foreground as marking the greatest effort of the Norwegian medieval period. As the cathedral in Chartres spoke to Charles Péguy, so the cathedral in Trondheim spoke its noble language to Fredrik Paasche, telling of things sacred and imperishable: "How precious it is for a nation, to be able to see that its soul at that time had raised itself to such a mighty work, the grandest proof our ancient history can offer of the power which lay within the longing to overcome isolation and poverty."

In the introduction to her version of the story of Thorgils Arrbeinsstjup (*Flóamanna Saga*), Sigrid Undset speaks of her debt to the twentieth-century generation of scholars in the field of medieval Norse studies. She expresses her deep respect for Finnur Jónsson, "the great master in Norse literary history" before them. "None of us who have been occupied in the study of the medieval literature and history of Scandinavia can measure the debt we owe to Finnur Jónsson. But when it is a question of evaluating the artistic quality of the old writings, the impression he gives is most often remarkably dry and conventional." It was precisely in this respect that the new generation enjoyed a great advantage. "They had a feeling for the works as examples of literary art." "Sigurður Nordal is an author himself; he has written poetry and novels. Magnus Olsen and Fredrik Paasche have a good deal of the artist in them. And these three became the leading scholars in their field in the generation which followed Finnur Jónsson." It was Fredrik Paasche who became her chief guide. It was he who directed her attention to the rich deposits in the *Diplomatarium Norvegicum*. With the laws, this collection of letters and documents—lawsuits, testaments, inventories and the like— became one of the sources she used most in acquiring an assured knowledge of medieval social conditions.

But Sigrid Undset was not reduced to following in the leading-strings of the professionals. "One might say that I was brought up in history" she can justly declare. She is herself a historian, engaged on independent research. Her essay *On Ballads* (*Om folkeviser*, 1921) and her great study in religious history, *The Conversion in Norway* (*Trosskiftet i Norge*, in *Saga of Saints—Norske helgener—*1937), present not only new and original points of view, but are also remarkable for her sure critical sense in the treatment of sources and, above all, for her ability to judge men and their conduct in relation to the age and society in which they lived.[1]

Her psychological penetration makes it impossible for her to accept the commonly-held notion of the splendour of the Viking Age or the equally superficial idea of the grandeur of the pre-Christian family-society. Her rejection of the latter is an essential factor in her attitude. The violence and bitterness of spirit in the mythological and heroic poems of the Edda appear to her to be the results of an attitude to life which is determined by the conception of a merciless

[1] *Norske helgener* was written after the novels which portray medieval life, but express the same fundamental attitude.

fate. It was, however, most decisive for her point of view, that the family-sagas showed her how the individual was confined within a society which, though possessing organs for legal process and judgment, yet required the execution of law by the individual himself. When, as we have said, she can speak of the reading of *Njáls Saga* as a turning point in her life, it is because she gained from it a powerful impression of the psychological pressure which the family-society exercised on the individual. She is, it is true, aware that the ordained chieftain in the harrowed Iceland of the Sturlung Age may often have transferred the conflicts of his own experience into the stories of men who stood powerless before two irreconcilable moral duties: the Christian claim and that of the family-society. But nevertheless there is "a line from the heroic poems continued in the family-sagas, when these generally make us feel that the ethic of the family-society resulted in repugnance, strain and misfortune for the individual; whereas they much more seldom reveal the happiness and security which must have been enjoyed by many, in the confidence that they lived in a social circle to which they were firmly bound, and that on their natural bonds they could implicitly rely" (*Saga of Saints*).

"To suggest that the outlook of the Norse peoples before their contact with Christianity was one of radiant and imbecile optimism—a kind of genial faith, shining and vacant, full of rude fighting vigour—is a pretty unimaginative misrepresentation." Although she saw the stunted growths in the old family-society, she was not however blind to its noble features and moral virtues, the passion of men in that age for law and justice and, above all, for loyalty. Regard for these virtues shines through the story of Viga-Ljot and Vigdis. But their tragedy was played out in a world which had no knowledge of "a door which leads to freedom for the soul of every human being, even though his deeds and the deeds of others have their inevitable conquences and defeat here on earth" (*Saga of Saints*).

The ballads were a primary source for Sigrid Undset's re-creations from the medieval world. The first part of *Kristin Lavransdatter* is full of their poetry. And study of the ballads, especially the comparison of Danish and Norwegian types, gave support for her favourite theory— that the Christian evaluation of life had struck deeper roots in Norway than in the other Scandinavian countries—a theory directly opposed to that maintained by Edvard Bull in *Nation and Church in the Middle Ages*.

From her childhood, she had had the impression of an essential difference between the Norwegian and Danish ballads. The Danish poems put a greater strain on the emotions of the reader. Passion burns more fiercely and is communicated more directly, the violence is uglier and more brutal. The Norwegian ballads have more of a far-away touch of fairy-land. The combats of the hero with other heroes and in the land of trolls relegate the whole to a fantastic and supernatural world. The impression given is often gay and pleasing, and pain is expressed with such full-toned lyricism that "the echo in the mind is sweet, not harrowing."

She shows every restraint in attempting to explain this difference, and objections to her theory have been raised by Sverker Ek and others. But it is a brilliant hypothesis and very characteristic of Sigrid Undset's view of the Middle Ages. She believes that too much emphasis has been placed on the immediate influence of natural conditions in the development of the ballads, and too little on dissimilar social and political conditions in Denmark and Norway in the thirteenth century, the period when the ballad-dance was generally introduced. In Denmark it was a time of bloody feuds, between king and nobles and amongst the great men themselves. In Norway, from the reign of Haakon Haakonsson to the time of Magnus Smek, there was, judged by medieval standards, a unique period of peace. There was nothing to foster the growth of the knightly ballad in Norway as there was in Denmark. The particular Danish contribution to the ballad-treasury of Scandinavia was the "hard tone" of this "chivalric" poetry. "It is as if Danish youth, at a comparatively early stage, began to take less interest in the hero's journey to troll-land, and more in the young man who rides to the home of his father's slayer or forcibly abducts his ladylove." In a way, the normal life in Norway at this time was too cultured, too much restrained by law and equity, to provide a suitable milieu for the ballad. It was natural for the Norwegian ballad-poet to translate his subject into a world of fantasy and to tell of his hero's struggles against trolls and giantesses. To a certain extent, Norwegians had grown out of the conditions and the mentality which are necessary if the true knightly ballad is to thrive.

In this connection, the place which the legally established kingship had won in the consciousness of the people was, in combination with Christianity, of vital importance. Saint Olav, she writes, must have contributed towards the firm establishment of the old loyalty of the Norwegian people to the idea of kingship—even when they took arms in support of various pretenders. "Judging by what we find in saga and poem, it seems that the people must have taken him more closely to themselves than national saints have been in other countries—for in our medieval literature, Saint Olav appears as thoroughly Norwegian in build and as truly sanctified as the stave-church itself."

She can justly point to the thirteenth-century literature of Norway as a proof of the high standard of culture amongst the upper classes,—a literature written in the vernacular and of excellent quality. She stresses, as a particularly characteristic feature, its rich selection of religious writing, in every variety from *The King's Mirror*, that *vade mecum* of the "Christian gentleman", to pure theology and Old Testament translation. "I can confess without difficulty that a great part of this Old Norwegian literature of edification seems to me still very edifying at the present day. I think that the newspapers, for example, in place of their usual Sunday meditations, might profitably print translations from these works. From the Homily Book (which dates from the end of the twelfth century) might be selected first-rate sermons, like those for Lent, Christmas, Holy Innocents' Day, All Saints' Day, or the one for the consecration of a church, along with the beautiful translation of the Lord's Prayer. Or there are the thought-provoking dialogues between fear and courage, body and soul, etc. They might at least give the people of our own day some conception of what the Middle Ages understood by a Christian way of life and a Christian point of view."

She demonstrates the close connection between this general didactic literature and the religious element which is also a characteristic feature of the ballads. She maintains that one fact at least is certain: that the finest piece of folk-poetry in our possession was composed in Norway, the visionary *Dream-Poem* (*Draumkvædet*). It has a power unparalleled in folk-literature. It "carries thought away on the pilgrim paths, which lead over wild mountains and through the passes set round with boulder-country and snow fields and white peaks, towards Nidaros and its lead-roofed church and the spire's gilded vane, the organ-roar and the perfume of incense and holy Mass sung in its pillared hall. And in the midst of the rushing concourse of sights, the visionary soul remains sound and safely balanced—in that, Olav Aastason might be Saint Olav himself. The *Dream-Poem* is the great ballad in the Norse language—after Brother Gamli's touching *Harmsól*, on the sorrow of the sinful and the mercy of God, after *Sólarljóð*, with its mighty picture of a soul's progress from the world of the Eddic poems into the light of God the Almighty, the One and the Three."

In *The Conversion in Norway*, Sigrid Undset remarks on the indifference or lack of understanding which for so long characterised scholarship, when it came to treat the history of Catholic Norway and Scandinavia. In a period which extended over nearly five hundred years of the nation's history, scholars had, until recently, left unconsidered "the most important condition of man's existence—his religion and the institutions which fostered his religious life". She emphasises the way in which historians have been fettered by the Protestant prejudices which accepted, as a matter of course, the tradition that the Reformation meant the victory of true Christianity over the dark and idolatrous corruption of the pure Gospel in the Middle Ages. Even in the work of scholars like P. A Munch, Rudolf Keyser and Chr. A. Lange, this attitude had had some influence. "Precisely when the moment came to speak of religious life in the Middle Ages, their Lutheran imaginations failed them." What it had meant, for example, to the people themselves when they "instituted a Mass or entered a monastery, could not be imagined by them without a sort of pitying prejudice". In other cases, students of the period were bound by an unhistorical rationalism, which judged the past according to the ideas of their own time. They were deluded by a belief in evolution, a theory which held that, in an era of science and technology, religion was a stage long past and happily overcome. Others were entangled in their romantic racial conceptions or in Marxist abstractions which allowed them unconcernedly to apply the contemporary ideology of class-warfare to the past.

Sigrid Undset spared no effort in acquiring as much factual knowledge as possible of religious life in the Catholic period of Norwegian history. She was not content with the story told by the visible relics—architecture, churches, monasteries, pictorial art—of the magnificence, brilliance and beauty which went with the Church's expansion. Her penetrating glance was directed first and foremost to the life of the common people and their relationship with religion. In this connection, unexpectedly revealing glimpses into the life of the common people were given by the literature of religious edification. In the aristocratic family-sagas, common life is either ignored or touched on only by accident, but in religious writings its appearance is not due merely to chance. There it results from a new value set on humanity, from a brotherhood between men unknown in the family-society. There was no lack of evidence to show that people understood that they belonged to a society whose bounds stretched far beyond life and the visible world.

Old folk-beliefs and customs showed how tenacious of life the heathen conceptions continued to be, but they were equally indicative of the power which the new attitude to life and death had won over the thoughts, feelings and conduct of the people. As I have said, Sigrid Undset attached great importance to the study of legislation. She regarded with the greatest interest the rules which men set up for themselves in ordering their social life, especially those laws which, in the medieval period, present the Christian point of view and the Christian ideas of justice in opposition to the old heathen forms. It had meant radical changes and must undoubtedly have had the effect of an upheaval on the minds of many; but each new decision stood there to remind every individual that he was now a Christian, living in a Christian society. "Against the parents' right to dispose of an unwanted child, a right always demanded by the heathen, Saint Olav set the right of the child to live as one of God's created." On the whole, the sexual morality of the Church was in many points fundamentally different from that of the older society. The Church protected the position of women. Marriage was an indissoluble union, and there could be no marriage without the consent of the bride. It was a new doctrine, this demand for loyalty in the man as well as in the woman. "That a man should be physically faithful to his wife was so novel a requirement and so fundamentally opposed to the customs of the time, that Saint Olav himself did not abide by it: the mother of his only son was the waiting-woman of his queen." Thus law was one thing and its practical application another!

For Sigrid Undset, as for Paasche, the great fact of Norway's medieval history was not the Viking expeditions, however bold and adventurous they may have been, nor yet the characteristic family-society and the country's isolation from the rest of Europe: but it lay precisely in the contact with the outside world and the acquisition of Christian civilisation. The essential fact was that Norway became an integral part of Europe. To Sigrid Undset, something worthy of real admiration and indicative of genuine strength was the way in which the people, without losing their national identity, were able to create in the two centuries which followed the official introduction of Christianity a highly cultured Christian society, such as we find in the twelfth and thirteenth centuries and in the first half of the fourteenth. In her essay, *The Conversion in Norway*, she writes that, in spite of the fierceness and brutality of the main medieval period, in spite of war, plague and confusion, stable institutions were created, which laboured for the cause of civilisation. And between battles, life was peaceful, spacious and attractive. After the dark centuries, a new illumination was shed on life.

The great age of medieval Norway came to an abrupt end. The Norwegian empire fell in ruins; the Lutheran Church came to replace the Catholic; darkness sank once more over the land. "*Tristia fuere prima reformationis tempora.* Sad was the Reformation's first age in Norway" are the words in a speech by Oluf Kolsrud, given at the University in 1937, when the introduction of the new faith was commemorated. In her essay *On Ballads*, Sigrid Undset writes, "The destruction of the Norwegian Church is like a symbol of the ruin of the kingdom's independence—the archbishopric cast down, the cathedrals neglected or simply demolished, the treasures of the churches sent to Denmark to be melted down, the bodies of Saint Sunniva and the Men of Selje, of Saint Halvard and Saint Olav, thrust into the earth, no one knows where. And in the same way, the royal graves of Norway were disturbed, so that there is now no trace of them to be found, and we know not where lies the dust of our ancient kings."

In her article, *War and Literature (Krig og litteratur)*, written during the second World War, Sigrid Undset points out that an author is most often impelled to write of historical events not by pride and jubilation in victories won, but by pain which fills him when the cause or person, in whom he has put his faith, is in danger or suffers defeat. It is then that the poetic genius awakens: it will not accept physical defeat. She adduces many examples from both Christian and non-Christian writers. This is a characteristic common to all mankind, but most especially to the Christian. The cross is the symbol of both defeat and victory. "Be of good cheer; I have overcome the world." She mentions the overthrow of the Christians in their struggle against the Moors. In that defeat was born the *Chanson de Roland*, which resounded throughout Europe. Already in her essay on the ballads, she had written, "The blast of Roland's horn, far, far away over the field of Ronceval, echoed and re-echoed through Telemark."

The medieval Christian period in Norway, its victory and defeat, had made an early appeal to both the historian and novelist in her. Her youthful dream of writing a novel about the later Middle Ages in Norway could first be realised, when she had achieved a vantage-point from which she could survey the whole field. It first happened when the Christian conception gave her the illumination which revealed meaning in both victory and defeat, that she was able to control the mass of material which lay before her, and gather the details into one great vision. Just as Dante in *The Divine Comedy* had to pass through hell before he glimpsed the heaven of eternity and understood that *la sua voluntade è nostra pace*, so it was necessary for Sigrid Undset to journey first through this world, in which modern and un-Christian humanity had confined itself, in order to become aware of its freezing cold and the loneliness of man. It was when she saw how an un-Christian civilisation either trod the spiritual life underfoot or unleashed demonic powers, that she first understood the language of the heaven-yearning Gothic forms. The Church was no longer "a picturesque ruin in the landscape", no longer even the expression of an age; it was the symbol of a reality in which she herself believed, and her recognition of her own contemporaneity with the Middle Ages was deeper and more heart-felt than was her feeling of kinship with the paganism of the modern age. She created from her own flesh and blood the account of the arduous and complicated, but still exciting, pilgrimages of Kristin and Olav. For this reason, her historical novels have a character completely different from those of Sir Walter Scott. They are novels which are symbolic of our own time, Christian literary works, more related in their inner life—despite all the dissimilarities— to those of Dostoievsky than those of Scott. Dostoievsky could use his own age as material for his prophecy of a world without Christianity. Sigrid Undset sought in the Middle Ages the material which would make Christianity visible to our time.

There is no essential difference between the leading motives in Sigrid Undset's medieval novels and those in her novels of contemporary life. In his book, *When Norway Became Christian (Da Norge ble kristnet)*, Georg Sverdrup writes, "With their utilitarian attitude, the northern peoples were chiefly concerned with what they demanded of the gods and not with what the gods demanded of them." The same attitude is found in the modern heathen, as he is portrayed in Sigrid Undset's novels of contemporary life. Even in the time when she herself believed in nothing, she was, as we have said, appalled when people demanded that God should be as they thought He ought to be. "Though she felt God was far away, and she was most willing to believe that He did not interfere in human affairs in the way people said He did, still, on the other hand, it seemed almost madness for anyone to say what God ought to be." It was different with the Christian of the Middle Ages. He might be overcome by self-seeking and covetousness and avarice for the goods of this world, he might raise himself defiantly against God's will, or bury himself deep in life's thorn-bush; but still he knew that his was the guilt, and that in the end there was no trust to be put in self-made ideas and dreams of how the world should be ordered. Medieval men might be besotted and slothful and almost dead in their faith,—but when they were roused, they had no doubt that the way which God appointed for them was the way they had to go, whether they wished it or not.

The impulse in all Sigrid Undset's medieval writing, in *Kristin Lavransdatter* and in the story of Olav Audunsson, is a fundamental conception, common to the whole Christian faith: the idea of man as created by God, made in God's image and called to be God's servant and fellow-worker in the world. Tension results from conflict between God's will and the self-will of man. Asbjørn the priest says to Olav Audunsson, "It is easy to be a good Christian, as long as God only requires you to listen to beautiful music in church and to obey Him while He caresses you with a fatherly hand. But a man's faith is put to the test, when God wants something the man does not want himself." The Church sanctifies the bonds which attach him to wife and child, family, nation and king, but above the laws of men stands the law of God. Every single human soul is raised up and given a place in a society where the slave has the same value as the lord. All men belong to the generation of God. All have their origin and their true home in a supernatural world, but equally all are called to be God's fellow-workers in this world. No one is so insignificant that he has no part in the struggle between the powers of good and evil. Every tiny action has cosmic repercussions. Both Kristin and Olav have learnt this in a language which children can understand. Brother Edvin, for example, explains it to Kristin, when as a little girl she pays a visit to Hamar with her father. The monk takes her into the church and shows her the pictures of saints and dragons. "The dragon looks very small to me," says Kristin; "it doesn't look as if it could have swallowed her up." Brother Edvin explains, "Neither could it, for it wasn't any bigger. Dragons and everything else which serve the devil—they only seem big as long as there is fear inside us. But if you hasten whole-heartedly to God and make some of His strength your own, then the power of the devil straightway suffers such a crushing defeat that his minions become small and helpless, and dragons and evil spirits sink down and become no bigger than cats and crows and gnomes. You can see that the whole mountain Saint Sunniva was in is not so big that she mightn't take it into the fold of her cloak." To Olav also, the Christian spiritual world speaks its plain and simple picture-language, although here it appears more dramatic and vigorous: "From the dawn of ages, there was a battle fought throughout the world between God and His enemies. And everything that had life and soul or the breath of the spirit was in the fight on one side or the other, whether they knew it or not—angels and spirits, men here on earth and men beyond the grave. And most often it was through a man's cowardice that the devil managed to entice him into his camp: when a man was afraid that God would require too much of him, make him speak some truth which he found difficult to utter, or make him deny some dear gratification, without which he did not feel strong enough to live—gain, success, wantonness, or the good opinion of other people."

Saint Augustine had struck the dominant note in the spiritual life of the Middle Ages, and it also marks the main theme in Sigrid Undset's medieval writing. Her text is,

Fecisti nos ad te et inquietum est cor nostrum donec requiescat in te (*Confessions*, Book I).[1]

Her first medieval novel, *Kristin Lavransdatter*, came in three parts, with a year's interval between each one, *The Garland* (*Kransen*) in 1920, *The Mistress of Husaby* (*Husfrue*) in 1921, and *The Cross* (*Korset*) in 1922. They make an artistic whole, deal with the same principal characters, and present in different shades and colours the same historical and social background. Each part has, nevertheless, its individuality, its own tone and feeling.

The action takes place in the first half of the fourteenth century, the period which saw the beginning of the decline of Norway's great medieval age. In each of the three parts, Norwegian history finds its peculiar reflection.

There is no direct connection between political events and the story told in *The Garland*. In the first decades of the century, peace and order were supreme under the firm rule of Haakon V. We are introduced to a peaceful world in the home where Kristin grows up, the farm Jørundgaard in Sel in Gudbrandsdal. Externally, life follows its quiet course, securely established by the work of generations on behalf of law and Christianity. Most people prefer to accept the good things of life without making any return payment, but Kristin's parents, Lavrans and Ragnfrid, are particularly pious. They go regularly to church, give shelter to the servants of God and to men who travel on the Church's business, as well as to pilgrims when they make their way up through the valley to Nidaros. They show the greatest respect for the parish priest. Lavrans is especially God-fearing. For him it goes without saying that, if God's kingdom is to advance here on earth, people must honour and love Him above everything else, attuning their will to His will. But Lavrans is no bigot: "a cheerful temper and joy

---

[1] " You have made us for yourself, and our hearts know no peace until they rest in you." Eugenia Kielland was fully justified in using these words as a motto for her essays on Sigrid Undset in *Ord och Bild*, 1926.

in life flowed in broad streams in the mind of this quiet man".
Now and then he may have had need of a celebration
between the continual labour and the strict fasts he kept. But
"it never occurred to him to drown his sorrows in drink—he
thought that a man ought to take his joy to the drinking-
table". In his youth, he had lived at the family-farm at
Skog in Follo, not far from Oslo, and then he had felt the
attraction of a monastic life. "Many things drew me the
other way, too. . . . But when I was out fishing in Botnfjord
and heard the bells ringing on Hovedø, then I thought that
they attracted me most of all." He does not complain because he did not choose this way: "it would be unmanly
to complain of the lot I have myself chosen". But with
every year spent on this life's journey, he has understood
better the significance of the example set by the monks.
"There exists no worthier occupation for a man, who
has been given the grace to understand a little of God's
mercy, than to serve Him and watch and pray for those
who still go with the darkness of the world's affairs before
their eyes."

Lavrans belongs to one of the great families, and he has
done homage to the king and become his man. But he plays
no part in national affairs and has no wish for it. Dearest
to him are his work and his home-life, in the company of his
own at Jørundgaard. His wife, Ragnfrid, is a member of the
old Gjæsling family from Sandbu in the neighbouring district of Vaagaa. The Gjæslings also have no part in political
life. Like Lavrans' family, the sons of the Law-man, they
belong to that section of the aristocracy which, in social terms,
are on the way to forming a kind of minor nobility, who live
more or less as farmers. It is true that they may model some
of their customs on the court-life of Oslo; but affairs of state
are remote—"No one spoke much of such things home in
the valley."

We realise that in this social development there lies something momentous for the future state of the country. Affairs

of state still weigh on Lavrans' mind. He will defend law and justice and the mere thought of foreign domination makes him belligerent. But he was not made to be a leader in playing the diplomatic game with the great men of Sweden and Denmark. His is an individual greatness, an inner strength which affects all who come into contact with it. In the portrait of Lavrans Bjørgulfsson, we perceive the peaceful, constructive Norway, which from earliest times had employed its strength in establishing the land. He has severe trials to undergo. His wife, Ragnfrid, and his daughter, Kristin, both shatter the faith and confidence he has put in them. But his trust in God does not fail. He has chosen his place amongst the soldiers of Saint Olav, and help is never lacking. In the concrete example of Lavrans Bjørgulfsson, the Christian man, the gentle, thoughtful and self-examining knight of Saint Olav, we see how the spiritual tradition of Christianity has settled, as a living force, in an individual mind, and from there has been transmitted to all that surrounds it.

Against this background is played the first act of the love-story of Kristin and Erlend. It is a story brimming with lyricism; often it has the emotional quality of a ballad. "This is what all ballads are about," says Kristin of her love. But never for a moment does the emotion overflow its proper bounds; it is kept inside the frame of historical realism by a firm hand, and there is such a perfect fusion of spirit and matter that everything, people and objects, landscapes and interior scenes, stands before us in plastic clarity, living and full of poetry.

Jørundgaard is the name of the first of the three sections in *The Garland*. Jørundgaard, the farm and all it stands for, is the social organism of which Kristin grows a part, protected by her mother and father and the secure order surrounding her. She has a vague realisation that outside there exists a dangerous and enticing world. When she was seven years old, she saw the fairy-lady. She was with her father at the summer-farm, and she lay on the bank of the stream, watching her own reflection in the water. When she lifted her head, she saw a beautiful woman. The fairy-creature coaxed her with a garland of chrysanthemums and wanted her to come with her. But the child was frightened and shrieked at the top of her voice for her father—she heard his voice above her and knew that she was safe. But Kristin did not forget the fairy-lady. She tells Mistress Aashild, a woman of the world, about her encounter. She learns that such creatures of the underworld are not so dangerous. "It was sensible to run away, since you were only a child at the time. But have you never heard of people who have taken the gold offered them by the dwarfs, and afterwards fettered the monster in rock?" The story of the fairy-lady suggests the self-infatuation which lies in wait in the child's mind, ready to ensnare it, unless it chooses to accept help from another will—a will different from that represented by the allurement proffered by Mistress Aashild.

The message of Christianity affects Kristin deeply, even when she is a child. From the time when she was a little girl, the Church has accompanied her as it accompanied everyone else. Eirik the priest had taught her what the holy words meant in Norwegian, so that she would find it easier to keep her thoughts on God when she was in church. She gets into the habit of remembering her Creator. With her father she visits Bishop's Hamar. Splendid and beautiful sights have a decided effect on her—they tell of the glory of God, and fill her with reverence and wonder. She does not completely understand the profound and noble words in which Brother Edvin speaks of the division in the human mind but the words remain with her all the same, and they come to the surface when life confirms their significance. "There is no man, Kristin, who does not love and fear God, but it is because our hearts are divided between love for God and fear of the devil and love for the world and the flesh, that we are wretched both in life and death."

Lavrans arranges Kristin's future marriage as it seems best to him. By verbal agreement and hand-shake, Kristin is betrothed, at the age of fifteen, to Simon Darre, son of the knight, Andres Gudmundsson, and heir of the neighbouring farm of Formo. Simon is a handsome and modest man, and Kristin has nothing particular against him, even though he is not exactly like the bridegroom she had imagined for herself. Young as she is, she has already had some experience of love's dangerous power—in the affection which her playfellow, Arne Gyrdson, had shown for her, and when she had to defend herself against an attempt to violate her by Bantein, a youth training for the priesthood. For her it is "a reality that she and all people had a sinful body of flesh, which enmeshed the soul and cut into it with biting cords".

Kristin's mind is troubled and alarmed. "Put me in a nunnery," she says to her father. A year with the sisters in Nonnesæter in Oslo seems a reasonable idea to Lavrans— she might perhaps regain some peace of mind before they drank the bridal ale. In Oslo she meets Erlend Nikolausson. She knew a little about him before—Mistress Aashild, his aunt, had said that he would be a fitting bridegroom for her. "You should marry a man, Kristin, who knows what chivalry and courtesy are." Mistress Aashild has only contempt for these high-born folk who sit quietly up in the valleys and let themselves moulder away in "farmers' ways and churlishness". Erlend is just the man Kristin had dreamed of. The intoxication of love carries them both away: they belong together, and swear to be true to one another. Erlend says, "May God forsake me if woman or maid ever rests in my arms, before I can possess you with law and honour,—you say it too." Kristin says, "May God forsake me if ever I take another man in my arms as long as I live." If he had shown a decent propriety, their marriage might well have been arranged. Canon law would not allow any maid to be forced into marriage against her will. And even though the agreement with Simon Darre is a serious matter, and it would be difficult for Lavrans to ask to be released from it in order to give his daughter to the unsettled Erlend Nikolaus-son—who, into the bargain, has a mistress, Eline Ormsdatter, and two children at home on his farm,—yet Kristin can console herself with the thought that her father would not use compulsion, just because a few parcels of land were conveniently close to one another. "Father certainly won't wish me to lose all joy in the world just because of that." But Erlend's chivalry is no deep quality. He puts aside all regard for law and honour and decent conduct. And Kristin lets Erlend do with her what he will.

Their marriage has to be carried through with scheming and defiance. But behind them the path is blood-stained: senseless and blinded by passion, theirs is the guilt in the death of Eline Ormsdatter. Fully aware of what they are doing, they dupe Lavrans, who learns only half the truth from them. Kristin does not want her father to know that Erlend had touched her before he made an honourable offer for her hand. "We have done so much wrong before we came here," Kristin says to Brother Edvin; "above all, my heart is wounded by the thought that I have caused my father so much sorrow." And she knows that she has dishonoured not only the family order, but the divine order also. When she and Erlend kneel during the wedding cere-mony—she with a garland, the honourable badge of maiden-hood—and she feels the baby leap in her womb, she prays silently, "Holy King Olav, I cry to you. I pray to you for help among all the host of Heaven, for I know that above everything you loved the righteousness of God. I call on you to watch over the innocent in my womb. Turn away God's wrath from this innocent one, turn it on me, for the Lord's dear sake."

The Mistress of Husaby and *The Cross* do not possess the dramatic tension of *The Garland,* nor its sense of life throbbing with youth and love and lyricism, but they are no less great as literature. In these two parts, the epic power in Sigrid

Undset's art is unfolded in marvellous wealth and vast amplitude, perhaps to an even higher degree than in the story of Olav Audunsson. Everything, great and small, finds a place—the whole of life, the everyday world, political events, love, marriage, household duties, child-bed and death-bed. Nothing is common; everything is seen in its cosmic relationship. Nature and landscape appear in a changeful light, following the rhythmic movements of the seasons. Human life is seen in its mutable phases, the long weary development in every man and woman, before they learn to love someone or something higher than themselves. All of them journey through life to the same common goal, "the judgment-seat, where every human being shall be judged as he *is*, and not as he appears in the eyes of others". All human life is seen in an eternal perspective, in relation to the divine order, the one absolute perfection, which is the source of all truth, beauty and wisdom.

The action in *The Mistress of Husaby* extends from the years following the death of Haakon V in 1319 down to the middle of the 1330's, when Erlend makes his unsuccessful bid at insurrection. This, it is true, is an invented episode, but one for which the actual historical situation provides ample warrant. There really was disquiet and anxiety for the state of the country, especially in connection with the union of the crowns of Norway and Sweden under the minor, Magnus Eiriksson. The regency government of his mother, Duchess Ingebjørg, inspired no confidence. At a great meeting of the court in Oslo in 1323, it was left to the archbishop, Eiliv, to appoint one man to direct affairs of state in Norway. He chose Erling Vidkunsson, who was given the title of Steward and invested with all the powers of government. In 1327 Duchess Ingebjørg married her favourite, the Danish duke, Knut Porse, by whom she had two sons, the elder named Haakon. In 1332, King Magnus was declared to be of age, and Erling Vidkunsson resigned his office. King Magnus was half-Swedish by birth and had been brought up in Sweden. He continued to spend most of his time there, and took little interest in Norwegian affairs. A national rallying-point was the archbishop's seat in Nidaros, under the leadership of the wise and able bishops, Eiliv Arnesson and Paal Baardsson. The great men of the country also realised that some action must be taken, if Norway was once more to have a truly national government. Matters came to a head in 1332, when an insurrection was led by members of the king's own family, Erling Vidkunsson and Jon and Sigurd, the sons of Haftor, in alliance with Ulv Sakseson. Only a few details of this rising are known. A compromise with the king was reached, but there remained dissatisfaction with the bad government which resulted from the personal union with Sweden.

All this is mirrored in the novel. The political events are brought closer to the lives of individuals. One day, un-expected visitors come to Erlend and Kristin at Husaby— Lavrans and Erling Vidkunsson and other good men. Mat-ters have gone so far that the sober Lavrans thinks that the King's men in the valleys should ride to Oslo and see to the King's interests—"They govern so ill for the poor young lad." There is a certain historical background for scenes of this kind, as there is also for Erlend's attempt at revolt.

Sigrid Undset in a letter to Fredrik Paasche writes, "It is an invidious matter, the invention of a hitherto unknown chapter in Norway's history." But, as we have said, there is nothing improbable in it. It accords with the actual political situation. At any rate, it ought to have happened, said Paasche. Erlend's plan was to make Haakon—the son of Duchess Ingebjørg and Knut Porse—king of Norway, and thus finally bring the personal union to an end. In carrying out his plan, Erlend is reckless and ill-advised. And only when he has suffered defeat, does Kristin understand the greatness of his intention. "God help me, I hadn't the sense to understand such important things. But ignorant as I am, with no sense for anything but looking after the home and the children, even I know that justice had far too long a journey to make, when a case had to travel so far to find this king, and then get home again to the valleys. I too have seen that ordinary folk in this country are worse off and live in harder times than when I was a child and the blessed King Haakon was our lord. Now I understand that my husband has taken up such a great matter that none of the other nobles dared raise it."

Erlend's revolt is only an episode, but it plays a part in the central story, which tells how Kristin is able to make amends for the harm she has done to others by her sin.

Kristin is mistress of Erlend's old family farm, at Husaby in Skogn in Orkdølafylke. She cannot refrain from making comparisons with Jørundgaard. It is not simply that the management of both house and farm has gone to rack and ruin, —Erlend and his mistress, Eline Ormsdatter, not having worried overmuch about such things. In a way, life there is certainly more in the style of the great; and Erlend is proud of his descent from Duke Skule, who had once owned the estate and lived there. Customs are much as they were in olden times, when people had male and female slaves. But it seems to Kristin that Erlend knows remarkably little of his dead forbears. Kristin's parents had told their children of their ancestors, but they had never prided themselves on their power and position. Erlend would doubtless be most willing to do without Kristin's ideals of self-discipline, self-denial and humility. He shows no special respect for the priest, and what the law says does not seem to mean much to him. He cannot refrain from mocking Lavrans a little, because Lavrans had seen to it that his household had learnt something of the law. "That must have been wonderful fun—everybody sitting and listening to the old fellow recite the laws, section by section. Lavrans is unlike other men in every way, then—otherwise people usually say that if the farmer knew the law of the land and the stallion knew his strength, both to the full, then the devil would be a knight."

But even if there is much that is pagan in the life at Husaby, it does not lead to Kristin's withdrawal from the Christian spiritual world: on the contrary, that world increases in attraction, though, it is true, there can often be more than a single motive for Kristin's feelings. She is obstinate, and what was regarded with honour and esteem at Jørundgaard must also be respected at Husaby. But her will to keep faith with Saint Olav, with whom she has made a pact in her heart, stays pure. She knows she stands in need of help from God and His saints.

The fact is that Kristin has a difficult temperament. Self-will, obstinacy and wilfulness fight incessantly within her against the divine will, the earthbound and instinctive against the liberating power of the spirit. She can never say of herself that she is saved, for selfish desires, conscious and unconscious, are with her continually, and they are opposed to love.

Kristin receives a forceful impression of the spiritual power of Christianity from Master Gunnulf, Erlend's brother. It corresponds to that which she had received in her childhood from Brother Edvin. Like his brother, Gunnulf has a craving for adventure, but, in contrast to Erlend—who, to use a figure from one of Sigrid Undset's essays, had chosen a gay gallop along the broad highway of sin,—he had preferred a tense progress along the narrow path of virtue. Gunnulf has been out into the world; he has studied in Paris and elsewhere, and is learned in all branches of knowledge. In his character is to be found a personal and conscious expression of the connection between Norway and the universalism of Christianity. Gunnulf's combination of religious passion and visionary power is related to the qualities which the poet of the *Dream-Poem* must have possessed. He is wholly seized by the expansive force in the Christian idea. He burns with zeal to carry the torch of Christianity to the farthest north; he speaks to Archbishop Eiliv about his plan to go as a missionary amongst the Lapps. The archbishop thinks that these sons of Nikolaus can never show moderation—"no matter whether what they have set their minds on is good or bad ".

Gunnulf becomes Kristin's familiar friend. No one can talk to her as he does of abasing self-will before the will of God. "You know that you must open your heart to His love. And then you must love Him in return with all the strength of your soul." He speaks in noble figures and pictures, which raise his preaching to the level of religious poetry. Sometimes his words are starkly realistic: "You have had two children, and have you never thought of this—that every child born is baptised in blood, and that the first thing that a human child breathes in this world is the stench of blood? Don't you think that, as their mother, you should do everything in your power to ensure that your sons do not fall back to their first baptismal covenant, but hold fast to the second pact, which they made with God at the font?"

The visual expressions of Christian culture in art and architecture make an impression on Kristin's mind. Here the high point is reached in the description of her first pilgrimage to Christ Church in Nidaros. She has made confession to Eiliv, the parish-priest at Husaby, but he had not the power to absolve her from her guilty share in the hapless death of Eline Ormsdatter. Only the archbishop can grant her absolution from that. She has longed for a remedy and is full of gratitude that her son, the baby she had carried in her womb when she was married to Erlend, has been brought into the world alive and healthy. Now she is to go barefoot to the grave of Saint Olav and there lay down the golden garland, which she had guarded so weakly and worn falsely. Her mind is prepared, ready to take in the sight which opens out before her when she gets to Feginsbrekka (the Hill of Joy), the hillside near Nidaros, where the pilgrims coming from Gauldal first catch sight of the city with its churches and towers, and where they fall on their knees and give thanks to God. The landscape lies before her in the golden evening sunshine: "But above the green land and the magnificent city towered Christ Church, so gigantic and resplendent that everything else seemed to lie at its feet. The evening sun struck full on its front and shining windows, as it stood there with its tower and dizzy spire and golden vanes, pointing upwards to the bright summer heaven . . . Overcome and sobbing, the young woman sank before the cross at the wayside, where thousands of pilgrims had lain and thanked God for the helping hands stretched out to mankind on the journey through this dangerous and lovely world." She goes towards the church and into the cathedral yard and looks up over the west front. The supernatural world reveals itself in sensuous form, speaking to men of God's greatness and their own insignificance. "Not of their own strength had men succeeded in this work—the spirit of God had worked in the holy Øystein and the men after him, who had built this house. Thy kingdom come, Thy will be done on earth as it is in Heaven: now she understood the words. A reflected beam of the glory of God's kingdom bore witness in these stones, proclaiming that His will was all that was beautiful. Kristin shivered. Yes, God must turn away in sorrow from all that was ugly—from sin and shame and impurity. In the galleries of this heavenly citadel stood holy men and women, so fair that she dared not look at them. The unwithering tendrils of eternity wound upwards in peace and loveliness, bursting into leaf on spire and tower, flowering in monstrances of stone. Over the central door hung Christ on the cross, Mary and John the Evangelist stood at His side, and they were white as if made of crushed snow, and on the white was the gleam of gold."

Now she sees how low she lies in the dust. But in her merciless self-examination and self-knowledge, there is also the will to mount up, so that she can accept the help she is proffered. "Yes, Lord King, now I understand. I am in sore need of your help, so that I do not turn from God again." She utters the prayer which Gunnulf had taught her to read from the Fiftieth Psalm: *"Cor mundum crea in me, Deus, et Spiritum rectum innova in visceribus meis. Ne projicias me a facie tua. . . ."*[1]

Kristin's remorse, self-examination and penance are honourable and sincere, but in the life that follows there is no jubilant feeling of salvation, no assurance of eternal bliss. There must be unceasing struggle and effort. For it is in the concrete life, in her actions, her relationship with husband, children and step-children, with her father and with Simon Darre, that she must show that her contrition is positive, encouraging her will to rise up and seek a new way forward.

Sigrid Undset's almost omniscient understanding of human nature reaches its highest level in the description of all these circumstances. Kristin remains the central figure; but all the other characters are fully illumined. They live their own lives, each one entangled in the complexities of his own mind, each one predisposed in his own fashion, each one with his own history.

The relationship between Kristin and her father forms a moving story. When Erlend sets off on his first journey from Husaby over the Dovre mountains to Jørundgaard, Kristin asks him to take this greeting with him: "Tell them at home that, every day since I left, I have longed to fall at the feet of Mother and Father and beg their forgiveness." Reconciliation with her father costs Kristin a great deal, for she is always stubborn. But remorse fashions in her a new heart and liberates imprisoned forces; it gives her new understanding both of herself and of her fellow-men. Lavrans knows however that she still has far to go. The scene where Kristin and Lavrans part at Hjerkinn, after her visit to her parents, is unforgettable. "Grieve no more for anything you have done to me which you must regret, Kristin. But remember it, when your children grow up and you perhaps feel that they

---

[1] "Create a clean heart in me, O God; and renew a right spirit within my bowels. Cast me not away from thy face . . ."

don't behave towards you or their father as would be fitting. And remember then, too, what I told you of my own youth. Your love for them is steadfast—but you are most stubborn when you love most."

Kristin re-establishes Husaby on a firm footing after the disorder which had reigned there when Eline Ormsdatter had charge of the farm. She is generous towards the step-children, even when it involves grave difficulties. With every child she bears—she has seven sons—her power increases to take a wider view and to thank God for what He has given her. But her relations with Erlend are the touchstone. It is not easy to bring her obstinacy to heel. Here it is hardest for her not to put herself in the foreground; here she remains closely imprisoned in her own ego. Is it not he who, fundamentally, is responsible for the misery in which she lives? She continually reminds him of his guilt, in violent outbursts and small stinging references. She is for ever digging up the past. "You don't do that from piety," says Erlend. It is not, we are told, that she willingly and intentionally harbours spite against her husband—she knows she was not small-minded in other things, but she is towards Erlend. Nevertheless, in spite of everything, God's love is at work within her. When she is on the point of losing what she cherishes, that love comes to life in her in warmth and goodness. When Erlend's unsuccessful revolutionary bid brings him to the prison-tower and the threat of death hangs over him, then she is in the same case as Gudrun in *Laxdæla Saga* and Vigdis in *The Story of Viga-Ljot and Vigdis*—she realises she behaved worst towards him because she loved him best. She understands what a debt of gratitude she owes Erlend, because he has loved her as much as his own life. Now she must admit to herself that it was she who, with her coldness and barbed words, provoked in him his restlessness and desire to be up and doing; it was she even who drove him to be unfaithful to her. She prays to Saint Olav that she may not be completely unworthy of the love she has been given. She too must share the guilt in what has happened. If she had followed the call to chastity of convent life, which as a girl she heard within her and which Brother Edvin had urged her to follow, she would have been spared her misery. The way to Heaven was marked plain with beacons before her: it was she who went grubbing amongst the briars, wandering in the waste land. "It is unworthy to complain of the fate one has chosen for oneself," says Kristin to herself.

Erlend is released from prison. Erling Vidkunsson pleads his case before the king, and Simon Darre is one of those who stand by him. Erlend and Kristin have much to be thankful for, as they begin the last stage of their life together.

In *The Cross*, the last part of the novel-cycle, we return once more to Kristin's childhood home. Erlend is deprived of his estate and has to be content with the succession to Jørundgaard. The action spans a period of fifteen years and the book ends with an account of the great plague, which harried every section of the populace, but had perhaps its direst effects amongst the ranks of the highly cultured clerics. The political events of this period play no part in the novel. We hear of the disturbances of 1338-9, when the nobles planned to depose King Magnus and set young Jon Haftorsson from Sudrheim on the throne in his stead—a feeble attempt. And up in the valley at Jørundgaard in Sel are heard only vague rumblings, for the most part mere rumours. "Kristin didn't pay much attention to the rumours she heard; she thought bitterly that they were only small folk now, and affairs of state were no concern of theirs."

The world has closed in round Kristin at Jørundgaard—not only in external conditions, but also in her mind, her inner life.

Nowhere is Sigrid Undset's realism more merciless and searching than in her account of the last years of Kristin's life. There is grandeur in this truthfulness which will not suffer any embellishment. She sees through the frailty of human nature, the wickedness of man and his divided will, the source of his disease. But this realism is not pessimistic in effect—it does not leave a character bound and helpless. It knows that escape can be made, that freedom does exist, that it is always possible to break through and win the strength which gives that freedom.

Everything seems favourable for Kristin and Erlend when they make a new start, after his release from prison. The danger hanging over their heads has brought them closer to one another than ever before. But it does not last long, and Kristin is once more in the clutch of evil powers. "She sat and made room for the old bitter thoughts, as if they were pleasant companions." She welcomes them almost with gladness, but she turns cold inside when she remembers Brother Edvin's comment on the damned in Hell, who will not be parted from their torment: "Their pleasure was in hate and sorrow—that was why Christ could not set them free." On one occasion she is at the summer farm, where she was as a child with her father, and remembers the fairy-lady she saw. Now, at any rate, she thinks, there is no fairy-lady who would want to tempt such a thin, worn-out woman. "No elfin-lady wanted to lay her child to these dried-up dugs." But creatures of the underworld are just as eager to catch Kristin now as then. Her youthful beauty is no longer the allurement they proffer. Now the monsters throng upward from the depth of her unconscious mind—"In the dark rise so many thoughts—like the dust-free plants down in the sea that wave and sway in such wonderful and bewitching loveliness."

She puts one obstruction after another in her own path, entangling her mind in a tight mesh of jealousy and self-righteousness and an insidious craving for self-assertion. She feels she owes it to herself to get even with Simon Darre, who lives on the next farm and is married to her sister. It is true that she likes her brother-in-law and is grateful to him for the magnanimity and kindness he has shown towards her and Erlend. But she thinks it is humiliating to take so much from him; she must make some return, not from gratitude, but so that she can feel that she has held her own. There is a grim description of the way in which she makes her repayment. Simon's son is dying, and to cure the boy, Kristin dares to go to the churchyard, alone at dead of night, to fetch a piece of turf from a grave. Simon lets her do this appalling deed, although he knows that his duty before God and man is to restrain her. He has become a healer by witchcraft—she likes that idea. She has won an advantage in the secret struggle between them. "She should share that secret with him—the fact that he knew that she had also seen him on one occasion when he had not stood so firm." She is finally reconciled with Simon, although most of the credit for it must go to him. He has a genial, harmonious temperament, and he is helped by his Christian faith. True, he does not think he has had much help from keeping the promise he once made to Lavrans, never "to miss Mass, save for the most pressing reason". But Lavrans' example has had its influence. Simon has been able to follow him at least some of the way, and, where sacred things are concerned, he has "a feeling which made him wish to express his gratitude in more heartfelt fashion than before".

Reconciliation with Erlend is, however, a more difficult matter. Again it is self-righteousness which enervates Kristin's love. She is forced to admire the superiority with which Erlend accepts his reversal of fortune, the alienation of his property, and the contempt of the local people. He is a man who lives for the moment, fickle perhaps and thoughtless and inconsiderate, but incapable of bearing a grudge. He feels no particular remorse for his sins, but nevertheless, in the last years of his life, he is further than Kristin on the road that leads to Heaven.

The feeling remains with Kristin that he does not properly appreciate how much help he has received from her. It was she who restored Husaby, she who ventured all in her efforts to save him when he was imprisoned. Hers too was the drudgery and exertion with their seven sons: now, it is as if he has taken them from her, for it is him they admire and honour. The stage is reached at which Erlend can no longer live with Kristin. He leaves her and settles down on a farm in Dovre,—unheard-of though it was "amongst Christian folk, that any couple legally united should separate on their own inclination". Erlend has not, however, shut himself up in the confines of his own personality. When Kristin finally comes to ask him to return, he receives her with open arms and absolute sincerity. He will not live with her at Jørund-gaard, "but whether you come by night or day, I shall welcome you as if it were the Queen of Heaven come down from the clouds to visit me". And then, he adds, we shall see which of us is "the more obstinate". Erlend returns to their district when local gossip takes Kristin as its target: the folk blame her because, they say, the father of the child she and Erlend now have together was not her husband. He protects his wife's honour with the loss of his life. "Kiss me, Kristin," he whispers in his last farewell. There is something like the lilt of laughter in his voice. "There have really been too many other things between you and me—than Christianity and wedlock—to make it easy—for us to leave one another—like Christian partners." Kristin thinks to herself that Erlend was no elfin-knight after all, but a Christian man.

Her Christian faith remains in a sorry plight. True, she reads her prayers and a part of the Psalter each Saturday and keeps the fasts laid on her by Archbishop Eiliv, when he gave her absolution. She gives alms, and when wayfarers come to Jørundgaard and ask for shelter, she attends to their needs in person—"But she no longer felt that a ray of light kindled in her heart as she did it." Nevertheless, a ray of light from the eternal source is shining within her. She *knows* that there is a light. In spite of all her severity and bitterness and in spite of her wilfulness, she possesses the desire for God. In reality, she has never forgotten that He saw into her heart. She had prayed that He would work "a miracle in her mind"—"For all the days of my life, I have wanted to do two things, one as much as the other: to go the right way and to follow my own roving paths."

The miracle first happens when she is left a widow: she removes her egocentric self from the foreground and can view her life in the light of God's love. In the end, the truth of Christianity is confirmed for her by life itself. "It dawned on Kristin Lavransdatter in a new way that the interpreters of God's word were right. The life of the body was irremediably plagued with troubles. In this world, where human beings interbreed, beget new generations, and, loving their own flesh, are impelled one to another by the body's lust, bitterness of heart and disappointed hopes must come as surely as the frost comes in autumn."

Almost as subtle as Sigrid Undset's account of the way in which Kristin's heart becomes enmeshed in selfishness is her description of how Kristin's heart is opened and her power to accept divine aid developed to the full. Through the strength of a will which she no longer excludes, a transformation takes place within her. We enter the realm of mysticism. "A will other than her own" is to be her guide. Sigrid Undset is careful not to portray Kristin's new life as full of the joy and delight of the blessed, after she has decided to leave Jørundgaard—where now, for the most part, she is only in the way of her daughter-in-law—and journey on the pilgrim's path to Nidaros. There she will celebrate the feast of Saint Olav and seek admission amongst the sisters of the convent of Rein—for the original sin of pride and disobedience is always lying in wait. But gradually, it seems as if a high, bright heaven arches wide over Kristin in the last years of her life. It sheds its beams with the wonder of a summer's day on her pilgrimage over the Dovre mountains, its brilliance breaks through the terrors of the Black

Death and gives Kristin strength in her work of nursing the sick—above all, it gives her the strength to be humble. The gigantic inspiration of the whole work finds expression in the last clear thoughts which pass through Kristin's mind: "It seemed a mystery to her, something she had not grasped but which she knew to be assured. God had kept her fast to a pact which had been made on her behalf, though without her knowledge, by the love He had freely bestowed on her. And despite her wilfulness and her dull, earth-bound mind, some part of that love had come to life in her, had worked in her like the sun in the soil, and pushed forth shoots which could never be utterly blasted, not by love's fiercest flame or love's violent anger. A handmaid of God had she been—an unruly and refractory servant, most often a lip-server in her prayers and unfaithful in her heart, lazy and neglectful, impatient under correction, unsteadfast in deed. Nevertheless, He had held her fast in His service, and a secret mark had been set on her, under the shining gold ring, to show that she was the serving-woman of God, owned by that Lord and King who now came, borne in the holy hands of the priest, to give her freedom and salvation."

In 1925, three years after the last volume of *Kristin Lavransdatter* was published, appeared *Olav Audunsson of Hestviken* (*Olav Audunssøn i Hestviken*), to be followed two years later by *Olav Audunsson and His Children* (*Olav Audunssøn og hans børn*). The setting of these stories is centred in the districts round Lake Mjøsa. We are to imagine that the farm, Frettastein, where Olav is brought up with Ingunn Steinfinnsdatter, is situated in Veldre in Ringsaker. From the farm can be seen the estate of Biri on the other side of the water. On the night of Steinfinn's revenge, when he kills Mattias Haraldsson and burns his farm, Ingunn, his fifteen-year-old daughter, stands with her mother outside Frettastein, watching the pillar of smoke from the burning buildings on the lake's further shore. Otherwise, we move chiefly in the districts which lie around the head of Oslofjord. Hestviken, the ancestral home of Olav Audunsson, stands on the eastern side of the fjord, beyond Oksen. As in *Kristin Lavransdatter*, the action often takes us to Hamar and Oslo. We are given a glimpse of conditions in Denmark, when Olav describes his stay with his mother's brother at Høvdinggaard. He is surprised at the arbitrary behaviour of the great men in Denmark—they show little regard for the law. We accompany Olav on his trading-voyage to England, and Sigrid Undset presents us with a finely executed close-up picture of medieval London.

There is the same fertile and sensuous depiction of nature as in *Kristin Lavransdatter*, and the same intimacy in the presentation of the historical background, although this now appears somewhat differently. The focus is on the struggle between the Church and the barons, but otherwise the action, which extends from the middle of the thirteenth to the early part of the fourteenth century, is only indirectly affected by political events. It is a comparatively peaceful Norway which is described, the Norway of the youthful years of Kristin Lavransdatter. All the same, the civil wars between Birkebeiner and Bagler, Sverre and Magnus Erlingsson, King Haakon and Duke Skule, are not very far away. It is said of the sons of Steinfinn, the forefathers of Ingunn, that they did not care overmuch who were kings in Norway. Some of them followed Magnus Erlingsson and Sigurd, the foster-son of Markus, but none of them supported Sverre and members of his dynasty more than they were compelled to: their chief concern was with the wealth and power of their own family. They came to terms with King Haakon. Steinfinn, Ingunn's father, has, shortly before the story begins, been with King Haakon on his last expedition to the Western Isles, and fought bravely in the battle at Largs. When the king lay sick in Kirkwall, he often kept night-watch over him, and it is his own opinion, at any rate, that the king showed him great favour. It has been otherwise with Olav's family, the men of Hestviken. They were ardent supporters of Magnus Erlingsson, Magnus the Crowned, as they called him. He was the rightful king in their eyes, and they had many personal motives for desiring revenge on Sverre "the priest". They were with Filippus, the Bagler-king, and Olav's grandfather swore loyalty to Benedikt, in Marker, who claimed to be a son of Magnus Erlingsson. In this family they do not easily forget.

Olav is still a child when his parents die, and he is fostered at Frettastein with Ingunn: their fathers have agreed between themselves that the two children should marry. All this makes no difference to Olav, who still clings fast to the political tradition of his family. It does not make him an extremist and he has not the least thought of disloyalty to the Sverre dynasty, but the fate of the men of Hestviken has, as it were, cast a shadow on times yet to come. They were an ill-starred family, not "lucky men". Precisely for this reason, Olav feels secret sympathy for them. It was said of one of his dead ancestors that he bore misfortune so well that no one could suffer adversity more nobly. And this was the measure of their "faithfulness of heart".

For the inner significance of the novel, however, this reflection of the civil wars is far less essential than the conflict between the legal conceptions of the old heathen family society and the new ideas which were working their way to the fore, finding expression both in the legislation of Magnus the "law-reformer" and in the struggle of the Church to assert and extend its position. It is conflict over both form and matter, touching both the way in which the law is to be applied and the values it is to defend. It goes deep into questions of custom and usage, and this conflict is mirrored in the struggles of which the novel tells. The removal of the law's execution from the individual member of the clan into the hands of the State authorities meant in reality that many were freed from the psychological difficulties and often unreasonable duties, which the demand for blood-revenge imposed on them. Nevertheless, the monopoly of the execution of the law by the State must have been felt by many as a humiliation, an insult to their self-respect. "I call these new laws rotten laws" says the self-willed Haftor Kolbeinsson, when the prior at Hamar tries to dissuade him from taking the law into his own hands, explaining that even a criminal enjoys protection under the law, and must be punished according to law and "not be made to suffer revenge with new lawlessness, which in its turn breeds new revenge, and so on in an endless chain". Haftor thinks that the new laws may be very suitable for weaklings, but for men who are jealous of their honour the old ones are better. When Olav is sixteen, he is present at the vengeance exacted by his foster-father in the slaying of Mattias Haraldsson of Biri. Olav feels no moral scruples about this. He and Ingunn both witnessed the degrading revenge which Mattias took on her father, and he consoled his foster-sister with these words: "Just remember that your father will take vengeance in his turn without fail. You can be sure of that. And then I think I shall go along, and show that Steinfinn has a son-in-law, even though his sons are too young to bear arms." There is hope in his words, but the "blood-night", the night after the killing, sees them turned to shame. The feast which is held after the work well done is strained with nervous excitement. A sombre, gloomy mood prevails, an unconscious feeling that their vengeance did not give the satisfaction they had expected. There is a hard and brilliant paganism in the old sword-dance which they begin, with its inciting words: "With swords we hewed—Hild's game we played—when we sent the Helsing men—to the halls of Odin—the sword could bite—when we lay in Iva." But none of them is quite sure of the steps of the dance or of the words of the old *Krákumál*. It turns into foolery. Insensate and half-drunk, Olav leads Ingunn away with him, and she submits to his will. It is a glaring contrast to their delicate and sincere meeting as young lovers on the summer-trip to Hamar, when they looked into one another's eyes, and it seemed "as if they became one flesh simply by the pressure of their warm hands together".

We see the decisive role played by the Church in the civilising process. Naturally there were differences between the ecclesiastical and secular lords, between Church and people and Church and State—differences which might find crude expression. They are not glossed over in the novel; but they cast no shadow on the spiritual fight which the Church is waging—which it was, in fact, waging at that time. Unquestionably, the simple idea that a slaying might be something to atone for in more than material fashion came from the Church. It seems that Edvard Bull is right in all essentials, when he says, "If the Northmen knew nothing of sin in heathen times, they had also no knowledge of remorse or penance for sin" (*Nation and Church*, 1912, p. 98). The Church's struggle on behalf of the Christian view of marriage, and its maintenance of that view by the decisions of canon law, also sprang from the respect which Christianity has for the individual. Despite all the struggles for power and the temptations they involved, the light of Christian humanitarianism was carried to the people by the Church.

The literary presentation of the Church's spiritual battle is one of the novel's great features, and here, for good historical reasons, it plays a larger part than in *Kristin Lavransdatter*.

The questions at issue are those which hinge upon the new doctrine of mankind's universal brotherhood and of man's need to submit self-will to the Christian ordering of things, the teaching which tells people to be content with law, permitting justice to be done but never taking its execution into their own hands. Deeply affected as Olav is by the new teaching, he is still aroused and moved to revolt when it points to a way other than that which he wishes to follow. "Flesh and blood in a man *were* like that." But the priests and monks loved the new order: "They delved deep into the laws, copied them and discussed the articles, disagreed with one another and disputed with laymen on their meaning—and they did so because they loved this law and dreamt that it would reform all men, until the time would come when no man would lift a weapon against his neighbour or maintain his right with violence, but everyone would be at peace, ready to hear Our Lord's new and mild prescript of brotherhood between all God's children."

The most notable churchmen who appear in *Olav Audunsson* are, in fact, imbued with the Augustinian ideals of Christian unity and justice. But for the most part, their activity is of a kind different from that of the roving Brother Edvin, with his child-like piety, or of Master Gunnulf, the ardent champion of the extension of Christ's kingdom. Bishop Torfinn of Hamar is typical amongst them. History knows little of him, beyond the fact that he was forced into exile during the regency government of the 1280's, which was hostile to the Church. In the novel, we learn to know him as a representative of the practical and organising side of the Church's work in accomplishing Christian unity, one of those who work to adjust the supernatural scheme to conditions of time and space and to life's infinite variety. Here we meet the wisdom of the Church, at once strong and meek. It is he who has to deal with Olav's difficult case, which is complicated by his childhood betrothal to Ingunn and their intercourse before marriage. There were no witnesses at their betrothal and, now that Ingunn's father is dead, her uncles will not hear of a match between her and Olav. They need a nephew with more power behind him. Having had a part in the slaying of Mattias, it is important for them to muster every ally against the men who are to take up that case, whether it is to be resolved by atonement or by other means. Olav's great desire is "to share a husband's bed with Ingunn" without more ado: then he could settle with her haughty uncles. But he hangs back, even though he has got Brother Vegard, his own and

Ingunn's confessor from childhood, "to bless the bridal cup and bed for them". But even then he had to hide from his confessor the fact that he and Ingunn had already lived in secret as man and wife. It is doubtful, too, whether anyone at Frettastein would take notice of any orders he might give. There is no way out but to follow the advice of Arnvid Finnsson, his loyal friend and a kinsman of Ingunn, and to lay his case before Bishop Torfinn: "In this affair, only Holy Church can judge." Olav is alarmed at the prospect; he had heard of this strict bishop, who is supposed to have said, "Better the death of ten men than the violation of one virgin." The conversation between Bishop Torfinn and Olav is characteristic. To the young, self-willed boy, insisting on the right which he thinks is his, the bishop explains the Christian idea of marriage and the obligations Ingunn and Olav have taken on themselves by entering the same bed without the consent of kinsmen and the Church's public blessing. Since they did it in the belief that the agreement between their fathers was valid, they have by that act given their own consent to their parents' decision (*consensus matrimonialis*), and they are bound before God to keep the promise they have made to each other. It is therefore possible for the Church to help Olav to a reconciliation with Ingunn's kinsmen. On the other hand, he has gained no right in the case by holding his wedding in secret, but rather, it is now his bounden duty to make atonement both to Ingunn's relatives and to the Church, because "marriage matters must be conducted openly". And if there is no reconciliation to be achieved, then he and Ingunn must go their separate ways: they cannot marry again without committing adultery. They are still bound to one another before God.

Against this background, where paganism and Christianity meet, is unfolded the life-story of Olav Audunsson, a psychological study without parallel in Norwegian literature, as searching as the story of Kristin, but even more piercing and profound. As Charles Kent writes, it is doubtless possible to argue at length as to how far Christianity had any real power over men's minds at that time; but if it possessed such power, its influence on Olav's mind would have been such as it is described in this novel.

There is no disloyalty in Olav. He is true of heart, like all the men of Hestviken, and it is not his way to give up a cause simply because it is lost—it can still have right on its side. There is no finer element in Olav Audunsson than this vein of pure gold, his faithfulness of soul. It is crystal-clear to him that God, as the Creator, is rightful lord of the created. It is equally obvious that Christ requires obedience and that He is worthy to receive love—He who gave His life for those who followed Him. This only provides confirmation, as it were, of the old morality. And the Christian world-picture is not only obvious; there is in it something urgent and incisive, something dramatic and full of power: there is a battle throughout the world.

The Church appeals to his sense of beauty and to his inborn desire for justice. The Dominican monk at Hamar, Asbjørn the Fat, has taught Olav a little mathematics, and explained to him how some part of God's essence found its reflection in *Arithmetica*. "It was like having a glimpse into one of the heavenly powers; suspended from the golden chain of numbers hangs the whole of creation, and up and down the links move angels and spirits. His heart was raised up in longing that his life might also come to rest in the palm of God's hand, like one of these golden links— that his life might also be an account reckoned without error."

Two things are difficult for him to grasp. The Church lays such an unreasonable stress on the value of the individual life—of old, no-one used to be particularly concerned on that account. And something even harder: God has such a desire for truth in a man's innermost heart that the thing is a burden. It is as if God goes with him wherever he stands or moves, never leaving him in peace and quiet, but always demanding that he should sacrifice something for His sake, even though it might mean sacrificing honour and respect. The justice of God is different from the justice of men, and it can entail a loss of prestige not to be endured by flesh and blood.

The psychological, moral and religious problem is more clearly formulated in *Olav Audunsson* than in *Kristin Lavransdatter*, and its universal human application is more directly evident. As contemporary criticism showed, a superficial reading of *Kristin Lavransdatter* could give the impression that Kristin's difficulties depended essentially on certain provisions to do with betrothal and marriage, which were only characteristic of the period in which she lived. It is not easy to make a similar mistake in reading *Olav Audunsson*. It is true that the description of the way in which the marriage of Olav and Ingunn is brought about plays an important part in the novel; but, unlike Kristin, Olav does not marry in a spirit of defiance or in opposition to the will of his parents. He is moreover willing to put his case into the hands of Bishop Torfinn. He understands little of what the bishop tries to make clear to him, but he yields to him as he yielded to law and king. And the manner in which the bishop wants to have the affair arranged with Ingunn's uncles does not conflict overmuch with his own wishes. In Bishop Torfinn, Olav believes he has seen a man who can lead him to all the things in the service and love of which he could find happiness and self-respect.

Before he brings Ingunn home to Hestviken as his wedded wife, Olav becomes guilty of both a slaying and a secret murder. The death of Einar Kolbeinsson is no great weight on his conscience. He did it in a moment of rage when he heard his friend, Arnvid Finnson, slandered. He can in fact abide by his deed and take his punishment without any loss of prestige. It is different with the treacherous murder of the run-away Icelandic theological student, Teit Hallsson, who

seduced Ingunn while Olav was in exile and is the father
of the child Ingunn is to bear. If he had struck him down in
open combat and stood by his action, then that might well
have passed off without any special loss of honour in people's
estimation. On the other hand, it might not have gone so
easily. It is clear that Ingunn simply made a fool of herself
over this Icelander. Even so, it has never occurred to him
for a moment to desert her: he will never play her false.
"He could save some poor remnant of respect for her."
Appearances might be kept up if Teit were out of the way—
but it must be arranged so that no one would know.

The central stress of the whole novel is concentrated in the
powerful description of Olav's murder of Teit. He stands up
there in the remote, deserted wilderness, where he has
persuaded Teit to follow him and where he has struck him
down. An endless white world of desolate snow-covered
forest stretches outside the poor hut where Olav and Teit's
corpse keep company. It is an ugly blood-chilling scene.
He smooths out the bunk and fetches the body, lays it down
and attempts to straighten its limbs. "Teit gaped hideously.
Olav could not get his mouth and eyes to shut, and he
covered his face with the old patchy and bloodstained fur-
cap." He burns down the hut. In the land of the living there
is no trace of Teit left, and no one will make enquiries
about him. Olav comforts himself with the thought that
this fellow has got his deserts—Teit "might have killed many
a better man in battle, and never taken it to heart". The
moral code of the old family society would probably not
have judged the deed to be very manly, but neither would
it have been much concerned over the fate of a man without
kin, like the run-away student. Olav Audunsson can indeed
try to make himself relentless: the difficulty simply lies in
the fact that he is no longer a heathen. Christianity has
planted some ideas in him of the value of the individual in
God's sight—of the rights which even this contemptible
wretch Teit possesses, since he too belongs to a society under

the sway of a law higher than that which men make for themselves.

There is a figure in modern literature who is not very far removed from Olav Audunsson. It is not, as some have maintained, Enok Haave in Garborg's *Peace (Fred)*, for Enok's feeling of guilt is a fiction, self-induced. It is rather Dostoievsky's Raskolnikov—despite the wide differences in period and mentality between the thirteenth-century Norwegian, deeply affected by the idea of Christ, and the satanic intellectual of the nineteenth century. The motive for Raskolnikov's murder of the pawnbroker is not the same as the motive which drives Olav to murder Teit. Much might be said to excuse Olav. Raskolnikov is seized by the demon of power: he will rule over men, and they shall bow before the will of their lord. But, on the other hand, the logic of the modern pagan, Raskolnikov, is not very different from that of Olav's heathen ego. Of what significance can it be, thinks Raskolnikov, if I the genius do away with a miserable louse of a pawnbroker? And in the background to the two stories there is a remarkable similarity. For Dostoievsky, the background is formed by a prophetic vision of the future. In Raskolnikov's ideal of life, Dostoievsky sees preparation for the modern paganism, the collective society and totalitarian state which swallow the individual. For Sigrid Undset, the background is the collective instinct of the old family society, from which the individual, by virtue of his contact with Christianity, is on the way to freeing himself. The dichotomy which results in the consciences of Olav and Raskolnikov, the guilt and the desperate need to make atonement, which they both experience, have then their origin in the same historical fact: the view of humanity which Christianity has introduced into the world.

It is a novel which deals with the tragedy of guilt-complex, wrote Sigurd Hoel. From the "pedagogic and psychological" point of view, he continues, Olav's fate may be considered as a warning example of one who does not "treat his own mind hygienically". Or it is possible to regard it more from a biological standpoint: "a mind like Olav Audunsson's will always have a tendency towards pessimism and despair; by nature it is disposed to melancholia, remorse and all that is tragic, whatever care may be taken of it". But Hoel understands clearly that Sigrid Undset is not entirely of the same opinion. From certain parts of the novel's construction, he has the impression that she regards Olav's "fixed ideas of sin and guilt" from a religious and theological point of view: Olav's fate is the fate of one who disobeys the voice of God. (*Nordisk Tidsskrift* H.4, 1928).

The religious and theological attitude is of course the heart of the matter. Without sympathy for this attitude, a reader will have difficulty in following with interest the psychological development of Olav Audunsson. It will be possible for him to enjoy the novel as the picture of a period, and to take delight in the descriptions of nature and interior scenes and in the richly varied characterisation of the numerous people involved, but the inner tension will not be felt. What in particular makes this book unique in our Norwegian literature is its description of contrition as a rejuvenating power in the human mind. "And remorse shall be cast out on God's green earth," says Vraal in Kinck's *The Man of Instinct* (*Driftekaren*), words which undoubtedly show that Kinck, with his biological and vitalistic attitude, regarded this mysterious phenomenon as something unhealthy, similar to Nietzsche's conception of remorse as a secret, assertive desire which, for want of a better object, fastens upon itself: "In times of peace, men of war turn on themselves."

Sigrid Undset is not the first Norwegian author in whose writing contrition, in the Christian sense, plays such an essential part. It is a leading motive in Henrik Wergeland and Henrik Ibsen. In *Creation, Man and Messiah* (*Skabelsen, Mennesket og Messias*), contrition is the redeeming power which liberates man from his animal nature: "With his first sin, man has begun to know himself." The motif runs throughout Ibsen's work. Solveig is Peer Gynt's redeeming angel insofar as she awakens in him the feeling of remorse, from its first vague stirring—"I've read something about remorse, if I remember rightly"—to the final shattering moment of *contritio cordis*, to use the theological term, the contrition which is the perfect form of remorse because it seems to have the inherent power to force out the confession, *confessio oris*.

But neither of these authors has seen so deeply into the nature of remorse as Sigrid Undset in *Olav Audunsson*, nor have they shown us how conscience, with all its imperfections, demonstrates the existence of an invisible order with which man is connected. Contrition is presented to us as the fountainhead of health—those stirrings of the conscience which are characterised by the desire to re-establish inner harmony by rehearsing before God all that is past. When Olav confesses to his friend, Arnvid Finnsson, and speaks of his remorse, the conversation is paradoxical but essentially Christian: "I never felt Our Lord to be so lovable beyond all measure as when I understood He had branded me with the mark of Cain."

All stages or phases of Christian contrition are described. Sorrow for his sin, the *attritio* of theology, haunts Olav. He thinks of the sons of Steinfinn: they were "lucky men" in a way, carefree and cheerful natures—struck by misfortune, they either spewed it out like poison or died from it. Fundamentally it was the same with poor Ingunn. Misfortune came on her like a fatal disease; she will never recover, he thought to himself. *The Good Fortune of Olav Audunsson* is the apparently inconsistent title of that part of the novel which tells of his married life with Ingunn at Hestviken, the period of almost uninterrupted remorse for the crime he has committed and for all the falsehood into which it has led him. It is some relief for him to be living on the family farm, in the countryside which is his home, and to be busy in restoring the property. He follows Duke Haakon on his expedition to Denmark, and his conscience grows lighter: "It was unreasonable to believe that the Lord should feel such great jealousy, because he had killed Teit." The carefree campaigning life can lead him to regard his own faithfulness to Ingunn with hostility—that too has become a burden for him, even though he loved her so much. It is as if he has sacrificed his youthful strength and unimpaired vigour so that "she might suck her health from his health". But it is impossible for him to forget. He does not escape from his remorse. "Olav Audunsson's good fortune was that he was made in such a way that he could carry on without it."

When Ingunn dies, he makes a serious attempt to tear himself away from the nagging past. His mind lives through a crisis on his trading-voyage to England. In the first place, the attraction of Christianity grows stronger. Nearby are the church of Saint Olav and the church of the Dominican monastery; for preference, he visits the latter. "As he knelt there during Mass in these early morning hours, memories of early morning in the cathedral at Hamar became so near and alive." He is moved by the proof given of the Church's universality. Here in this foreign land, where a barrier seems raised between him and other men and where a language is spoken which he cannot understand, the Church's voice is unchanged—it is the same voice which he has heard in childhood, youth and manhood. He knows that if he should voyage to the uttermost ends of the Christian world, wherever he came to a church and entered, he would be received by the same voice, and that everywhere the Church would proffer its help with open hands. He thinks there is still something to live for. It is like coming home to his mother, after a long journey which has brought him loss and injury rather than honour and gain. It is as if she said to him, "Not even the unluckiest man has lost the battle which is still unfought": as if he heard a voice in the stillness which said, "Because you still love me, I seek after you.

Because you yearn for me, I follow after you. I pursue you because, even as you flee from me, you call on me."[1] He feels that he quickens again; his life shall shine once more. He has wandered outlawed so long on the borders of the kingdom of God's mercy that now he will rise up and "serve his Lord with hymn and prayer and contemplation". But the contemplation, the self-examination, demands too high a price. The path he must follow proves too narrow, the burdens God has laid on him too unreasonable. He leaves his "lucid hours" behind him.

He can still make his own solitary way in the wilderness. There is always something to live for—there is the farm and the children. He can ensure that the wiping out of his own failure does not entail the ruin of his family and their inheritance. He can harden his heart. But immediately, with this resolve, the "good fortune" of Olav Audunsson is at an end. The farm prospers and provision is made for the children. Olav has taken Eirik, the son of Teit and Ingunn, to himself, and the local folk believe him to be his child. Eirik loves and admires him, but Olav cannot return his affection. His mind freezes over; all joy seems at an end. And if he retains any feeling of gladness—it is "almost a cold joy"—it is because he can still see that he is in the wrong and that God is just. Though he may turn in revolt, the world still rests in the hands of Christ. He feels his apostasy, but still will not let himself be counted amongst Christ's enemies. The description of this phase of Olav's contrition is called *Winter*.

Because he has become cold and hard, he thinks he is no longer capable of remorse. His will seems crushed; he no longer has the power to choose; he lives under duress: "He could no longer feel remorse, he had no more love for God, he had no wish to retrace his steps. Now he would rather go on wandering and wandering away from God on his own

[1] Cf. Francis Thompson's *The Hound of Heaven:* "I fled Him down the nights and down the days."

paths for ever. It was Hell, the land of eternal pain—he knew it—but the world of suffering had become his home."

What is it that prevents remorse from breaking out from under his brooding grief to become the complete contrition, which in itself contains the power to make confession? It is not fear of God but fear of the judgments of men which keeps him from confession. A full confession, not only of Teit's slaying but also of all the falsehood, all the petty deceits, which have followed it, will result in a *satisfactio operis*, which must make plain to the world that he is no more than a despicable murderer. With the advent of Christianity, the old conception of loyalty must be lifted up onto a higher plane, and the old conception of honour must be elevated in the same way.

Time after time he is on the point of going to confession. When Ingunn dies, he is very near to doing so. He cannot bear to be parted from her without first winning release from the tight mesh in which he has entangled both their souls. He has dragged her down the road to Hell with him. At that time, the hardening of his soul has not advanced so far. He is on the point of breaking out of his prison and accepting the help which God waits to give, not to punish his sin but to wipe it out. He is seized by a passionate determination "to fall at the feet of God", and to raise Ingunn and himself out of their misery. In his dream he sees himself renewed; it is as if "the sweetness of their freshest youth" has returned. But it remains a good intention and a dream. His dread of men's opinion holds him back.

After long and bitter years, in which he grows ever more hard, his remorse suddenly bears fruit. There is some warmth in his heart—love for his daughter Cecilia and for Eirik. Despite his hatred for the son of the murdered man, "the avenging son", there is something in him which yearns for the boy. But the past stands like an invisible wall between them. His children detest their father; Eirik lifts a sword against him and would kill him; his daughter cannot bear his presence. All at once, Olav sees clearly that he is dragging Eirik and Cecilia into the slough where he himself has blundered. He says to Cecilia, "Don't believe that you benefit your children by being hard in heart and soul"; as he says it, he knows he is passing judgment on his own wasted life. "He should have flourished like the oak-tree, been as patient and wide-embracing, giving shelter and light to all who came to him." Instead, he has become a man who suffered from an inward "leprosy". His intellect cannot comprehend the reason why it is impossible for him to be at one with any human soul, without first being at one with God. Nevertheless, he knows that such is the case. There is only one thing to do—fall at the feet of God.

By any non-Christian interpretation, the description of Olav Audunsson's confession must seem infinitely sad. Of what use can it be that the dying Olav finally decides to cleanse his soul—something which might perhaps have helped him to get a grip on his life, if it had happened earlier? It is all too late. He is suffering, moreover, from a stroke, so that he is unable to articulate the words of his confession. But from a Christian point of view, the ending gives no cause for grief. True, it is a sad thing that Olav Audunsson, who had yearned so passionately to be the faithful warrior of God, should receive only too late the strength to carry the cross amongst men and battle in its cause on earth. But in Olav's perfect remorse, his heartfelt contrition, there is release for himself and for those nearest to him, for Eirik the avenging son and for Cecilia. Contrition has restored to life a continuity which had seemed irreparably broken. Olav's experience of the true nature of this continuity and consistency breaks out in a flood of joy in the last prayer which springs up in his heart, as, on that early summer morning, he creeps out of bed and sees the sunrise. Before his eyes he sees the innocence of nature, in his heart he feels the guilt of man. All he sees seems a reflection of God's splendour, and everything seems to be waiting for the contrition of the fallen.

Echoes from the Psalms of David are mingled in this wonderful hymn, which tells of the creature's longing for the righteousness of God. "All the trees of the forest shall rejoice in the face of the Lord, for He comes to judge the earth with righteousness; the waves shall clap their hands. Olav knew that they were waiting now, the trees that grew on the hills of his land, everything that sprouted and grew on the estate of his inheritance, and the waves moving in procession in the bay—all were waiting to see judgment passed on their dishonest and unfaithful master. It was this which the earth awaited every single hour, but it was only in the trembling dawn that the earth, beautiful and betrayed, sighed so audibly—sorrowful and merciless, it waited, like a maiden shamed, to see justice done on those who appeared before the seat of judgment. The sentence fell every minute and every hour; it was the password which one day called to the next, and which every night whispered to its successor. Everything created by God sang the hymn of praise—*Benedicite omnia opera Domini Domino*—and he too had known it when he was young. But those whom God set as lords and princes over the earth were false to Him and fought against each other, betraying God and their fellowmen."

The tone of Sigrid Undset's medieval novels is characterised first and foremost by great calm. We seem to be carried along on a deep stream, appreciating the pictures which pass before us as if they were direct sensations. She once wrote of Emily Brontë's power "to discern the delightfulness of every object," and the words apply to her own faculty: "Things are seen in the same way as children and the very young see nature—in happy moments when every tiny, insignificant thing beneath the open sky reveals its delight to our jaded senses. Whoever, through the years, has the power to see in this way, is a poet, even though that power may never be productive."

She had known how to reproduce her impressions of Oslo and its commonplace quarters, Welhaven's Street and Therese Street, painful in their beauty, Blaasen and Nordmark, as well as of Rome and the Campagna, all in such a way that the reader felt it as his own experience. Now she reveals the same power in her description of the external medieval world—landscapes, buildings, churches, monasteries, saints' days and working days, fights and feuds, the life of labour and the festive gathering, human conduct in all life's relationships. She could identify herself with the man or woman of the Middle Ages, sense with their senses, and consequently experience their emotions and think their thoughts. It is one of the great miracles in the history of creative literature, and even when the religious concepts of the novels mean nothing to the reader, this other aspect does not fail to fascinate him.

There is no sorcery in Sigrid Undset's art. Hers is the eternal realism, the realism of Homer and the Bible, of the sagas and the great novels of the nineteenth century.

In Sigrid Undset's writing, as in that of her contemporary Olva Duun, the saga-realism is united naturally and organically with modern realism and gains in strength thereby. Her use of word and action to suggest character indirectly is related to the method of the family-sagas. And the individual's family connections backward in time, which the sagas only introduce by a list of names (though this is often stylistically effective), receive in her writing a deeper significance, determined by not only the heathen but also the Christian belief that all is not at an end between living and dead.

To these features of presentation, and in harmony with modern literary realism, Sigrid Undset adds her powerful descriptions of background. She has been called the Zola of the Middle Ages. Her aim, however, is not to show the medieval man and woman as products of their age and environment, but rather to reveal the play between the external and internal, the life of the soul in the whole of its material and organic context. Her medieval novels are not peopled by ethereal beings. The primitive earth-bound side of human nature, the life of instinct, impulse and passion, provides fundamental characteristics in most of them. We see them grow up from the soil whence they first spring. But there is always a keynote heard from Heaven, a note struck by the longing of the created for the Creator.

The definite historical setting, and even more the precise localisation, may perhaps increase the impression of reality for Norwegian readers; in any case, they add to the enchantment of her writing. One likes to hear the old familiar names of farms and counties, valleys, towns and churches, all the way from the head of Oslofjord northward through the country round Mjøsa and on through Gudbrandsdal, over the Dovre mountains to Trøndelag and the cathedral of Nidaros, with glimpses still further north to the remotest outposts of Christian civilisation. But this precise localisation has charm also for foreign readers. Tourists inquire the way taken by Kristin Lavransdatter on her pilgrimage over Dovre to the tomb of Saint Olav, just as many a Norwegian reader of Scott's *Waverley Novels* or of Runeberg's *Fänrik Ståls Sägner*—as Knut Liestøl writes—thinks he has arrived in familiar historical places, when he travels in the Border country between Scotland and England, or amongst the scenes which he knows as the background for Runeberg's historical stories.

The question whether the reality in her novels corresponds to actual historical conditions is, from a purely æsthetic point of view, quite superfluous. Literature has its own life, possesses an inner truth independent of historical fact. But respect for the material, the external matter from which her world is constructed, loyalty to tradition and accuracy in the treatment of fact—these, like her impressions of nature, are nonetheless an integral part in the process of artistic creation. The historical realism of these novels is inextricably bound up with their ethical and spiritual message of the eternal which dwells in every man and woman and her revelation of the common stuff of humanity which is coloured, shaped and changed in the shifting tide of time.

It may be said that History is Sigrid Undset's muse. No one since Snorri Sturluson has presented medieval Norway with such power. Her inspiration is not simply Norway's past, but the history of Europe and Christendom. None of her contemporaries has heard the voices of the past as she has done; but neither has any of them seen further into the future and been more aware both of the darkness which lies before them and of the way through to the light beyond.

CHAPTER VII

Between the Wars: The Battle for Christian Civilisation

Soon after the first World War, in 1920, Hans E. Kinck, one of Scandinavia's most gifted intellectuals, published a collection of articles which he called *Helmsman Overboard* (*Rormanden overbord*). They were written during and after the years of catastrophe and, though they deal with a variety of topics, have in reality a single theme: the brutalising effect of war on men's minds and the consideration of what can be found in the prevailing gloom on which to rely and build. He writes that the dark days may last a long time. Those who are young now and who may have to take the "middle watch" are in for a "bad spell on the tossing vessel". The life of European culture is ebbing; it has been struck in its central and vital nerve—respect for the individual. "In every walk of life it is the individual who, in one way or another, is in jeopardy, while the taste of the masses gains control." In this connection, we can disregard Kinck's racial Romanticism. When it came to the point, he was an intellectual in the best sense of the word. One feels unconsciously, he says, that "in the end the decisive factor is mind" (*Helmsman Overboard*, p. 224f.).

The strongest mass-movement of the time was determined ideologically by the new Marxism. Its newness lay in its emphasis on the dynamic character of historical or dialectical materialism. Historical development is determined in the last resort by economic forces, class struggles which go their predetermined way according to the compelling laws of nature. "The Historical Process" is the catchword which is now continually repeated; one might call it the mystical divinity, whose power nothing can resist. In the "process" itself, the individual makes little difference one way or the other. His value is assessed not from a theological or metaphysical standpoint, but according to his importance for that particular stage in the dialectical evolution in which he happens to find himself. In reality, materialistic philosophy in the form of Marxism has undergone a metamorphosis significant for the history of the world. It has gone down into the dim depths of German Romanticism and returned armed with the cunning weapons of Hegelian logic.

An old phrase has it that, when the gods are driven out, the devils move in. The Fascist and Nazi reaction against Marxism was born of the same perplexity which threw people into the arms of the Communist masters: the ends were different but the means were the same. Hitler's doctrines of race-biology went perhaps even further than dialectical materialism in their contempt for the value of the human being. Meanwhile the three movements were at one in demanding the total subordination of the individual to the collective unity, to the state of the socialist society, or to the race or *das Germanentum*.

There appears a type of paganism hitherto unknown in the world. T. S. Eliot, the European poet who best represents the period between the wars, characterises it summarily in *The Rock*:

*Men have left GOD not for other gods, they say, but for no god;
and this has never happened before
That men both deny gods and worship gods, professing first Reason,
And then Money, and Power, and what they call Life, or Race, or
Dialectic.*

It has often been said that Norwegian thought in the years between the wars was, as elsewhere, stamped by a sterile, rootless and disillusioned intellectualism. "It was seldom that we glimpsed any sense of firm guiding values, any conscious realisation of human worth and a sustaining ideal of life" are words from the so-called *Cultural Letter* (*Kulturbrev*) of 1945, where some of the leading intellectuals of the time reckon up the period's salient features.

As far as literature is concerned, this judgment is only partly correct. "Firm values" and a "sustaining ideal" could be more than glimpsed not only in Sigrid Undset's work, but also in that of Olav Aukrust, Arnulf Øverland, Johan Falkberget, Olav Duun, Inge Krokann, Ingeborg Møller, Sigurd Christiansen, Ronald Fangen and others. Several of these authors give conscious expression to the Christian point of view.

Sigrid Undset is in a special position. In none of the other writers of the period do we find such a fundamental revolt against the materialist interpretation of life, with a criticism of contemporary culture so firmly based in point of principle and inspired by so clear a religious ideal. This applies both to her controversial and historical writing between the wars and to the novels of contemporary life which she also wrote in this period, particularly *The Wild Orchid* (*Gymnadenia*) and *The Burning Bush* (*Den brændende busk*).

Sigrid Undset's cultural roots go deep into Norway's past, and her writing stands in an intimate and organic relationship to the Norwegian cultural scene. Nevertheless, it was not from Norway but from England and France that she received the strongest impulses during the years after 1918, when she was engaged in her struggle on the cultural front.

After the first World War, her connections with France were strengthened—indeed there was in Norway at that time a general movement in this direction. Contact with the intellectual life of France was more influential than it had been for many years, though it was less strong amongst radical thinkers, who were mostly led by neo-Marxism or psychoanalysis to Russia or to the research and philosophy of Germany. But in the circle of neo-Humanists, the study of modern French thought had a liberating effect and presented a much wider horizon to their view. An inspiring impulse came from Peter Rokseth, who was deeply affected by the intellectual renaissance amongst French thinkers. Amongst his pupils were the brilliantly gifted Anders Wylle and Carl Vigo Holst, who both died young. Anders Wylle lived and breathed in the great Christian tradition of French intellectual life, and felt himself called to interpret to his countrymen the Christian humanism of France. From that source he received an essential impulse in his work for the Nansen School, which he hoped to transform into an institution capable of giving expression to a fundamental attitude to life, opposed to the materialism of the age in all its forms. He took his doctor's degree with a thesis called *Paul Claudel: A Christian Poet*, and was at work on a book about Charles Péguy.

In a little article which pays tribute to Jacques Maritain, Sigrid Undset gives a short and striking characterisation, of the French philosophical outlook which is here in question. For her, an essential point of contact lay with the French Dominicans, who had begun work in Norway immediately after the first World War. Of these, the strongest influence flowed from Father A. J. Lutz. From these Dominicans, she writes, one received confirmation of the fact that the Catholic Church was no antique relic, tied for ever to anachronistic social forms to which no one could ever return, but an active movement which pressed on with the times, possessing social awareness and a highly developed intellectual life, always preaching the same unchanging message, but with the power to present it according to the needs of the age. What was needed was an introduction into the religious way of thinking. It was no accident, she writes, that just such an impulse should come from France. By no one had the promulgation of the materialist idea, man's revolt against all the links which bind him to the supernatural world, been made with such eloquence or with such beguiling clarity as by French philosophers. But on the other hand, spiritual realism had nowhere been established with such insight, wisdom, simplicity and enthusiasm as in France—and amongst the first there, by Jacques Maritain. He and his allies urged us not simply to defend but to attack.

There were extremely few who were as well fitted as Sigrid Undset to take up the struggle against the paganism of the twentieth century. It is rare that one finds such a combination of sympathies as she possesses, fully conscious as she is both of the past and the present. It is even more seldom that one finds this dual awareness based on such a wide and confident knowledge of all aspects of culture— archaeology, folk-lore, the history of religion from its most primitive to its highest forms, the history of ideas and of literature, as well as psychology and sociology. In her essays, as sometimes in her novels, the mass of material can weigh heavy; but it means, on the other hand, that her controversial writing is most solidly founded upon knowledge of actual conditions. And she possesses both wit and humour —she enjoys fighting for a cause which is reckoned lost by the masses and the super-intelligent, or taking part in a "hopeless struggle" against evolution or the Historical Process.

Christianity, as she herself says, is "an urgent summons to spiritual warfare". She takes courage and hope from the fact that hitherto the Church has not only survived all its attacks from without, but has also been raised up anew after the periods of decay, which were due to its own error and sin—as, for example, after the degeneration of the tenth century and the papal corruption of the Renaissance, periods which always give good ammunition to any debating-society polemic against the Church. This inner regeneration of the Church is for her a miracle. "At any rate, no one who is otherwise a believer has been in a position to explain in reasonable terms how the Church could have survived the tenth century and then raised itself up once more, unscathed and strong, to a life fuller, richer and finer than ever before" (*Saint Olav, King of Norway: Hellig Olav, Norges Konge*).

During the first World War, she realised that European civilisation and Christianity are inseparably bound together. Now she sees forces asserting themselves who set themselves the express task of severing the vital link which join these two. If this succeeds, she writes, no one can see what form will be taken by the civilisation then to be created, but the totalitarian state can give us an idea. If the people of Europe cast off Christianity, the spiritual source of their life will dry up. "One may just as well believe that a tree whose roots are chopped away will continue to bud and bear fruit and flowers."

She emphasises that what is fundamentally at issue in the cultural struggle of the age is the battle between the ideologies which desire the total secularisation of mankind and complete severance from religion and those accepted by men who neither wish nor are able to free themselves from the Christian ideal—the ideal which claims that no society worthy of humanity can be established on earth, unless it finds its support in a power not of this world. Without such a mainstay, the individual is doomed. No wonder, she writes, that the masses, to whom the effects of an un-Christian civilisation have been brought home most nearly, should cry, "Let the State take us!"

The new Catholicism, with which Sigrid Undset is associated, is adjusted in principle to democratic and social forms. Maritain writes that in its innermost essence democracy is an inspiration of the Gospel. And Sigrid Undset writes, "That element of democracy which is in Christianity is the only one which cannot be argued out of existence. Against all talk of equality, there remains the irrefutable objection that human beings are not equal—one is a coin of copper, another of silver. Christianity meets this objection by maintaining that all of them are minted with the king's picture on them." Democracy is not an end in itself, it is one of the means to be used in protecting the human person. But as long as dictatorship does not accept the inviolability of the human person as its norm, democracy is at its mercy. That norm is an ideal which has never in the history of the human family received more elevated expression than in the Christian doctrine that man is created in God's image. And with that there is created an authority superior to the mundane order.

The criticism which Sigrid Undset levels at the Lutheran Church is based essentially on the submission of that Church to the mundane authority, the State. This is clear from the controversies in which she was engaged with Bishop Jens Gleditsch, just after her conversion, and with Pastor Sigurd Normann and Archbishop Nathan Söderblom, a year or two later. It is to be found especially in three articles, *The Inheritance Which Must Be Accepted (Arven som maa løftes), What Catholicism Thinks of Luther (Hvad katolisismen mener om Luther),* and *The Lutheran Spirit and the Catholic Spirit (Lutherdommens aand og katolisismens aand),* together with the little book, *Catholic Propaganda (Katolsk propaganda),* first printed in Ronald Fangen's periodical *Vor Verden* in 1927.

At that time, there were stronger prejudices to overcome than at present, if one was to undertake a cultural struggle on behalf of Catholicism. The controversy over state support for Lars Eskeland's Folk High-School had shown, for example, that Protestant legends about the Catholic Church had been fostered and developed just as far as the corresponding Catholic legends about the Protestant Church, and very often further. Work like that of Sigrid Undset's in the essays mentioned above was intended to educate, and, even if it was particularist in approach, could in the long run only serve to strengthen Christian unity between

Sigrid Undset

Protestants and Catholics. It was important to make clear what elements in Lutheranism had helped to clear the way for the totalitarian conception of the State.

The controversy was occasioned by certain considerations, published by Bishop Gleditsch in the newspaper *Aftenposten*, on the motives which lay behind the conversion of Sigrid Undset and Lars Eskeland to the Catholic Church. He thought it only natural that, in a time of chaos, they should seek some spiritual foothold. But when they looked for it in the Catholic communion, it was because they allowed themselves to "imagine" that the Reformation had set them outside the Church—"disinherited them". For the rest, it was a matter of idealisation and fantasy, corresponding to "the literary movement to which we usually give the name of Romanticism." This Romanticism in Sigrid Undset's work could not be disguised by the fact that her writing was otherwise realistic in style.

Sigrid Undset's reply does not give the impression of one who has turned to the Church as an asylum for romantic æsthetes. And in her contribution to the controversy, she takes a far-reaching historical view.

She shows that Luther must accept no small share of the responsibility for the process of secularisation which has been in operation since the Renaissance. Whatever one may think of Luther as a religious personality—and Sigrid Undset does not take kindly to him—it is still impossible to escape the fact that he not merely broke with the Church, but made his new church-establishment submissive to the German princes, that is, to the State. With this, the evangelical Lutheran Church lost its spiritual sovereignty and, in Germany at least, became a prop for the absolute State. She maintains with irrefutable logic that if, moreover, in a democratic society a political party came to power which dismissed its "handmaid", that would be the end of the established church. As a supra-national and universal spiritual organisation, the Lutheran Church had capitulated in principle. In her view, the Protestant Church only retains rudiments of the spiritual society and living tradition which form the vital part of the Catholic Church.[1]

Sigrid Undset has adopted the Catholic conception of the Church in all its richness and spiritual profundity. She is not surprised that in Protestant countries the houses of God are shut and locked when the priest is not there. Christianity has become a "preaching religion". It is as if the sacred no longer has its dwelling in the Protestant churches. It is of some small help, perhaps, that Bible-reading has been given a more prominent place—but, she writes, "when I was fourteen or fifteen, I already thought it a grotesque idea that God the Almighty, maker of heaven and earth, father of past times and peoples as well as of the centuries to come, should make the home-coming of His children to their Father's house depend on the achievement of proficiency in reading." To her the Protestant Church is no longer a Church at all, and she thinks it has ceased to be so for a steadily increasing number of Protestants. Its place has been taken by the prayer-house and chapel, where religion runs riot in revivals, prayer-meetings, public witness and confession of God, and foundation of brotherhoods and sisterhoods. She speaks of this with no contempt. "I understand that the ordinary man must turn to the wild growths of this religion in order to find food, since for centuries the common human need for religion has been starved by the Lutheran Church."

She is opposed to Luther's degradation of the ideals of chastity, virginity and celibacy, but chiefly to his doctrine of the bondage of the human will, as it is developed in one of his principal works, *On the Will Enslaved.* Here it is

[1] Grundtvig put life into these rudiments more than any other thinker in Scandinavia. Apart from his hymns, his teaching seems scarcely to have been of significance for Sigrid Undset. From the point of view of church history, however, it is interesting to note how strongly Krogh-Tonning (*Memoirs of a Convert: En konvertits erindringer*, 1906, p. 51) emphasises the impulse towards Catholicism which he received from Grundtvig's ideas. He further characterises the Grundtvig school as "a nursery for Roman Catholic sympathies."

especially her little book *Catholic Propaganda* which is important. This is one of the most illuminating of her controversial writings, and at the same time it is one of those most deeply inspired by her faith. It was written while she was still at work on *Olav Audunsson* and may to some extent be read, especially in that part where she speaks of remorse and of David's "tempest-tossed" Psalms, as her commentary on the novel. Chiefly however, this book is concerned with the divine dignity of mankind. Luther's doctrines of the total depravity of human nature and of salvation by faith alone are absurd for the Catholic Christian. Sigrid Undset's reasoning is in accord with Christian philosophy and with the *philosophia perennis* as a whole. There is a resemblance between God and man, an *analogia entis*, as Thomas Aquinas calls it; and in fallen man the image of God is not completely destroyed. Man's freedom consists precisely in this, that he has the power to choose whether he will be as the divine nature has intended, or whether he will try to escape from this intention, even though he knows that punishment is not an excluded factor —punishment not in the form of vengeance wreaked by a white-haired divinity, but as a necessary consequence of man's own choice to place himself outside the divine order. "No human being shall be saved unless he wills it so himself, and none condemned unless it is his will, choosing this rather than allowing his will to harmonise with the will of God."

It is evident to Sigrid Undset that Protestant theologians have not drawn the full conclusions from the theory of human nature's total depravity, any more than Luther himself had done. Neither does Archbishop Söderblom, in his elaborate reply to Sigrid Undset in *Vor Verden* (April 1927), go deeply into the matter. He says only this: "It cannot be helped— God and man are incommensurable, and the divine life can never be introduced into human affairs on this little planet of ours without conflict and imperfection." But this very conflict is the theme of all Sigrid Undset's writing. And she is surely right in maintaining that Luther's anti-humanist ideas of the enslaved will and mankind's utter depravity are amongst the causes of the opposition, often apparent in Protestant countries, between the Christian life and the secular cultural life, between the "spiritual" and the "worldly". Sigrid Undset tells a little story from a Norwegian country district, where offence was taken by the "regenerate" at the "unspiritual" way in which the pastor's wife walked. Less amusing examples could be supplied from the efforts of those in favour of Folk High Schools, or from Grundt-vigianism and the liberal youth-movement, not to mention instances from the experience of those who have practised art or pleaded its cause in societies dominated by Protestant pietism. A feeling for beauty, as an attraction towards the divine, is not seldom regarded in pietist logic as a devilish allurement.

As we have seen, Sigrid Undset's opinion is that people today are more taken up with themselves and more ego-centric than at any other epoch. To a large and essential degree, her novels of modern life presented a psychological analysis of this phenomenon. The criticism of contemporary culture which she makes from her Christian point of view follows the same course. The Renaissance, as well as the Reformation, must be given a share in the responsibility—a just allotment, for the movement which goes under that name in the history-books heralds, in reality, the self-worship of our own time. Then began in full earnest the "egocentric cult of the personality". Even so, its appearance at that time was only sporadic and the Christian community was still unbroken. "The men and women of the Renaissance fought and loved and intrigued and enjoyed all that life could offer in the way of mental pleasure, art and beauty and sensuous gratification, but nevertheless the old Catholic feeling of humanity's fundamental solidarity remained more or less untouched." (*Stages on the Way: Etapper, Ny Række.*)

In the nineteenth and twentieth centuries, however, the egocentric attitude to life becomes dominant. It lies at the heart of Rousseau's cult of the naturally good man, "the noble savage", whom society has depraved. It is equally fundamental in forms of secularised liberalism, in that dream of a blessed socialist society, for example, and in mystic longing for the beatitude which will come, if only the sexual life can succeed in finding an unrepressed development. Sigrid Undset suggests that everything of this kind is a disguise, more or less attractive, for the cult of the self and for wishful thinking.

The unveiling of this egocentric cult, in all its forms, hidden and revealed, direct and indirect, is the dominant aim in a whole series of her best essays. As she does in *Confusion of Ideas*, so here she often takes as her starting-point something which seems to her especially typical of the fallacies of the age. We find this, for instance, in her essay on spiritualism called *Blasphemy* (*Blasfemi*). Spiritualists' ideas of a life after death are regarded by her as the result of egocentric dreams, the longing for fulfilment of all their earthly hopes. Something similar is apparent in the attempts of liberal theologians to construct the historical Jesus in the form of "an amiable young preacher with special gifts for moving women's institutes" and generally speaking in all attempts to fashion a modernised Christianity (*Samtiden*, 1935). Especially worthy of notice is her essay on D. H. Lawrence, written with sympathy and deep feeling for his work. She is fully aware of the greatness of this tragic writer of the period between the wars. He felt the failings and the pain of his time as his own. He is a voice crying in the wilderness, she writes. "The widespread fear of the consequences of the mechanisation of existence—a slow death from the loss of our vital warmth—is given shape and voice in D. H. Lawrence, in poems and descriptions which gush out like the spurt of blood from a severed artery, in intense animated pictures of life in conflict." But the cure he ad-

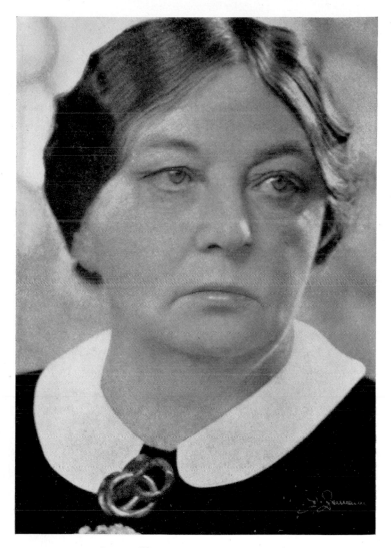

SIGRID UNDSET IN THE LATE 1930'S

vocated was no more than a poor substitute for religion. His "eternal circuit round the sexual act, which for his sensitive soul means communion"—this was the dream of a sexual mystic, a dream of life's renewal through "the blood", not unrelated to the racial and biological mysticism of the Nazis. "Much that happens in Europe today, and even more that is likely to happen, is the brutal reaction of humanity in the mass against those problems which the exceptional man, the genius D. H. Lawrence, perceived, contemplated and fought against in his way." (1938).

On the warriors of the Christian faith, its heroes and heroines, Sigrid Undset has written a whole series of essays. Controversy steps into the background, but even here her writing constitutes a refutation of the new paganism and its idolatry. She has to make clear to her readers what a saint really is and what is really implied in his veneration and invocation, to explain that it is not a question of a disguised polytheism or of old local divinities decked out in Christian trappings, but of a living communion with those men and woman who had "heroic love for God" and have gone furthest in the execution of Our Lord's command, "Be ye therefore perfect, even as your Father which is in heaven is perfect." She maintains that there is one element in hagiolatry which every spiritually-minded person should know how to value: it teaches one to assess life by spiritual standards. "The saintly cults exclude the cult of success— of worldly and temporal prosperity and of those people who have had luck with them here on earth. This is not to say that a person who has apparently always enjoyed good fortune and has lived a happy human life is necessarily a worse Christian, one who must needs expect a painful reckoning with his God and Judge. But it does mean that the Church, with its veneration of the saints, stands firm against the idea of a religious business transaction, the idea which has led people to believe that the material prosperity of individuals and nations is a sign of God's special pleasure in them, while in misfortune and defeat they always see God's judgment."

Veneration of the saints depends on a human need which it seems impossible to eradicate. "For lack of anything better, we have practised the hero-worship of match-kings and gangsters, sportsmen and artists, film-stars and dictators." "Some figures we must set up on pedestals in order to admire something of ourselves in them. But only with the saints can we find an outlet for our craving for hero-worship, where self-worship does not creep in" (*They Sought the Ancient Paths*).

It is the picture she presents of the saints and their lives, and not any kind of controversial apology, which is most important in these biographies. In them she displays her rich powers as a historian, portrayer of character and writer; she translates the saints' lives into a modern idiom, closely related to the transformation she effected in her historical novels. Usually, there is an extensive and detailed presentation of the whole social and historical background, but, from this, the personality and the Christian idea and its realisation within the framework of the assumptions and demands of the particular age emerge with even more convincing power. She shows, for example, how in the thirteenth century a certain Ramon Lull, or Raimundus Lullus, could be transformed, by virtue of his mystical experience of God, from an idler into a man of action; and how Angela Merici, in contrast to the egocentric fulfilment of life demanded by her Renaissance contemporaries, could find precisely through her love for God a source of spiritual energy, which directed her craving for action towards other ends than self-worship. As we know, "the mystical bride of God" was a pioneer in various kinds of philanthropic work, especially in nursing and education, and an organiser with a gift for administration, who founded the famous order of the Ursulines. Sigrid Undset has given her essay on Saint Angela Merici the controversial title of *A Woman of the Suffragette Movement.* She gives her a place amongst those cultured women who made their influence felt in the life of medieval society, thanks to the Catholic Church's recognition of the right of women to develop their intellectual powers. According to Sigrid Undset—and her view is probably correct—even the Renaissance women who took a hand in politics, patronised art and learning and were themselves artists and blue-stockings, found one of their essential preconditions in this tradition of the Church. But "we all know that wherever Lutheranism or Calvinism came to set their mark on the culture of a country, women were educated in the course of a few generations to accept the idea that they existed only for the sake of men. Thus, when the emancipation of women came in those countries, it usually went hand in hand with the emancipation of the whole people from their religious traditions" (*Stages on the Road*).

Sigrid Undset fostered a quite exceptional affection for what she calls "the Church's epic in England", the struggle of the Church against the ecclesiastical policy of Henry VIII and against the persecution of English Catholics, the so-called Recusants, in the sixteenth and seventeenth centuries. Sigrid Undset is not the only one to have seen a parallel between this struggle and the life-and-death conflict of our own time between intellectual freedom and the totalitarian state. Realisation of it has, for example, inspired Rose Macaulay's novel, *They Were Defeated*, and the biography of Thomas More by the historian, R. W. Chambers, published in 1935. Chambers writes that More is the hero of the Catholic because he gave his life "in and for the faith of the Holy Catholic Church". Chambers adds that he should be the hero of all men of good will. "I am not forgetting . . . that his blessing belongs of right to those of the faith for which he died, and that the rest of us can only have such blessing as poor Esau claimed, who had lost his birthright: 'Hast thou but one blessing: bless me, even me also, oh my father'."

Sigrid Undset has not often spoken of men like Thomas More and Cardinal Fisher, who also suffered martyrdom for his faith. But Thomas More was always close to her heart. She was once asked which historical personage she most admired. Her unhesitating answer was Thomas More, the Christian humanist who at the block uttered the proud words, "The King's good servant, but God's first."

She writes of the less famous, often almost forgotten, soldiers of Christ, like the priest, poet and martyr, Robert Southwell, who was brought to the scaffold not because of rebellion against the throne, but because he could not bring himself to obey the order of the government that he should not administer the sacraments to his co-religionists according to the rites of their Church. Or she dips into letters and diaries, as in the essay, *Cavalier*, which tells of that dauntless recusant, William Blundell. The gem in this group of essays is, however, the one called *The Greatest Power* (*Den sterkeste magt*), on Lucius Cary Falkland, who first supported Cromwell, but later, when he saw fanaticism gain the upper hand, went over to the king's party. He was fighting on two fronts, desirous both of change and conservation. Sigrid Undset's suggestion, that he was related in spirit to the optimists of later times who have believed in "the victory of the good", may, as far as it goes, be true. But it is also true that his optimism had a more solid foundation than had the nineteenth century's radiant faith in evolution. The eventual victory of the good depends on whether the "wills of individual men and women are directed into an effort to do God's will—even if in life they have not been able to hold fast to that line without wavering, deviation and interruption." Moreover, the optimistic evolutionary faith of the nineteenth century has, as she says, its source in "an illumination which is no more than the reflection of what appears to the modern un-Christian world to be the sun sunk down behind a hill."

Sigrid Undset's most important historical writing is her account of the first introduction of Christianity into Norway and of the men who did most to further its cause. On this subject, there is her brilliant scholarly essay, *The Conversion in Norway*, and her biographies of the medieval Norwegian saints, studies which were collected and published in the monumental work, *Saga of Saints* (*Norske Helgener*, 1937).

From the purely academic point of view—and as far as one considers sympathy with the subject to be a benefit to the historian—Sigrid Undset's presentation of these personalities has the great advantage of being made by one who is herself a Catholic. Her attitude thus conforms to the conception which, with other motives, must have been a powerful impulse in the formation of the legends concerning these saintly figures. *Saga of Saints* represents something new, precisely because her treatment was based on consideration of the history of ideas and she had the ability to see the historical events in the light of the ideas which brought them about or, at least, played a part in producing them.

Her discussion of the figure of Thorgils Arrbeinsstjup in *Flóamanna Saga* is typical of her critical attitude towards source-material. From this story, it is possible to get the impression of a man's conscious choice, determined by religious factors. Thorgils will not let himself be frightened by Thor, and in all his trials answers that "he chooses Him who redeemed me with His blood." But one must remember, she writes, that Thorgils was an ancestor of Bishop Thorlák the Saint, and that this fact has certainly influenced his presentation in the saga. Nothing is further from her than romantic idealisation, but on the other hand, as George Sverdrup has pointed out, her psychological insight guards her from the facile destructive scepticism of many modern historians. Sverdrup thinks, however, that at times her scepticism is carried too far. (*When Norway Became Christian*, 1942, p. 96f.).

The most important thing in this essay is her discussion of the relation in which the old Norse religion stood to the new illumination of Christianity. In connection with her medieval novels, we have already mentioned her criticism of the nationalist-romantic ideas, especially those fostered in Germany, concerning the old mythology. It was fancied that this had been created by some mystic "folk mind", which possessed an intuitive knowledge of the original genius of the Germanic peoples and their mission in world history— ideas which re-appeared in the *nordische Religion* of the Nazis. A religion, similar in type to the "instituted religions", was constructed on the basis of the Eddic poems. The fact that these were the creations of individual poets was overlooked, and it was pure fantasy to consider them expressions of the "folk-mind" in the Romantic sense of the word. After all, the old Norse religion was in reality "a genuine folk-paganism—a conglomeration of beliefs and concepts and ideas which the people had gathered together through thousands of years."

Occupying a central position in her presentation of the conversion is, as we have said, the clear definition of the antithesis between the exclusive family society and the Christian universality, and between the belief in fate and the Christian conception of freedom, "the message of man's free will to choose", which breaks through the determinist conviction of the unshakable powers of destiny. These antitheses are fundamental. It is simply naïve, she writes, to wonder that neo-pagan ideologies in our own time should create closed societies and dictatorial governments, both hostile to freedom.[1]

Her emphasis on the realism of Christianity is also characteristic. "The realistic daylight of the Gospel was set against the primaeval mist of the myth." The new religion was historical. "It was founded by a Man whose life and death

[1] Cf. H. Bergson, *Les deux sources de la morale et de la réligion* (1932), on Christianity as the "open" religion.

could be reckoned in time, and of whom there are written records; the faith was passed on from age to age and from nation to nation, by apostles, martyrs and bishops, and professed by men and women in spite of persecutions, perils and the sentence of death—the saints, of whose life and death men also had written evidence." Probably she is also right when she maintains that the strongest impression made by the saints' lives on the northern peoples was not the result of the marvellous embellishment, nor yet the fact that the saints could remind them of the old swarm of heathen gods, but simply depended on the contention that these men and women had really lived in such-and-such a place at such-and-such a time.

She considers much more than the differences between Christianity and the older faith. As a good Catholic, Sigrid Undset has a deep respect for the general religious sentiment which finds expression even in the most primitive beliefs—in a feeling for the sacred, the idea of sacrifice and communion with the dead. The Church does not simply imply a radical break with the past—on the contrary, it lends support to whatever seems to be reaching towards the divine reality and adapts the old forms to fit the new content. "The old festivals connected with spring-time and harvest and all the work of the farming-year were brought under a heavenly Ministry of Agriculture, and so continued, cleansed of their coarsest heathen features and sanctified by Christian ceremonies and devotions."

Neither could there have been a clean break between old and new in ethical matters. Loyalty was the virtue in which everyone believed and which was glorified in the old poetry. "At the heart of the veneration of the saints lay the same glorification, transferred onto a higher plane and applied to those warriors of whom Christ had said that they were those who had endured with Him in all His tribulations. And even the people who had neither the desire nor the courage to follow too closely in the footsteps of Christ and His saints admitted that the holy men and women were the flower of Adam's kin, those who had succeeded in achieving mankind's goal in the world."

It is from this point of view that Sigrid Undset writes of the holy ones of Norway: Saint Sunniva and the Men of Selje, Saint Olav, Norway's King, Saint Halvard, Saint Magnus, Earl of Orkney, Saint Eystein, Archbishop of Nidaros, Saint Torfinn, Bishop of Hamar, and from our own time, Father Karl Schilling.

Of the long series of literary portraits of Saint Olav, from the Middle Ages down to our own day, Sigrid Undset's is near to being the most sober. The biography in *Saga of Saints* seems almost dry in comparison with Fredrik Paasche's heartfelt account of Olav and the Olav tradition, or Harry Fett's brilliantly imaginative view of Olav as typical of the European crisis-period round about the year 1000, or Olav Aukrust's mystical poetry in Olav's honour. It has none of the religious fervour which marks the little essay she wrote on the occasion of his nine-hundredth anniversary, *Saint Olav, King of Norway*. In *Saga of Saints* she tells his life from the available sources, weighing the value of these one against another. There is no question of idealising Olav's character: she does not conceal his meanness and his lust for power and revenge. But as far as she is concerned, the problem to be faced is not primarily the personality of the historical Olav. She seeks rather to explain how his reputation could attain such enormous power, how it was that, after death and defeat, his influence could begin to have real effect. Who was Saint Olav? Naturally, she writes, the rumours of Olav's sanctity made excellent propaganda material in the hands of those men who wanted to rid themselves of Svein Knutsson's rule in Norway. Nevertheless, the belief in Olav as God's instrument on earth and a mighty saint in Heaven did not come to life as an element in a struggle for political power. It is a fact that the oldest sources we have on which to base an assessment of Olav's reputation,—as it was shaped immediately after his enemies had cleared him from their way,—are *Glælognskviða*, by the scald Thórarin Loftunga, and a few liturgical texts. Motives are mixed in every human action, but there was nothing here to suggest that the political factor was of primary importance. Thórarin writes his poem in honour of Svein Knutsson; but he says that King Svein must rule in such a way that the holy king in Heaven will not grudge him the kingdom. Both for Thórarin and for the Office of Saint Olav, it is an essential point to be made that Olav fought the good fight—"sinless he had saved his soul". It was the Church which glorified Olav's cause as the cause of victory at a time when, in the general view, it had still not recovered from its material defeat. In itself, of course, there was nothing novel in praising a man who had suffered defeat, as long as his personal fame lived after him. The Vikings had understood that as well as anyone. Here too was to be found a connecting link between the mental attitude of the Viking Age and the Christian point of view. But the Christian view had a perspective which was eternal—and for this reason, the man Olav Haraldsson became Olav the saint.

Amongst the other lives, her version and interpretation of the legend of Saint Halvard must be specially noticed. It is a work of art, simple and moving, inspired by the legend's power to make the Christian message of brotherhood amongst all men concrete and graphic. One understands why Knut Hagberg chose this legend as Sigrid Undset's contribution to his great anthology, *The Christian Idea. From Augustine to T. S. Eliot* (*Den kristne tanke. Fra Augustin til T. S. Eliot*, 1947).

Her vast educational work concerning the Church and the history of Christian ideas and their relation to our own time was continued in her brilliant contributions to Cappelen's history of culture—*The Church of Sogne* (*Sognekirken*), *On the Pilgrim's Path* (*Paa pilegrimsferd*), *Monastery Life* (*Klosterliv*)

—and in the little essay, *The Idea of a Monastery* (*Kloster-tanken*), which appeared in the periodical, *Fritt Ord*. This is cultural history of an inspired kind, full of accurate and striking information, steeped in her profound familiarity with the material, and illumined throughout by her Christian attitude to life.

Important as Sigrid Undset's controversial and historical writings are, it is only in her new novels of modern life that we really become acquainted with the whole spiritual emphasis of her criticism of culture in the post-war world. For, after all, she is first and foremost an artist.

CHAPTER VIII

New Novels of Contemporary Life:
Madame Dorothea

I N HER first novels of modern life, Sigrid Undset portrayed characters for whom, with a few exceptions, religion was of little importance—or, at least, of little conscious importance. Religion exists in them in rudimentary form or it is open to them as a possibility. Ideas they have gathered from religious instruction, from Church and Christianity, may have a momentary influence, but relationship with God or with an objective truth never becomes a decisive factor in their lives. But when she now returns from medieval to modern themes, the position is altered. There is no question of her books' being religious propaganda—Christian literature, as that phrase is commonly understood,—but the leading motives are religious.

She is no less a realist than before, and no less a realist than other contemporary Christian novelists, like François Mauriac and Georges Bernanos in France and Graham Greene and Evelyn Waugh in England. But, once again, she must be placed in a separate category. The psychological penetration of a writer like François Mauriac, for example, fastens above all on the evil in man and his wretchedness without grace. In this series of her modern novels, Sigrid Undset is chiefly occupied with man's inherent tendency towards truth and virtue. Sin and the sense of guilt, remorse and penitence, which were vital elements in the medieval novels, continue to play an important part, but another aspect also claims attention. In the medieval novels we meet the Augustinian type of Christianity. In the story of the conversion of Paul Selmer, in *The Wild Orchid* (*Gymnadenia*) and *The Burning Bush* (*Den brændende busk*), we find another type, which the French philosopher, Etienne Gilson, calls Thomist. Thomism, he says, is the doctrine which teaches that man's pure nature needs the Christian faith as a guarantee for its full development. In Paul Selmer, we see how the "pure nature"—i.e. his inherent tendency towards the true and good—is repelled by the worldliness and lack of perspective of modern culture, and how it is drawn towards a Church which does not sacrifice the eternal for the immediate.

These books contain some biting satire. It tends to be somewhat stylised when it is aimed at the Protestant clergy, especially the liberal theologians; but it is mercilessly accurate when it touches such things as the boom-mentality, baseness and superficiality, which prevailed amongst large social groups in Norway during the first World War. Equally sure and unsparing is her exposure of the self-satisfaction and fatuity of the un-Christian middle-class, or, as in *Ida Elisabeth*, her exposure of idealistic self-deception and the "nature-idyll".

The satire remains of minor significance, and here, as elsewhere, her greatness lies in her powers of self-identification with ordinary people. She had possessed that faculty from the beginning, but her ability to share in the life of others has perhaps never extended so far as in her portrayal of such "anonymous" characters as Lucy Sippen in *The Wild Orchid*, Ida Elisabeth in the novel which bears her name, and Nathalie in *The Faithful Wife* (*Den trofaste hustru*). This activity of her imagination has gained new strength from the Christian attitude, which conditioned the creation of these novels.

In the novel-cycle *The Wild Orchid* (1929) and *The Burning Bush* (1930), she describes Paul Selmer's development from an agnostic or free-thinker of the modern type

into one who believes in God and the vitality of Christianity
as objective truths.

Essential stages of Sigrid Undset's own development seem
to be reflected in Paul's progress, and, as far as that goes,
one can speak of the work as autobiography. But in external
circumstances there is no similarity—apart from the fact
that they are both children of the same epoch. The similarity
exists on the purely spiritual plane, and they are alike in
intellectual make-up and in temperament. Paul Selmer
has the same scepticism as his creator, and the same blend
of cool logic, sense of reality and tender sympathy.

Not that Paul has any very spectacular gifts, although it
is true that he has something of a bent for geology and has
taken his honours degree in that subject. But he gives up
his studies and goes into business, at first with a friend and
then on his own, running a small stone-works. We are not
concerned with any far-away fantasy: Paul has both feet
firmly on the ground of practical life—or, as people often
call it, "real life".

The action in *The Wild Orchid*, the first part of the cycle,
spans the period from about 1905 to the outbreak of the
first World War. The mentality of that period is marked
by an optimistic faith in life and the future, and this outlook
prevails in the home where Paul grows up. His mother,
Julie Selmer, lives on the traditions from the 'eighties:
in her eyes, that was the great age when people here in
Norway were liberated from all the prejudices which the
Church and Christianity had set in the way of progress
and the free development of the personality. She has broken
away from her marriage to Selmer, the conservative office-
manager, unable to stand it any longer; they were just not
suited to one another. For the rest, Julie Selmer has engaging
qualities; she is courageous, energetic and independent.
She has made an attractive and pleasant home for her
children. She insists that they learn to show respect for
everything frail and small. She loves flowers. "'I'm so

excited to see if the gymnadenia I planted here last year will come to anything.' 'Gymnadenia?' said Paul; 'isn't that a kind of orchid?' 'That's right—white and with a lovely scent. I got a few bulbs from Ringebu last year, but you can never be sure how they'll take when you plant them out.' Paul thought the name was so beautiful. He lay on his back in the grass. 'Gymnadenia,' he whispered softly. . . . He imagined tall stems with luminous wax-white flowers under the dark juniper-bushes. He saw where they stood and shone over the grass, there where it was finest and shot through with patches of light. They must smell like the butterfly orchid. 'Gymnadenia,' he whispered, as if it were something which lay outside in life, waiting for him. 'Gymnadenia—so lovely. . . .'"

Paul cannot help feeling a reaction against his mother. Young as he is,—he has just matriculated,—he seems to sense her spiritual sterility, something sharp and cold in her. The other "liberated" souls make the same impression on him. They declared that they were on the side of the future, evolution and the "new dawn". "But once folk were 'liberated', they became so intolerably circumscribed." When they dreamed of a new order for the world, it was as if they were making a fetish of themselves. "It might very well be that there was a need to extend the circle. I merely think that the circle has not been made wider in this way, but that it has been rubbed out and only a point left, the little ego, the heart which once beat and was full of warmth at the centre of at least a small circle. They chatter about duties and aims and how happy society will be, when everyone has advanced as far and they all hold the same views as themselves."

Paul's fellow-students talked of socialism, the new morality, the materialist interpretation of life, the abolition of religion. Socialism might easily carry away the masses, he thought—until some new call to arms was heard. And most of the young people, "while they let themselves be carried along by the stream, seemed to imagine that they were dancing in front of the ark". The abolition of religion? For one who had never had a religion, that could be of no interest. As for an outlook on life, he restricted himself to a couple of brief maxims: never believe something because most other people believe it; and never yield to the temptation to argue in this way—if others do it, then so can I.

The events of 1905 make a profound impression on Paul. It is a religious emotion which he experiences on June 7th[1]—religious insofar as he knows what it is to be lacking a God to turn to. He pulls a face at the words of his brother-in-law, Halstein Garnaas, who says, "You can count on it that there are thousands—millions—of hearts which are lifted up towards the high place today." But to himself he admits that it is only the way Halstein puts things which he finds repellent —for today there should have been a God. "As he came along in the brougham, he could have knelt down and folded his hands. There ought to have been someone to whom he could give the praise and honour—with all his heart, and from some source deeper yet within him, from the profoundest depth of his whole being. There should have been someone whose blessing he could pray for. This evening, he understood why people needed something of this sort— a God with whom they could hold communion." There are other political events in that year of which he does not approve. He has to ask himself if there has not been a fatal flaw in the whole thing from the beginning. It is worst for him to meet those who will not agree that the autumn retreat has been a humiliation.

Paul's first contact with the Catholic Church is accidental. In one of his early years as a student, he rents a room in Schwensen's Street with a family who turn out to be Catholics. But there is nothing accidental about the way in which he accepts their acquaintance. In the first place, he has none

---

[1] On this day the Norwegian Parliament declared that the country's union with Sweden was dissolved.

of the Lutheran antagonism towards Catholics; and in the second place, he is completely free from the prejudices of the "liberated". There is no pride in Paul Selmer, and he has not thrown himself into the arms of any of the new paganism's substitute religions—Progress, Science, Evolution, Socialism, and the rest. But his scepticism has not entirely destroyed his spiritual life—on the contrary, it has provided soil for the delicate plant within him, his craving for the eternal, his longing for something more than the daily round can give, that part of him which desires to meet his Creator.

He has qualities which make him well fitted to understand the Christian spiritual world, which he now gradually learns to know. His contact with it is made both through the simple, ingenuous piety of the people he stays with, the Gotaas family, and through the deeply considered appropriation of Christianity which he finds in the young intellectual converts, Randi Alme and Harald Tange. He has to revise the opinion, which he has heard so often, that the Catholics use all sorts of tricks in order to get people into their toils. He talks to the Catholics he knows. Old Gotaas speaks to him unaffectedly and nobly of the mystery of prayer, on one occasion when Paul says flippantly that he finds it hard to understand how he can always have something to pray for. "Paul had a tiny glimpse into a mystical life of devotion of which he knew nothing. It had never in fact occurred to him before, that prayer was not simply a matter of asking for something God might do for one."

He feels he would like to attend a Catholic church. There he finds much that is strange and incomprehensible, but all the same, he is gripped by the devotion he can recognise there—he has never seen anything like it in a Protestant church. Here people have come together, not to listen to a sermon, but to worship an invisible being. "It was impossible for this service to have any other meaning. The priest never turned to the congregation and busied himself with them; it was rather as if this man at their head was the leader in an act of worship. And for the first time in his life, he thought he could see some point in a church service—in this silent adoration, he could feel that there was a Being present who welcomed the souls as they came. It was obvious that early Christianity, with its power to achieve such a colossal expansion, must have had such a form as this—and in this form also it must have come first to this country, before it was turned into a preaching-religion."

He comes across a little book containing the old Latin hymns, *Te Deum* and *Miserere*, with a German translation, having known only the first words of both. The *Te Deum*, he had fancied, was a kind of howl of triumph which the Catholics uttered when they made merry over Saint Bartholomew's Eve, while the *Miserere* was usually sung when they burnt heretics or shut up unruly nuns. "But, as it was, they were quite breathtakingly beautiful. He had least of all expected that the *Te Deum* should close in a humble prayer—'Vouchsafe, O Lord, to keep us from sin this day'—or something like that. 'Day by day we magnify thee; have mercy, have mercy upon us—in thee have we trusted, and thou wilt not put us to shame for ever.' That was something like the ending. But the *Miserere* ended, not exactly in triumph, but still on a curiously resolute and cheerful note—something like 'Then shall my mouth acknowledge thy praise'—and something about Sion's walls, 'they shall be built up again, and the people will bring sacrifices to the altars!'"

The impulse to seek after the giver of all good gifts and to return thanks to him has, in reality, always been with him. He felt it out in the world of nature, strongest of all, up in the mountains. "All of us Norwegians have a religious feeling when we are face to face with the mountains." The feeling can come over him, whenever he stands before some strange and wonderful thing; and he cannot be satisfied when the objects he marvels at remain, as it were, anonymous.

He wants to know to whom he may offer his devotion, who has given him his feeling of humility: he not only sees the sign, but realises that there is one who intended it for a sign. A friend asks, "Why is it absolutely necessary for you to put your finger on the miracle-maker?" Paul answers, "Why? Because I have really always thought that, when I get to the top of a mountain for instance, it would be more natural to build an altar and perform some sacrifice there, rather than add a few stones to the cairn or put an empty bottle on it with a list of names inside. If I felt like taking the butter from my tin and spreading it on the stones and making an offering to the sun in that way—that's an action I could very well take pleasure in; my religious feeling would have found some expression. If only I didn't know that the sun got no satisfaction from the grateful sacrifice of my butter! My religious feeling tells me that it is perfectly natural to worship the sun and to offer it sacrifices—as long as people haven't realised that the sun is quite unconscious of us and of the good it does us. It's the same with all nature-worship—it's inevitable, but only until we understand that Nature has neither thought nor feeling for us."

In this search for the objective truth, to which both his heart and mind aspire, it is a matter of course that Paul should seek guidance from the followers of the Catholic faith. He wants to find out what it really teaches, what its dogma and ceremony signify.

Gradually, he becomes acquainted with a set of standards which are totally different in kind from those of the anthropocentric ideology of progress in which he has been brought up, without ever truly believing in it. He sees the opposition between belief in an evolution which sends mankind now in one direction, now in another, and the conception of God as the Creator and man as His created, man called to co-operate with God in the realisation of His world-plan and not of the wishful fantasies of humanity. The antithesis between the theocentric and the anthropocentric view of life becomes clear to him. An outlook which depends on the conception of God gives meaning to life itself, gives it moreover a logical place in the universal scheme. Above all, it satisfies Paul's longing for the eternal. Maybe the idea of God is also an illusion—but, in that case, we must accept everything as meaningless. Experience, on the other hand, seems to him to confirm what the Church has taught. Even the doctrine of original sin, which is enough to make modern pagans see red, is not perhaps the invention of the theologians. Harald Fangen says, "Perhaps you know what we Christians believe—that once, in the beginning of time, there was a catastrophe: it was human nature that suffered —it was given a wrench—we call it original sin— and ever since it has been in utter confusion." Nevertheless, the type of Christianity which Paul learns to know does not teach that life is evil in itself, or that the delight of the world is the Devil's snare, even though it may be used by him to persuade men to disobey God's will. "Nothing makes our desires and passions or any part of our nature sinful, except that all the elements in it are flung pell-mell together, everything is chaotic. And that was why God took our nature—to re-establish order in it. But then perhaps you know too that we learn that grace does not change our nature—it makes it perfect again."

Paul is in love with a young girl, Lucy Arnesen, or Lucy Snippen as she is called, after the tiny place she comes from. She is an assistant in a shop in Bogstad Street. It is his relations with her that open the flood-gates to his suppressed realisation of a divine reality. He loves Lucy so completely that he can no longer keep back his questionings as to whom we must thank for life and love. When he grasps the Christian or Catholic ideas concerning chastity and marriage, everything he has experienced with her is given substance and significance: the occasion, for example, when they were up by Lake Hurdal and he wanted them to bathe naked —Lucy, who was not exactly an inexperienced girl, had shown such wonderful shyness and modesty. Marriage does not, then, simply mean that two people are merged into one person,—it means rather that two people respond together to a call. He comes to understand what is implied when marriage is said to be a sacrament, a means of grace. It is a form of assistance which men and women accept in order to fulfil a mutual and common responsibility towards all that is conceived by them as eternal and divine. Why the marriage ceremony? he questions; and the priest answers that, if a man were perfect, he would not need it. He continues, "But no one can tell if the time may not come when everything in you tempts you to betrayal,—yes, even if you pray God to help, you may think He has not heard, because He does not give His help in the way you want. But then it is at least some help if you are bound by your own word and your own honour. We men are like that."

But all this is "nothing better than the black Middle Ages", says his mother, when she discovers her son's sympathy towards the Catholic Church. It was bad enough that her daughter, Tua, married Pastor Garnaas—but, at least, he was one of the liberal theologians. But Catholicism? why, it's prehistoric! Have people really advanced no further?

Paul fears that war is brewing out in the world. He thinks that what Pastor Tangen says is not wholly unreasonable: that when men, as individuals or as states and nations, have no basic aim other than to snatch for themselves as much of the world's goods as possible, then war is inevitable. Perhaps too, there was something in what Randi Alme told him to think about—how the Church had shown the way to lift human pugnacity into the supernatural realm, men being fighters in their inmost nature, unable to live without strife. If we do not fight with the world, the flesh and the Devil, then we fight with one another for a place in the sun. But Mrs Selmer says, No, war is impossible. Progress has reached that stage, at least. We all want peace. In any case, we have our international social democracy! So war *is* impossible!

In *The Wild Orchid* we are not told of Paul's reception into the Catholic Church. He has however penetrated far into the spiritual world of Christianity. In a moment of mystical vision, he grasps the significance of the Incarnation. God had revealed Himself to man in nature—"The heavens shew forth the glory of God"—that was one way. But in Christ His essence was revealed in a way which allowed it to be grasped by human understanding. "If it was true that He was present in this way, *here* and on thousands and thousands of other altars—then He must also be present in another way, present everywhere and always: an eye which took in the world's beginning in space and the constituents of the atom and the secret thoughts of men, all at one glance, with no before and after, no great and small. Everything was no more than His thought—everything simultaneous, equally clear and equally precious. . . . If this was the truth, the whole of life was inconceivably richer, more marvellous and more perilous, serious beyond words, of far greater worth than he had ever dreamed. Then he had glimpses of paths which led away into a great gloom and his thoughts could not stretch to conceive it; so onward into a light, and this he scarce dared allow himself to apprehend."

He has accepted the Christian faith and does not doubt that it is the truth. Either truth is *there*, or there is no meaning in anything. But then something happens which seems to imprison this witness to the faith inside him. He is engaged to Lucy Snippen and it is his intention that Pastor Tangen should marry them. But without warning, she writes to tell him that she is not the right person for him, and that everything must be over between them—she is going to marry an agent named Løvstø. Only later does he learn of the touching motive which lay behind her decision. His immediate reaction is to feel that he has been

Sigrid Undset

wronged,—he can see it in no other way. The "little flame, bright and alive", seems extinguished. As soon as God will not let him have things as he wants them, he follows his own course. "Three years later," we are briefly told, "Paul Selmer was married to a young woman called Bjørg Berge. How it had happened remained something of a mystery to Paul himself." Bjørg is a superficial creature, pleasure-seeking and intensely self-centred. They have children, but otherwise have little in common. Even so, Paul cannot be untrue to her. He has thrust away his apprehension of the divinity, but it was something more than a sentiment or emotion. In spite of everything, the wild orchid has taken root in Paul's soul.

Like *The Wild Orchid, The Burning Bush* is also set against the contemporary historical background. The storm, which Paul and others realised was on the way, has now broken. It was a sudden shock for everyone, but most people bothered little about the real meaning of the catastrophe. Not unreasonably, they thought of the things that concerned themselves. Bjørg was in Oslo in the first days of August 1914, and wrote home to Paul,—they were living in Trondheim then—sending an unmercifully long list of things he was to buy for her store-cupboard. "I shall only say that it is *terribly* serious—no one knows how difficult it will be to get things in the autumn." But time went on. There was money to make. People seemed gripped by a sort of market-day atmosphere. They had a vague feeling that the great "business concern of progress" had gone bankrupt, and that now "the hard and bloody exploitation of poor and unsuspecting modern man" was soon to begin. Civilisation had been run over by its own motor-car.

In this chaotic period, Paul's life and reflection lead him deeper into the Christian faith and he is prepared for the decisive step, reception into the Mother Church. He does not experience crises and fierce spiritual conflict; rather an inner growth and ripening, in accordance with his nature's deepest needs. The wild orchid, the delicate plant which has begun to shoot, continues to grow. Its roots have gone so deep that it is no longer possible to dislodge it. He is confirmed in his scepticism about the "reverend and aged banality", which said that religion was a kind of substitute for sex, and which is now declared to be the new truth of psychology. He becomes convinced that precisely the reverse is true. It was religion which he expelled when it no longer suited him. Fundamentally he believes in God, and although he may for a time have thought of not taking God into account, not reckoning on Him as the daily bread without which he could not live, and feel that God could not be alpha and omega for him, he still has enough imagination to conceive what a godless world would mean. It is given concrete expression for him. When he stands before his little child, he asks himself, "Dare you take your child in your arms and say, I do *not* believe? No. Even if by doing so, I could win for my children all the glory which the world can give—face to face with them, I could not."

The flame kindled within him cannot burn without fuel. "What thinks and feels in him is a soul longing for its Creator." He cannot be content to found his faith on subjective experience. It seeks the support which an objective truth can give, a reality outside himself. Christ and the Church, the martyrs, saints and great mystics, all are guarantees of this spiritual reality, something beyond his own confines, the fire which burns of itself, eternal and inextinguishable, the burning bush before which Moses stood.

Ever since his childhood, he has sought "with a kind of spiritual sense for some reality which was alive within the physical world, like a body inside a cloak". He knew it first as a kind of pantheism, a wonderful feeling of content which flooded through him when he experienced intense natural impressions, a feeling that Nature was good and kind. It was as if "new emotions sprang to life within him at every point—wonder, delight, good will, deep thankfulness". Later, he was capable of a sense of connection with something supernatural and timeless; he could feel "that something burst into bud within him, or that a light from outside sank into him, as sunlight sinks into the sea". Or he would stop in the middle of a ski-run, listen to the whisper of the woods and look around him: "Then it comes at once, a feeling that time is a moving staircase, and one seems to recall the sensation of first stepping out onto it from the timeless."

At such moments, he felt as if God, real and invisible, were close at hand; he did not doubt that all men were created so that they might be filled to overflowing with the love of God. But was this anything more than a subjective mood and feeling, anything more than self-suggestion? Or was his faith a witness not to be influenced by a passing mood? Did it concern the acknowledgement of an objective reality? The conformity in the experiences of the great mystics seemed to point in that direction. The *Revelations* of Juliana of Norwich, one of the classical works of English mysticism, have an overwhelming effect on Paul. It is five hundred years since the anchoress from Norwich asked the questions which are always pertinent, and received the answers which are as valid now as then. He cannot bring himself to believe that the harmonious union of *vita activa* and *vita contemplativa* could be the result of auto-suggestion. It is impossible, he says, that auto-suggestion could turn anyone into an organising genius or visionary, or make men and women, who are chronically sick in mind and suffer the gravest symptoms of nervous disorder, think of everything and everybody except themselves. The only explanation in which he, at any rate, can believe is that there is a reality which has come within the grasp of these people, in communion with which they live—a personality outside their own mortal selves. Even though all men have the possibility inherent within them of becoming mystics and saints, the true mystics and saints are still exceptional human beings. But if then he goes into a church and asks, "God, are you here?"—does he not find a means of connection, a communion, which even the wretchedest of men could use? Christ is the guarantor of the reality of the spiritual world. "He had realised that there could be no absolute authority other than that of the author himself—*Jesu Auctor vitæ,* as He is called in the Litany." He sees the whole of existence in a new light, and everything is given meaning. "It had been as when on some fine day an unexpected light falls on an old picture on the wall. Suddenly one discovers it as a unity—the two or three details, which were all one had noticed of it before, fall into place and become elements in a composition. Things that had happened to him and thoughts he had had years before rose up in his memory and were given a meaning in the new context. It was just like the poems he had had to learn by heart at school—then he had not even tried to understand anything in them, for after all they were only exercises to be learnt. But it sometimes happened that, when such a poem came to mind after he had grown up, it returned illuminated by a whole chain of meanings, while beneath lay a whole treasury of unutterable thoughts."

Paul Selmer's reception into the Catholic Church does not mean that he has achieved complete tranquillity and the certainty of salvation. In a certain sense, he is still in search of God. Pascal's statement of this paradoxical relationship— "Thou wouldst not seek after Me, if thou hadst not already found Me"—is valid for Paul also. But now he enters on a different kind of search. His faith lies in the firm assurance that he has been granted a glimpse of the objective truth relating to God, but he is by no means convinced of his power to hold on to what he has won or to penetrate beyond it. It is a perpetual struggle to gain deeper "insight into God", and to carry out the command: Seek God, not with the heart of the body but with the heart of the soul, which is the will.

The fact that he has become aware of the fundamental antithesis between the modern paganism and the Christian spiritual world implies a break, a personal choice. Paul is homeless in a godless world in a civilisation which makes nothing of the thought that man is intended for eternity. "It is incredible how the way one thinks of the future,—whether as time in the ordinary sense or as something timeless and endless,—makes a difference to one's opinions and outlook. It is a difference which affects one's attitude even in the smallest trifle. For Paul, this was a discovery to which he was not yet properly accustomed."

But the idea of mankind's eternal destiny does not float away into romantic vision. The service on Good Friday illustrates for Paul, almost too drastically, the "unbending realism" of Christianity. The description here marks a climax in the novel, a passage which illuminates all the rest, since it allows the reader to perceive exactly what kind of apprehension of reality is at issue in Paul Selmer's life, an apprehension totally foreign to the mentality of the age in which he has grown up. The distance which lies between the faith in humanity, at once idyllic and arrogant, of the evolutionary optimists, and the Christian view of man, could scarcely be demonstrated more clearly than in the ceremony where the symbolic significance of the Crucifixion is revealed to him. The token of God's image in man, crucified afresh in man's every sinful thought and deed, forces him to see himself as one who shares in the guilt of the revolt against God's will.

He can indeed at times feel the desire to have done with God. It is a nuisance to have to consider everything in relation to a will higher than his own inclination,—as when Bjørg "contracts a love-affair" and leaves him. It would have been easy to let her go her own way, in company with her shameless philanderer. If he had not been a Christian, he would have left her to her own devices, without the slightest hesitation. But now, that is impossible for him. When she returns, disillusioned and abandoned, he takes her back. He experiences a real crisis when he meets Lucy again and love for her burns up afresh in him. Then he feels a veritable nostalgia for the time when he believed that the world was nothing beyond what he could see and sense, and that every human being was his own centre of the universe, with no one to present an account to except himself. But he has learnt to take a different view of his neighbours in the world. He is moved to revolt and defiance, but he knows that God exists and that he can pray for help, and he accepts the guidance he is given. It is not a bottomless pit of misery. We catch sight of a way out, and we feel that the harmony, which he has himself destroyed, is re-established. A spark of the divine love has lodged in Paul, and that love has the power to raise up and restore. He has not merely let himself drift with the times. Like Kristin Lavransdatter, he too can say that something has come to life within him. "Beneath the surface there would always be a depth which no disturbance could reach. Fear and anxiety and bitterness might chase one after another across the surface; but love was heavy and sank down and down."

Paul's social conscience grows with his development as a practising Christian. He has never believed in Utopian dreams of an Earthly Paradise. Still, before his conversion, he only reckoned on two possibilities: either one got a grasp of the durable and then let evolution follow its perverse path; or one must join in the demolition-work and then build anew on entirely different principles. Presumably that was what the Communists wanted. But, as far as he could see, there was nothing in their new principles which could provide a solution to the fundamental problem—the fact that men are men. If Communism were accepted, it would only lead to a time when some talented leader would assume control over the masses and sacrifice them to his own ends.

But now he knows that a third possibility exists. In the end, it is Christianity alone which seriously believes that the individual human being is of an intrinsic worth, which it is vital to protect against both capitalist and Communist exploitation, as well as against those who, while plundering the people of their liberties, persuade them that they govern themselves. Paul believes in the Christian social movement, which sees as great a danger in the state-ownership of the means of production as in their accumulation in the hands of fewer and fewer private persons. It is essential to safeguard small independent businesses, the autonomy of the home and the rights of parents against any form of state encroachment; otherwise, the prospect is one of slavery for all of us. The objections which he has encountered to this programme have always revolved round the contention that it resists progress. And in a way that is true—for where men have no metaphysical foundation on which to build, there is nothing to be done, except give oneself over into the power of evolution. But Catholicism, Paul maintains, means precisely that—a man has a metaphysical foundation.

He himself practises "distributism". As Pastor Tangen once told him, in social life, as in everything else, there is only one thing which counts—"living one's faith".

Living in a non-Catholic community, Paul Selmer has a feeling of isolation. But that feeling counts for next to nothing compared with the wealth and joy and strength brought to him by his membership of the militant Church, which, in spite of betrayal and weakness and unfaithful servants, is for ever renewed and raised up to fight for the eternal in man, in a world which wants only to be of this world. "There was a free company of soldiers, who took their watchword nineteen hundred years ago and have never changed it for another."

The Wild Orchid and *The Burning Bush* were not very warmly received. The critics paid particular attention to the delightful love-story of Paul and Lucy. Carl Nærup wrote, "I think the story of Lucy Snippen contains one of the loveliest feminine portraits in Norwegian literature."

But the Christian ideal which shines through the story was for the most part ignored or discounted as Catholic propaganda. Nevertheless, the Finnish writer, Jarl Hemmer, could say, "I know people for whom *The Wild Orchid* and *The Burning Bush* became a kind of new Bible." This novel-cycle has, moreover, qualities which give it a markedly individual character as a work of religious edification. It is inspired by an apprehension such as we find in the great Christian mystics. But the mystic power, the religious intuition or "insight into God"—to use the writer's own phrase—works in an intimate and organic union, such as is only found in the great portrayers of humanity, with her powers of observation, analysis and reflection.

The figures in Norwegian literature who resemble most closely a character like Paul Selmer are to be found in the works of Sigurd Christiansen. Helge Gran and Jørgen Wendt, the two most notable characters in his novels, are also in search of the absolute. The religious ideal is the deepest motive in their intellectual life, but it takes a shape which is only conceivable in the Protestant milieu from which they come. For the High Lutheran Church Helge Gran has feelings similar to those of Paul Selmer, when he comes into contact with the Catholic Church. It has the power to preserve the sacred at a certain distance, to protect it from any cloying emotional reaction and the atmosphere of the prayer-meeting. "Perhaps they spend their lives in a more distant relationship to God, he thought. But for these people, He lives in Heaven rather than here. They haven't made a monopoly out of Him. He is supreme over the whole world, over men and animals and plants, over sea and land. He is far-away and great." There is a strain of the eternal Catholicism in Helge Gran—the recognition of God as the Absolute Other. But neither he nor Jørgen Wendt receives any help from the Church in his quest. Apart from their own subjective experience, they have no guarantee or authority for their faith.

There is much besides in the best writing of the twentieth century which treats of the waste land in which mankind wanders, and the crushing and brutalising effects which result when the factor of eternity is disregarded. But the other theme, the rediscovery of the eternal, is also present. Both the loss and the rediscovery form notable elements in the works of poets and writers like Paul Claudel, T. S. Eliot, Kafka, Mauriac, Aldous Huxley, Ronald Fangen, Pär Lagerquist and Arnulf Øverland. *The Wild Orchid* and *The Burning Bush* were inspired not only by the Christian faith but also by a universal religious impulse. Lagerquist has stated it in concentrated form in these fine lines:

> *O evighet, rör med din mörka vinge*
> *vid denna värld som glömt dess brus,*
> *vårt liv ånyo en mening finge*
> *om du det höljde med stjärneljus.*
> (*Oh, touch with your dark wing, eternity,*
> *This world oblivious of its sound;*
> *Our life again would find significance*
> *If you would spread your starlight over it.*)

Sigrid Undset is not then alone in handling this motive. What distinguishes *The Wild Orchid* and *The Burning Bush*—what makes them indeed unique—is her way of handling it. Scarcely any of her contemporaries have had the power to illuminate, in such a concrete and realistic, one might almost say, commonplace, way, the opposition between the paganism of the modern world and the Christian conception.

The novels, *Ida Elisabeth* (1932) and *The Faithful Wife* (1933), mark a new departure in Sigrid Undset's realistic treatment of modern life. In none of her other books is the everyday quality of both material and method so intimately connected with the whole idea of the novel and its artistic unity. Nevertheless,—or perhaps for this very reason—women characters like Ida Elisabeth or Nathalie in *The*

Faithful Wife are endowed with monumental greatness. They are like Olav Duun's Ragnhild: "I can't just be thrust here, then, without any kind of purpose or control." Their greatness is revealed in their relationship to the common round of life. They neither flee from it or nor are they swallowed up by it. They are loyal souls, and extract gold from the dross of everyday life. In a chaotic world, they stand for something stable; while the world totters on its supports, we find in them that which, in the final count, holds everything together. The art which portrays Ida Elisabeth and Nathalie is as far removed as can be from the art which idealises and embellishes, but in these characters we are given a glimpse of the eternally feminine, the prototype of womankind, in the Christian sense. There are things in these novels which remind one of Goethe's *Hermann und Dorothea*.

Although the religious idea is the essential impulse in both these novels, it does not appear with such clarity and directness as in *The Wild Orchid* and *The Burning Bush*. Their construction depends on the opposition between those fundamentally different adjustments which a person can make to life—the natural on the one hand, the supernatural on the other—the antithesis, that is, between man's ineradicable need of the transcendental and that other view of life, which sees human beings as citizens only of this world.

In a controversial exchange of articles with Ingeborg Maria Sick, in 1930, Sigrid Undset had developed the Christian conception of marriage and weighed its merits against neo-paganism's various types of sexual romanticism. Whether love was conceived as essentially an impulse towards physical contact or towards spiritual contact—"a kind of spiritual embrace"—both versions were, in the last instance, equally anti-social and anti-Christian. The Christian idea of marriage is realistic. Its premises are in the realities of everyday life, although at the same time, "it reaches far and high in its extension into the spiritual world".

This keynote is struck with delicacy and restraint in the opening chapter of *Ida Elisabeth*. Ida Elisabeth has been to the doctor in Bergen with her child, and now she is on her way home in the coastal steamer. Her husband, Fridtjof Braatø, is a good-for-nothing, and altogether she has little to look forward to. It is on the eve of the Feast of the Epiphany. She has not given it a thought until an acquaintance, Cis Meisting, who is a Catholic, happens to mention the day. "I've always thought Epiphany is such a wonderful feast," says the girl, "the story about the star always seems to fill me with so much longing." She quotes a charming translation of an American poem about the three kings and a poor woman, who has no gold, incense or myrrh to offer—only the gold of the moon, the smoke rising up from her home, and her own heart: "But these you shall have, With all that they hold of memories".

Ida Elisabeth says nothing, but the conversation has not been lost on her. "Follow a star which showed a way which led out of all this—that was all very well for those who could." For a moment, she too is full of longing. She has two children. "For their sake, she would gladly journey far, as far as any star would lead her, if only in the end she might find a place where she could make an offering like the woman in the poem. The smoke which swirled in the wind over their home, and her heart, with all the bitterness she could remember, for myrrh."

Ida Elisabeth is a simple and natural woman, neither rapturous nor sentimental. She has not grown up in an intellectual atmosphere. Her father was a sailor, and neither he nor her mother worried overmuch about her education. But her father was violently angry with her, when he heard how his daughter—then no more than a schoolgirl—had behaved with Fridtjof Braatø. He loaded her with coarse and brutal abuse, but there was a certain nobility in his bitter sorrow because his child was "disgraced, shamed and dragged in the dirt". Ida Elisabeth was furious with him, but something in his behaviour struck her. She knew that, in reality, there was truth in every word he had bawled at her, when he said that it was not whether "she had one child or two or none at all which made the difference"—what really mattered was that he had lost the only thing in the world he still believed in: "the last pure and lovely thing he still looked up to and loved." In the end he had flung his arms round her: "Oh God, it would have been better if you had died, Ida Elisabeth! A dog that's spoilt,—a man will shoot it if he's got a heart in his body,—but no one can do that to his child." Ida Elisabeth feels that in some peculiar way she is under an obligation to her father. She must not fail him: "It was like an inheritance she had received: an obstacle she had not been able to clear, but which she must keep trying to surmount." Some years later, she marries Fridtjof Braatø. There is a certain element of defiance in it: she will prove that what had passed between them was no mere lapse, but real love. And the fact that Fridtjof now wants to marry her means perhaps that he intends to prove that the feeling which drove him into "the bewildered sin of boyhood" was one he could stand by. But Fritjof is adolescent and remains so. There may have been some biological reason for his infantile mentality, but the upbringing, or the studied lack of it, which he has experienced, could scarcely have helped to counteract his weakness. In effect, he has never learnt anything more than that he, Fridtjof Braatø, is the centre of all existence; beyond this childish stage he never advances. The Braatø family was "weaned on the idyllic and on the idea that all this about the two sexes was no more than basking in the sun". "It is no use trying to go against Nature!"—they lived on such phrases: the idea was their religion. Fridtjof and all the others were "as they had to be,—with the disposition that was in them, and with no thought that there could be a real need for discipline and restraint where Nature was concerned".

Ida Elisabeth accepts the situation in which she has landed herself. She runs a small business and supports her husband and child. And in the end, it is she who has to take care of the "nature-idyll", the Braatø family. It would have been natural enough to let Fridtjof go his own way, once she had understood what he was really like. Her marriage was, after all, only escape into fantasy in an effort to avoid the truth. But she stays where she is, shutting her eyes to everything and "sliding round unpleasant facts". However, she cannot go on doing this when she discovers that Fridtjof has been unfaithful to her with another woman, at a time when she was pregnant with her fourth child. He does not want a divorce, but now she is absolutely resolved to be quit of the whole business. "I've felt that, if the devil is riding pick-a-back, you can't do much but carry him. But when the devil is obliging enough to jump off of his own accord, you can hardly imagine that anyone is stupid enough to bend down straight away and ask him to jump on again, please!"

Ida Elisabeth starts a dressmaking business in a valley in the east of the country and recreates a home for herself and the children. Everything and everyone flourish around her— she flourishes herself. "She had the boys and they were healthy and bubbling over with high spirits, sharing with her the discovery of the new world to which she had brought them. When she put her arms round them and felt the warmth of their young bodies, she thought to herself that 'there are many others who make do like this, and are glad to be alive.'" A lawyer, Trygve Toksvold, a fine, loyal man, as sound and clear-headed as Ida Elisabeth herself, falls in love with her. Their love is happy, full of charm and sweetness, and they plan to be married. But then Fridtjof and the Braatø family reappear on the scene. She has had a premonition that her past is lying in wait for her. When it does present itself, she cannot thrust it aside. The poor wretches need her help; Fridtjof is ill and must go to a tuberculosis sanatorium. She can only accept the situation. Despite the divorce, and despite her love for Trygve, she sees that her children are inseparably bound to their father, and that therefore she is bound to him too.

The final scene in the novel is a masterpiece—the description of Fridtjof's death-bed, where Ida Elisabeth sits and listens to the dismal strain of the harmonium:

> *From that mighty tribulation*
> *Comes the band of heroes home.*

Fridtjof as one of the band of heroes! The scene might have appeared blasphemous, if satire had been the only aim. To Ida Elizabeth, the scene is more than comic. May there not be a reality behind the things they are singing about?—even if their performance suggests that it is all nothing more than "sentiment and startings of the heart". Is there perhaps something firm and secure behind the vague clouds of emotion? Something inside her, or something present with her at that moment, tells her not to judge. It is not her affair. When Fridtjof is dead and she sees his face, he seems so handsome that she has never met anything so difficult to fathom before—"a kind of token that the unfathomable should not perhaps remain so for ever".

Ida Elisabeth has been carried through life by her loyalty. To have something to which she might be faithful—that is the star she has followed. As far as that went, there was no question of going against Nature. But it has been a sort of obstacle race. That impulse in her which she has never betrayed has demanded that she do more than simply follow her desire for happiness. It has been as if she grew in stature with every obstacle cleared. The apprehension of the divine, which dwelt within her as a potentiality, is finally realised, because she has carried the burden taken up of her own accord, and made her way forward to a place where there is someone to whom she can make her offering.

She has given her heart, and her oblation becomes a thank-offering. Ida Elisabeth is *anima naturaliter christiana*, a soul Christian by nature.

Religious faith, as tendency, possibility or potentiality, is also the theme of *The Faithful Wife*. From the psychological point of view, it is concerned with the conditions which bring about the suppression or realisation of such a tendency. The theme can also be stated in the question asked by Sigurd Nordgaard, the engineer who is the chief male character in the book: "Is this faith no more than a relic from old times? Or does it exist because there is a force exerted on us,—like gravity, for example?" Nathalie, Sigurd's wife, the central woman character, has grown up in a home where a somewhat sham left-wing idealism prevailed. Both her parents were credulous, simple people, romantics as far as the future was concerned. Bjørnson, Sars, Steen, Sivle and Aasen were the household gods. Christianity represented a stage of development which was long past and done with. Nathalie remembers that her father never let an opportunity slip for an attack on priests and the Church. True, he supported the liberal theologians: "But, doubtless, that was simply because he thought that everything which called itself liberal and broadminded must belong to his own party." Her mother was not one for the Church either, although she did hold fast to the historical Jesus. "She maintained that He was a pioneer of the suffragette movement, while the priests and the Church had never done anything but keep women in subjection." To the children home was almost a matter of indifference. Their parents were so occupied with all kinds of "causes" that they never seemed to have time for anything else. Ragna, Nathalie's sister, says of their mother, "You would think that every now and then she had found her children by accident in the waste-paper basket after a committee-meeting." This household is a variation of the similar type found with the Braatøs in *Ida Elisabeth* and the Selmers in *The Wild Orchid*. But in this novel, the milieu from which Nathalie has sprung is far in the background. We find ourselves in the middle 'thirties, and it is Communists, Fascists and Nazis who are active. Compared with them, Nathalie's parents were "a pair of sweet, innocent and warm-hearted human beings". They had declared that belief in authority must be beaten down, and that then a generation freer and more independent would arise. But precisely the opposite took place. The new generation was so "hungry for authority that they would willingly swear loyalty to the devil himself, only because his personality is undoubtedly that of a great leader".

Nathalie's husband comes of a farming family somewhere in Østerdal. Sigurd Nordgaard has the solid good sense of the countryman, a certain wisdom and thoughtfulness. People live in such a tremendous rush nowadays, he thinks, that they wither before they are ripe. He has a decided distrust of all those who have their "humble opinions" as to how the world should be managed, whether they are simpled-minded idealists like his parents-in-law or arrogant radicals, who think they have fathomed the whole of the "historical process". "Any reasonable person can understand that there must be factors in operation which cannot be known at the moment; whether anyone will be lucky enough to discover them later on is impossible for us to say— at present, we can do no more than recognise their existence."

It is impossible for Nathalie, nurtured in the irreligion of her home, to have any predisposition for religious ideas. But she is heartily sick of all the substitutes for religion which her parents played with, and she gets on wonderfully well with her Sigurd and the thought that the two of them are "as anonymous and unimportant in the world as anyone can be". Like him, she possesses the family-instinct. She is by nature the faithful wife. Nothing could be more obvious than that she just belongs to him—for ever. Loyalty may turn even growing old into something fine, she thinks. When they first met, she had understood that things were so: they had really received that rare gift of great passion. But even these two have attempted, to some extent, a modification of the family institution, in that she has a job outside the home. That was natural and proper as long as it was necessary, and since she has no children it is reasonable for it to continue. But Sigurd does not wholly like the arrangement: now, when they no longer need it, it is as if her business takes her away from the home a little. Another thing he has found unsatisfactory is the fact that they were not married in church. They had lived together before they were married, and the only difference now is that their relationship has been given a legitimate status in the eyes of other people. They have other small innovations. They have agreed, for instance, that neither should be forced to cultivate the other's circle of acquaintance further than likes and·dislikes reach.

The reason for Sigurd's unfaithfulness does not lie in these circumstances, even though they do not provide the most favourable conditions for their married life. All the same, his unfaithfulness comes as a shock to them both. Nathalie's heart is broken. "A broken heart! It had always seemed a ridiculous picture to her. She had thought of glass or something similar which breaks to smithereens with a crash. But now she felt as if her heart was crushed inside her—like a hand crushed to pulp in a door. I have given up, thought Nathalie. I surrender to the young eyes—oh so young—of Anne Gaarder——" The shock is no less for Sigurd. Is he really like that? So weak? He who had been so confident of himself? He loves the girl and she is to bear his child. But still it is with Nathalie that he belongs.

The decisive factor in this story is the girl herself, Adinda as they call her. She will not marry Sigurd, and she will not agree to the plan that her child should be taken away from her. It does not mean that she is not in love with the man she has become involved with: it is just that she cannot do this. Her parents are Christians and Catholics; they do not recognise "the divine right of grand passion". She cannot do what she pleases with her own life and the new life she now carries in her womb. She understands this herself. She has entered upon something which, at bottom, she knew conflicted with her religious convictions, with the ordering of life which, she knew, had its source in a love greater than hers. She too is weak; but the best in her receives support from an order outside herself. She grows strong and can take the consequences of her failure. She cannot detach herself from the child—but she can disappear from Sigurd's life.

With these events, religious faith, which has never been completely lacking in Sigurd, comes to life. The shame he feels and, above all, the wonderful constancy shown by Adinda, arouse him. Before, when he heard people discuss the crisis in modern culture, or when someone had tried to enlist his support for this or that movement—the classless society or Nordic Man or the spiritualist doctrine that "banality is stronger than death"—he had always thought that what they were really seeking was only something to believe in; and now the truth of his opinion is confirmed for him. Ultimately, the crisis of the world is a religious crisis. "One *must* adjust oneself differently here on earth according to the faith one holds." In every one of life's relationships, a man must adopt a different attitude if he believes there is a divine authority, "instead of thinking that he himself is the highest authority, or that society or the State is absolutely supreme".

His marriage with Nathalie is restored, and now for Sigurd it is not merely a social institution, but a sacrament where God and man meet. Nathalie does not properly understand his religious ideas, or what he means when he says that nothing can succeed, if the essential realities which surround one are ignored. "Realities?" she asks a little scornfully. "Isn't your religion more a matter of wishful thinking?" Sigurd answers, "If you'll be honest, Nathalie— don't you think that many of the people you have known who say they don't believe in God, in fact wish that He existed? Existed as a reality which, like a hand, grasps everything else that is,—and nothing we desire or invent can help us to slip out between His fingers." No, she must admit, God is not what she longs for. And she cannot conceive what satisfaction Sigurd gets from being a Christian in this way. But she is so happy that her separation from Sigurd is over that it must be "wonderful to have someone to thank".

In form *Ida Elisabeth* and *The Faithful Wife* are ordinary realistic novels of married life. The method is basically the same as in the experimental novel of the Zola school. But the Christian experimental novel certainly comes to very different conclusions from those of the naturalistic type. The Christian outlook counts on man's freedom. It is perhaps for that reason that the poetry does not fade away, and one feels it throughout as an undercurrent, a vital source, or as an effluence permeating the whole. Latent in these two novels is a hymn in praise of the ideals of virginity and Christian marriage and in honour of the traditional Christian institution of the family.

Eleven Years appeared in 1934, midway between *Ida Elisabeth* and *The Faithful Wife*. It is not a novel, but a fragment of autobiography, a record of everything which Sigrid Undset, in her fifties, could remember of the first eleven years of her life. The limit she sets is not a chance one. As we recall, Sigrid Undset was eleven when her father died in December, 1893: "She had loved no one as much as him." In other ways too, the conscious connection with her father is emphasised. We remember that his Christian name was Ingvald. Ingvild was also a name that ran in

his family, and he wished to give it to his daughter—but to
the Danish family it had seemed altogether too odd.

In Norwegian literature, *Eleven Years* is a unique volume
of memoirs, recollections of past life which have their origin
in a mental process of the kind described by Henri Bergson
in *Matière et mémoire*. He calls it *mémoire pure*—memories
which can well up when some chance sensation sets in
motion a mental life which has, as it were, lain dormant.
Marcel Proust's *À la recherche du temps perdu* is undoubtedly
the most striking example of how a writer can in this way
recall "lost time". Olaf Bull's autobiographical poem of
recollection, *Memoirs (Memoirer)*, is of the same kind. He
sits on a bench in Kierulf's Square and suddenly recognises the smell of newly washed cotton blouses, such as he
wore when he was a boy:

> *And now the mandrake's plucked ! From the grave of time*
> *A morning rises, distant, low and bright*— —

Memories from her earliest childhood in particular are
recalled to Sigrid Undset's mind by some relevant sense-
impression. The first thing she remembers, or feels she can
remember, goes all the way back to when she was eighteen
months old. She lay grubbing in the earth of her grand-
parents' garden in Kalundborg. The baby revels in the
summer-heat, still and intense, scratching away luxuriously
in the sun-warmed soil. Then someone comes, picks her up
from the little hole she had made for herself, and puts a
doll with a smooth, hard porcelain head in her arms. She
lifts it to her mouth—no, she doesn't want it, and throws
it out onto the grass. They bring it back to her and speak
to her in a different tone from usual. The doll gives a little
creaking noise which amuses her for a second, but then she
heaves it away again, this time much further.

She happened to see this little scene with the doll as if it
were real, when years later she came back to the old garden.

"She knew of a definite place on the edge of the lawn: I was sitting there. Behind there was an old box-hedge with tall bushes, and one bush had leaves like raspberry-leaves—it was a branch of that which had nodded to her."

Memories from later years can return to her in the same way, as when, for example, the sight of the weather signals, the cone and square on Sankthanshaugen, calls to mind her childish emotions with their religious colouring, of which we have spoken earlier; or when the smells in Keyser's Street awaken memories of the years she spent as a child in that distinctive quarter of the town.

Her memories are not otherwise built up on the basis of such involuntary recollections. In her mind lie clear memory-pictures, like "brightly illumined patches in a land of darkness", which are gradually enlarged to form a connected whole. To reproduce these she needs no external stimulus.

A conscious desire to be objective is one of the characteristic features of these recollections. It is shown, from a purely external point of view, by the fact that they are written in the third person. But essentially the objectivity lies in the control exercised by the author over her remembering self. It is a matter of remembering accurately, or of distinguishing between what she really remembers, what she only imperfectly remembers, and what others have told her. In *The Faithful Wife*, Nathalie reflects on Søren Kierkegaard's definition of the difference between remembering and recollecting. Following the distinction he makes, recollection must mean the distillation of "a kind of intoxicant from what she remembered", whereas memory consists of no more than a series of fluctuations between remembering correctly and incorrectly. As far as *Eleven Years* is concerned, it is primarily memory, as defined by Kierkegaard, which is in question. In every point where the recollected material is capable of control, it is found to be remembered correctly also.

With all its concrete objectivity and despite the absence of "the intoxicant of recollection", *Eleven Years* is none the less a work of the creative poetic imagination, and it is this which makes it such a remarkable study of child-psychology. An academic psychologist can observe and describe the same facts about a child, but only a writer has the power to fit them into a real and concrete whole, the complete context of which they form part, and then interpret them in relation to this totality. We see the child's world come into being: the intense egotism, contact with an outside world, dawning awareness of things and people and of an external will which interferes and against which revolt is made. We see the reactions, negative and positive, towards parents and towards reprimand and punishment; the world of religious ideas which is built up; the first acquaintance with sex; and the child's instinctive reaction against being prematurely snatched out of its feeling of security by adults. We see all the small events, in themselves insignificant, which can make a child intensely happy or intensely unhappy, the wounds which may never heal in a whole lifetime. And finally we see the home as a living organism, an integrating unit, where almost imperceptibly the child learns to understand what it is that gives substance to life.

Madame Dorothea (*Madame Dorthea*, 1939) is a historical novel. In this book she writes not of medieval people but of figures from the eighteenth century, the age of enlightenment, a time when the Middle Ages were regarded as a period to be ashamed of, caught as it was in the toils of utter superstition, ignorance and barbarism—spiritual darkness, which still cast its shadow over life, but which, now at last, was to be driven out by the clear daylight of reason.

What can have prompted Sigrid Undset to absorb herself in this period? It may have been an inner affinity, for with all her powers of imagination and feeling, she is pre-eminently a rationalist. She has a deep respect for reason,

the natural light in man, to use the language of the eighteenth century. "Reason carries, as it were, the light for
our actions," wrote Ludvig Holberg in his *Moral Issues, or
an Introduction to Natural and Public Law (Moralske Kjærne
eller Introduction til Natur- og Folkeretten,* 1715): "Its discern-
ment is called Conscience." It is binding on us, "since
God has given such laws to human kind and commanded
man to be obedient to them by virtue of the light innate
within him."

Even if a Christian cannot believe that it is possible for
him to be "obedient" to God's laws through his own
strength, he shares with the theistic philosophy of the
eighteenth century the belief that God's laws are written in
the hearts of men.

On her mother's side, the family tradition provided a
living and unbroken connection with the eighteenth century.
Living contacts with that age were her mother and, perhaps
even more, Moster, who was born in 1814 and died in 1905,
mentally alert and lively to the end. Moster told legends
and fairy-tales which had come from her father, Dean Vilhelm Adolf Worsøe, and he had them from his Norwegian
home, the glass-factory of Nøstetangen, where his father
had been overseer. The setting of *Madame Dorothea* is the
glass-factory at Biri, but nevertheless it was the tradition
from Nøstetangen which played a prominent part in the
book's creation. The old stories, which had been told in the
overseer's house at the glass-factory here late in the eighteenth century, were brought back to Norway by the little
girl who sat and listened to Moster's tales a hundred years
later. Not that *Madame Dorothea* is a repetition of Moster's
stories, but they were of essential significance for the inner
life of the novel. In the tradition they represent there was
no trace of "reason" or "enlightenment". Here was contact with the popular and unliterary, a different world from
that irradiated by "the clear daylight of reason".

Around the first glass-factories there must have grown up

a little community wholly individual in character. It was a new industry that was to be set in motion. It demanded personal initiative and a patriotic will to work; it also needed men with a technical knowledge not to be found inside the country, so that by far the greater number of skilled glass-blowers had to come from abroad. With difficulty and great expense, the company's agents recruited technicians from England and, more especially, from Germany. It was important to ensure that they did not leave their employment before new men had been trained in the craft. Most of the foreign workers had grown up and been educated in the Catholic faith, and they asked for the spiritual ministry which their belief and tenets required. The overseer at Nøstetangen requested the board of management to discover whether a Catholic priest might be brought to the country. It took some time before the royal permission was obtained, but in 1761 the Catholic priest, Casparus Dentzmann, visited all the glass-factories in the country and performed the necessary offices. His visit was followed by several others. The meeting between Madame Dorothea and the Catholic workman, Scharlach, a glass-blower, is thus not an idle invention.

In *Madame Dorothea,* as in *Kristin Lavransdatter* and *Olav Audunsson,* characters develop out of the cultural and social conditions of the period in which they live. This realism in the setting, authentic in small things as well as great, serves here, as in the medieval novels, to emphasise the fact that human nature changes very little or not at all. For the most part, there is no more than ripples on its surface.

The description of social conditions amongst the workers, of the labouring life and scene, occupies little space in the novel. On the other hand, the reader is brought close to life in the careful presentation of the daily round, kitchen utensils, clothes, the customs and manners of working days and holidays. We come to see and have experience of things and people, not through description, but through the feelings and reflections of the characters themselves. The tone of speech is slightly affected by eighteenth-century usage, without imitation of the style of letters, diaries and other literature. Only occasionally does a single expression or turn of phrase serve to create the period atmosphere; they occur naturally, and the author's use of them is careful and sparing. Quite without effort, we are surrounded by the atmosphere of a vanished age.

The portrait-gallery holds a rich and varied collection of characteristic types from every layer of the population. All of them show something which is peculiar to the age, but they are never conventionally conceived. Each one is a human soul with an individual existence: the enthusiastic tutor, Dabbelsteen, talented but degraded; Madame Dorothea's husband, Jørgen Thestrup, active and patriotic; the maternal grandmother on the estate at Lunde, domineering and greedy of life; and many others. The description of the cultural background reaches a high level in the account of the wedding at Lunde.

But *Madame Dorothea* is not merely the resurrection of a vanished age. It is inspired by a conception closely akin to the fundamental motive in all Sigrid Undset's writing.

The action takes place in the course of a few months some time in the 1790's. Jørgen Thestrup, Madame Dorothea's husband and overseer of the factory, has suddenly been lost. He has ridden out at night and in a snow-storm to search for his two half-grown sons, who have gone for a drive with their tutor, Dabbelsteen. The boys and "that much-to-be-pitied youth", their mentor, return safely, but their father does not return.

The reaction to this shocking event throws light on an essential characteristic of the period. People seize on it almost with avidity. The clear light of reason is no defence against their impulse to abandon themselves to superstition and fantastic stories. "How strange it is, this popular taste for horror-stories," thinks Madame Dorothea. "Conversations had dealt with almost nothing else but murder and executions, magic and witch-burning and omens—it was as if everyone wished to compete in capping one gruesome story with another." Yes, there were some who could tell that Jørgen Thestrup had himself confessed that he had had inexplicable experiences in the lane by the churchyard and in the factory itself at night-time.

Madame Dorothea knows well enough that superstition has flourished out in the kitchen and amongst the workmen in the factory—"After all, many of them were Papists." But it is new to her to find it so widespread and deep-rooted. She is not an incredulous sceptic; in the spirit of the age of enlightenment, her rationalism is religious, coloured by Christianity. In reality, it is the same natural piety as Ida Elisabeth possessed, or Nathalie in *The Faithful Wife*. She represents the same feminine type as they, motherly, unselfish and devoted. But, in contrast to Nathalie and Ida Elisabeth, Madame Dorothea's natural religion is consciously based on principle. She has no doubt that virtue, mankind's moral nature, is binding because of its divine origin. She teaches her children to say their prayers regularly every morning and evening. And she herself prays to God that He will fulfil her desires and that her husband may return in safety. But for any kind of "enthusiasm", she feels *dégoût*. She has loved "the blessed daylight" with all her heart. But now in her grief and with a future of uncertainty before her and the children, she receives little help from her religious faith. She has no connections with the Church; for a moment she is prompted to see if the priest could offer consolation—but she draws back at the thought of the jargon he would use. And what of the gipsy-woman, Sibilla? People have said that she can see hidden things—why not ask her? Perhaps she could tell her something of what has happened to her dear Jørgen. She cannot resist the temptation, but she feels it is degrading—

she is, then, no different from the common folk! When she finds the blessed daylight cold and cheerless, she too seeks refuge in superstition, and tries to shut out darkness with darkness.

She meets a ray of light when she talks with the pious workman, Scharlach—a light not the antithesis of reason, but of which the light of reason is itself a part. When she was seized with terror at the thought that the boys and her husband were not coming back, she went to Scharlach instinctively and immediately. There was something extraordinarily calm in the way he had organised the search for Thestrup. "But we mustn't lose heart, little Madame. We must leave it in God's hands,"—they were the words he used. She had always done that, she thought. But if such a terrible thing had happened, "then it wasn't so easy to leave everything in God's hands." It is no easier for Madame Dorothea than it was for Kristin and Olav to pray, "Thy will be done."

She has given no special thought to Scharlach in the months of tension and shock that have followed. But at last, when she and everyone else is certain that Thestrup is dead, she meets him again. One evening she meets him by chance as she enters the sitting-room. It is the time of evening prayers, and some of her children are present. She listens to their prayers. They are in praise of the Lord and in German: "Dich ziemt Lobgesang auf Sion, O Herr, und dir soll man Gelübde zählen in Jerusalem, erhört mein Gebet; zu dir soll ja alles Fleisch kommen." And they pray for the dead: "Die ewige Ruhe gieb ihnen, Herr, und das ewige Licht leuchte ihnen." She hears them praying in Norwegian for the dead man: "We pray thee also, dear God, have mercy on the soul of thy servant, Jørgen Thestrup; cleanse his soul from all sin and graciously grant him thy redemption, that he may enter into the blessedness of Heaven. Grant him eternal rest, O Lord." And Bertel, one of her sons, answers in a clear voice, "And let the eternal

light shine before him. May he rest in peace. Amen."
Madame Dorothea feels herself poignantly moved. She says
to Scharlach, "Religious fanaticism—on no account will I
have my children inoculated with such stuff." A conversation ensues between this intelligent woman representative
of eighteenth-century rationalism and the old glass-blower,
the spokesman for the spiritual realism of the Church, which
binds living and dead together in supernatural fellowship.
"Reason is a good thing to have and use," says Scharlach,
"but it's still only a part of our soul,—just as the day is good
and blessed, but still only a part of the twenty-four hours."
Madame Dorothea does not understand what he is aiming
at. He can't live in a completely visionary and fanatical
world, when he sets store by "God's blessed sun and the
lovely light of reason". But the sun must set each evening,
he continues, "so that we can see how many stars there are
in the sky, each of them a sun as big and as beautiful as our
own, so I've heard tell. True, there are dangers and many
an evil thing to threaten us in the darkness—but it also
brings coolness and refreshment, comfort to everything
that grows and lives here on earth." He tells her to think
how many there are who only use daylight and reason to
afflict and deceive their fellow-men. "The Devil and his
angels are on the move both night and day, and they never
take rest, never slumber." Dorothea admits inwardly that
there is perhaps something in what the old man says. But
does he believe in the Devil as well then? No, she will not
think about it, she will not "look into the Janus' face of
night". An uncanny breath seems to flow over her; it has
come both from the world of superstition—"from the
beastly mouths of old witch-wives"—and in reality also
"from the starry heaven of the pious old devotee". She
feels as uneasy about the one as about the other. Everyone
is blessed in his own faith, she said to Scharlach. No, that
was not his opinion. But he adds, "This I believe for certain—
that with your faith you will never be completely unhappy."

Madame Dorothea is only the beginning of a novel. We expect a sequel. We should like to hear more of this faithful wife and mother and her sons. Something has happened to her in those few months since the disappearance of her husband. A restlessness has come upon her. Perhaps she too has had a glimpse of new horizons and the presentiment of an interdependence between living and dead, of which she had known nothing before.

CHAPTER IX

The Struggle Against Nazism: War and Exile

IN 1929 Sigrid Undset published a little Christmas meditation in German, *Und wäre dies Kindlein nicht geboren?*, and a year later she wrote another on the same theme, *Das Weihnachtswunder*. They are reflections on God's embodiment in the flesh, the Incarnation as doctrine and as historical reality. "We can celebrate the Christmas miracle on any day of the year. For it means the breakthrough in time of the eternal reality."—"Light—*Lumen de Lumine*—the light which the darkness comprehended not" radiates from the child in the manger.

The earlier of the two meditations is more significant. In it, the sacred story is given palpable clarity. She emphasises the paradoxical in Christianity. "Is not the final and innermost cause of joy at Christmas the fact that the world was made to stand on its head, as it were?"—that God comes to the world in the shape of a helpless child: "If we look at it unsentimentally, it is not even pretty—the head too big for the tiny body, the limbs too small and thin, and it screams dreadfully with its wide-open toothless mouth." If it is our child, we love it, it becomes a precious treasure, the heir, the future of the family. But if it is not ours, then what importance can a tiny baby have? Why not kill it if it is unwanted, or if it might be thought to stand in the way of ourselves and our children? Or perhaps it will vitiate *die Kraft der Rasse*? "In fact there is no reason why we should answer this question in the negative, no reason except the whole of Christianity." Everywhere the same paradoxical touch—"His words were as distant and enigmatic as the starry sky and as ordinary and gentle as the wayside flowers." The incarnate God, who has set in "motion the eternal roundelay of all the worlds, lies flat on His face in blackest darkness and prays, and sweat like drops of blood falls from Him to the ground." And what sort of people are they, the friends and disciples He has chosen for Himself? Not learned, not brilliantly gifted, no great talent or genius amongst them, but men from the common folk, dull fellows, slow to grasp anything. "Of course, they were easily moved —they were deeply touched that evening when He established the new covenant and talked to them. But even so, they have not understood enough of what was going on in the Master's soul to keep them from sleeping, although He had asked them to watch with Him: a stone's throw away they lie fast asleep."

The Virgin Mary and the Christ-child—where she is excluded, the ghost of Herod slips into the dreams of people, asleep or dozing. "The old visions return again, of goddesses who have charge over the cycle of nature, of birth and decay, the budding and falling leaf. Each one of them presses her own child to her breast, ready to fight for it against others. The child of Leto once more bends his bow; there is no mercy for the children of Niobe." The meditation ends with a summons from the great medieval Christian hymn:

Adeste, fideles,
Læti triumphantes
Venite, venite in Bethlehem . . .
Venite, adoremus Dominum.

Begegnungen und Trennungen. Essays über Christentum und Germanentum (1931) follows the same trend as the two Christmas pieces, but is different in form. It is not religious instruction, but a series of reflections on history and religious psychology. Apart from the Introduction, which forms however an essential part of the book, it consists of essays

which had previously appeared in Norwegian. It opens
with a translation of her memorial article on Saint Olav,
written on the occasion of the nine-hundredth anniversary of
the battle at Stiklestad. It now has the title, *Olaf der Heilige.
Christentum und germanisches Naturheidentum.* It is followed
by *Rückkehr zur katholischen Kirche*, a translation of *Catholic
Propaganda*; and finally there is *Christentum und Neuheidentum*,
which in its Norwegian form had simply been called *Letter
to a Parish-priest (Brev til en sogneprest*, originally in *Credo*,
1930).

Collected in this way, these articles are endowed with new
force. They appear as a powerful apologia for Christianity,
just at the time when one of the most aggressive anti-
Christian offensives ever known in the history of Christendom
was about to begin. The Introduction emphasises the
contemporary situation and gives historical perspective
to the whole.

She points out the similarity between the present situation
and that of a thousand years ago, when the northern peoples
were making their first acquaintance with Christianity.
Now, as then, there are many who have lost their traditional
faith. Now, as then, there are some who think they can
put their trust in their own strength, their own "might and
main". But some could accept Christianity at that time,
so strong was their desire for light and clarity. In one way
or another, the old paganism was reaching out towards a
God. And Christianity did not wage war on man's religious
belief as such, his belief that he depended on divine supernatural powers. Christianity fulfilled his basic religious
need. But the similarity between past and present in this
case is only external. We cannot become pre-Christian
pagans over again. The paganism which flourishes in us
when Christianity is cast out is something quite different
from the paganism of our ancestors. "The old paganism
was a love-poem to a God who remained hidden, or it was
an attempt to gain the favour of the divine powers whose

presence man felt about him." The new paganism is a declaration of war against a God who has revealed Himself. The new mythology is most concerned with fabling God out of the world by new declarations of man's power and achievement.

The point at issue is that we must hold fast to Christianity as a revealed dogmatic religion. "Sentimental clinging to this or that feature of the individual parts of the Christian tradition is of no use at all. Break branches from a tree in the countryside and put them in vases to decorate your rooms— and see how long they stay fresh."

The logic of her argument was confirmed by Hitler's assumption of power and the subsequent elevation of the biological mysticism of race to the level of religion. Religion is opium for the masses, was the catchword of the Marxists. That of the Nazis was: Christianity is an oriental poison in our Germanic blood. "Nothing will prevent me from eradicating Christianity in Germany down to the last root-fibre," said Hitler. "Against the Christian teaching of the eternal worth of the individual soul and of personal responsibility, I declare, ruthlessly and with absolute definition, another doctrine of salvation—the doctrine which maintains that the individual is insignificant, is nothing, compared to the immortality of the nation in this world."[1]

In 1935 the refugee publishing firm in Lucerne, Vita Nova, published Sigrid Undset's first direct attack on Nazism, the article *Fortschritt, Rasse, Religion*, her contribution to a larger anti-Nazi publication which appeared under the title, *Die Gefährdung des Christentums durch Rassenwahn und Judenverfolgung*. The contributors included Protestant and Catholic clergy, scholars and thinkers, amongst the last Nikolai Berdiaev. He writes that both Nazism and Marxism are pseudo-scientific hypotheses or mythologies, which have arisen in an un-Christian and godless world. They represent

[1] Quoted from Edmond Vermeil, *Hitler et le Christianisme*, London, 1944, Preface.

a determinism and fatalism which cannot be reconciled with Christian doctrines and which must lead to war against Christianity. Nazism is the "destiny of the blood, which rules over the individual, an expression for paganism, pagan naturalism, pagan worship of nature".

It is also in opposition to the mythical ideals of modern man—Nature, Progress, Race—that Sigrid Undset maintains the Christian ideal, which represents the only human fellowship based not on illusion and wishful thinking but on the recognition of human nature as it is and on the hope which Christ has given to mankind. The Christian hope is open to "all men of good will and of every race and religion on earth—to all who have the courage to believe in an eternal life and are humble enough to seek the society of their Creator, instead of remaining isolated in their fetish-worship, their cult of the ideas and objects they have themselves created. Self-worship cannot stand—that cult leads to disintegration and death."

Sigrid Undset had a large reading public in Germany, and her denunciation of Nazism could not fail to attract attention. "Her works shall no longer be found in German papers, German libraries and German bookshops," wrote the *Westdeutscher Beobachter*. "We make this declaration our own," wrote the Norwegian Nazi newspaper, *Fronten* (May 15th 1937), and added, "What Sigrid Undset publishes is not merely foreign and offensive to us,—it is hostile. Sigrid Undset is certainly Nordic by birth, but her attitude of mind is most un-Nordic. . . . People have been quick to lose the capacity to react against anything at all—and forces outside the State are given free scope." Of these "forces outside the State", the Catholic Church is "one of the most corrupting". The author sighs for a new Luther. "But where have we any Lutheran priests?"

On April 6th 1940, Sigrid Undset gave an address in the Student Union in Oslo, on the same platform where, twenty-six years earlier in March 1914, she had spoken on the Fourth

Commandment, on "the first seed-leaf of civilisation—man's awareness of his obligations". On that occasion she had taken her text from a biblical commandment which, like "so many other biblical commandments, has been written in the hearts of men, irrespective of religion or race"—*And fear not them which kill the body*. Her theme now is not very different: Christianity and our time. The manuscript of the address has been lost and there is no report available. But one remark is remembered by many. We are well on the way, she said, to replacing the Christian maxim for life, "For what is a man profited, if he shall gain the whole world, and lose his own soul?"—with the following: "What is a man profited if he gain the highest standard of living and ruin his digestion?" Her lecture was received with extraordinary attentiveness. The war going on out in the world, the fate of Finland, the tense situation in Norway, all had led to an increased understanding of what Sigrid Undset and many others had found themselves forced to consider the vital problem in the crisis which Europe was and is suffering, the crisis of which the second World War was a symptom.

On the morning of April 9th 1940, Sigrid Undset returned to Lillehammer. She had three Finnish children at home in Bjerkebæk and she must look after them. She saw her two sons, Anders and Hans, just for a short time before they left for the war. She never saw Anders again. He fell in action some weeks later at the Segelstad bridge. On April 20th, when the English and Norwegians had to retreat from their positions at Brøttum, the station immediately south of Lillehammer, and the Germans were approaching the town, Sigrid Undset was ordered by the Norwegian military authorities to get away with all speed. It was feared that the Germans would force her to speak over the radio, on the "correctness" of their behaviour. She went north through Gudbrandsdal. At the Folk High School in

Hundorp, she met with other good friends, Fredrik Paasche and Stina, his wife, and Anders Wyller. They helped in the Norwegian government's broadcasting service during the retreat through Gudbrandsdal. On April 21st they suffered a heavy raid in Dombaas and took to the woods for shelter. When the sky was clear, they went into a hotel. She sat there and emptied the snow from her shoes; then there was a new alert. "The rest of us," says Fredrik Paasche, "rushed down to the door, but she still sat there. I called to her and told her to come along. But she only turned round and said, 'No. If they come again, I really shall get angry!'"

In *Kristin Lavransdatter*, Sigrid Undset has described the beauty of Gudbrandsdal as no one else. All the same, it seemed as if she now discovered it for the first time. Spring was slowly coming—again the story is from Paasche —and she pointed out the small grey cottages: "I have never noticed how lovely they are before. How lovely everything is."

They came to the burning town of Aandalsnes, so on to Molde, and from there out to Bud near Hustadviken. It was a question of reaching Northern Norway, which was still free. In a fishing-boat, with six bunks and thirty-six passengers, they sailed northwards. Day after day the sea lay clear and calm, night after night the red glow of sunset and the faint light of dawn were seen together. "Every moment, I think, we all said the same—it is unbelievable that anything so lovely can be real" (*Return to the Future*, 1942, p. 41). The plan was to reach Tromsø, but some miles south of Bodø they learnt that it was unlikely that they would be allowed to land there. There was nothing to be done but sail some distance south again, to Mo in Rana. From there it should be possible to get over to Sweden. One evening in May, they started on their journey over the border-mountains. It was twenty years since Sigrid Undset had had skis on her feet, and with a fur-coat for a skiing-outfit, she found it rather heavy going. She was glad to be given a place with a sick man they had with them, on a ski-sledge with six active lads in front.

In Sweden she met good friends and warm understanding. "All my Swedish friends had the same attitude towards the Nazis as I had," she says in *Return to the Future*.

One episode during her stay in Sweden must be mentioned. Ever since her earliest youth, Sigrid Undset had looked on Carl Linné as a kind of "lay patron-saint". Botany had always attracted her; her knowledge of flowers—and of birds—was impressive. She had to take the opportunity of visiting old Hammerby, Linné's estate outside Uppsala. While she and a friend wandered about in the simple, elegantly furnished rooms, in which the great eighteenth-century naturalist had lived, Carl Linné and his work became of symbolic significance. He spoke to her of the victories which mean more than victory in war, he spoke of science in the service of peace and reason. But she could not avoid thinking also of his religious philosophy, as he set it down in the reflections on *Nemesis Divina*, which he wrote for his son when he was himself a dying man. "Success made him neither an optimist nor a pessimist," she thought; "Baron von Linné knew what he had always known—that God governs the world with a hard and just hand. Sooner or later, His vengeance will fall on all who have been guilty of lies and injustice." The woman with her told the anecdote of an old Swedish woman, an author, who, after a dinner given in honour of Ibsen, had kissed the cloth where the master's hand had lain—a gesture not exactly to Sigrid Undset's taste! "But I did the same myself, I kissed the writing-desk where Linné's hand must have rested so often. Afterwards we sat outside under the trees, and the conservator's wife served us with coffee and bread-and-butter. It began to rain, a fine close rain, and we inhaled the good smell of wet earth and new grass. And Alice whispered the quotation from Linné which had been in my thoughts all the time: 'The defeated have still a weapon—appeal to God'."

The war news which came while she was in Sweden was, as we know, not encouraging. Some days before May 17th, she got the message that her son Anders had been killed. On Independence Day she wrote an article full of light, inspired by love of her country and her Christian outlook. She never gives up hope "that one day our children will be able to live as free people in a free Norway, that the red-crossed flags will one day stream again through our towns and villages. And on that day we can go joyfully to meet our dead—the dead from olden times, our forefathers, and those who have died this spring."

One message they received gave new grounds for hope— the decision of the King and his government to leave the country and continue the struggle "somewhere outside the frontiers of Norway". She asked herself, "How many in their heart of hearts share their faith that it is worth while? They must believe, plainly and simply, in a superhuman justice which in the fullness of time will prevail."

On July 14th her travels began again. With her youngest son, who had come to Sweden after the fighting in Norway had ended, she went by air via Tallinn, Riga and Veliki Luki to Moscow. She spent only fourteen days in the capital of Soviet Russia. She had never fostered any illusions about conditions there, but her impressions were more dispiriting than she had expected. They confirmed what she had imagined—that the new Russia was only the old Russia in a different guise. After the war, she writes in *Return to the Future*, she will perhaps drop her mask and come forward openly as "a nationalist and imperialist state, ruled by a clique under the thumb of Josef Stalin."

From Moscow the journey went on through Siberia to Japan. The country's fairy-tale beauty, the grace, dignity and friendliness of the people, the delicate colours of their dress, the innumerable things which witnessed to a highly developed artistic culture, all fascinated her so much that for once she had to give way to wishful thinking. She could not believe that Japanese Fascism could be an expression of the Japanese people. There could be no connection between Japan as an imperialist totalitarian state and the true character of the people—they had fallen a prey to a small group who wanted all the power in their own hands.

The journey's end was of course America. She landed in San Francisco on August 26th and left immediately for New York in order to start on a series of lectures she was to give there. She stayed at first at the Algonquin, on 44th Street, Manhattan. The people who had arranged for her to have apartments there, says Arne Skouen, presumably thought that this well-known artists' hotel would be a suitable place for the famous author. "Perhaps they were counting on someone fond of artistic company, a bon-mot-producing Nobel prize-winner, who would stay and be seen in the city's literary society in years to come." Meanwhile, Sigrid Undset found herself an apartment in a more unassuming and less central district, at Columbia Heights in Brooklyn, and there she stayed the whole time she was in America. In her first summers in the United States, she went for preference to a little country town, Monterey in Western Massachusetts, and worked there for three or four months. Other places of resort were also dear to her—she stayed with Willa Cather, on her estate in the north of New York State, with Marjorie Kinnan Rawlings, who had an orange-plantation in the depths of Florida, and with other American friends.

Both the country and the people were different from what she expected. "We come to America," she writes, "with the completely mistaken notion that the whole enormous country is dotted with great towns and huge industrial plants and clusters of chimneys, everything connected by arterial roads with a continuous stream of lorries and cars passing over them, as if they were on conveyor-belts—and we think there is never a glimpse of open country to be seen." She thinks it may be because the American literature we have mostly known gives an extremely one-sided picture—a rather "hard-boiled" literature, superficially romantic or anti-romantic, never particularly realistic. "It was only just before the outbreak of the war that books by Thomas Wolfe, Willa Cather, Marjorie Kinnan Rawlings and one or two more, had aroused in us the suspicion that America was still a continent which had vast sparsely settled territories and a mighty and varied natural beauty. Of course, Robert Frost's poetry conveyed New England to our senses, but then, he was so little known amongst us."

She was often surprised when she went by train in America because people very rarely looked out of the window at the country they were travelling through. They were usually absorbed in magazines or a book, or else they settled down to sleep. But she soon learnt that it was wrong to think that Americans had no feeling for the beauty of their native land. "At least, I was lucky enough to meet many American men and women who loved their country and their own districts the feeling and character of air and sky and contour in the places where they had grown up, the animals and trees, the creeping-plants which make any wood in America a wilderness, even when it is no bigger than a copse, the bird-life and the flowers—they knew and appreciated all these as happily and deeply as I knew Vestre Aker and Nordmark and the countryside round the little Danish town where I used to visit my grandfather in my childhood holidays." She writes this in an article with the title *Beautiful America*, after the opening words of the American song, "America, the beautiful . . ."

Sigrid Undset wrote about her impressions of the country and its inhabitants in newspapers and magazines. For the most part, they were random observations, but occasionally she made from them small character-sketches and close-up portraits, as in *The Beauties of America, My Street, My American Garden, American Literature, Common Ground,* and others.

She does not neglect to draw attention to the fact that America represents a culture which stands in its own right, rich and manifold, individual and vital. But it is what we have in common, above all the love of liberty, which she feels most strongly. She writes that the Germans and Russians have never understood the preciousness of freedom. "That is a fact which the Atlantic powers must never forget, if the Allies win this war."

As she travelled through parts of this gigantic country— the impression of its immensity was especially strong in the Middle West—it was not difficult for her to understand that, to the average person, the war and all the misery in Europe must seem remote and almost unreal. Even her own experience of bombs and machine-gun fire could be thought of as something she had dreamt. It could irritate her to hear people speak of the war against Hitler as merely another of the usual imperialist wars, which were started more or less regularly by the ambitious European states, but this never weakened her feeling that Europe and America were branches of the same tree. "The more I see of America, the more I admire the men who, on the basis of a group of British colonies on the Atlantic seaboard, created the United States, and the more knowledge I should like to have of them. The foundation laid by 'The Founding Fathers' is without doubt one of the great wonders of the world. . . . Sometimes when I hear Americans ridiculing 'the old school tie men' from other countries, I cannot help thinking of Washington and Jefferson and their nearest contemporaries—all men of the same civilisation and tradition as 'the old school tie'—and of what the world owes to the careful fostering and education of their genius or talent." If the "American dream" still has a spiritual content, it is due to impulses from these men (*American Literature*).

Sigrid Undset came to feel great affection for America and the Americans. "There are good fellows in every country"; but, generally speaking, it seems that her chief impression of the individual American was that he was throughout less self-centred than other people—frank, hospitable, helpful. When one talked to Sigrid Undset on the subject of Americans, her heart warmed immediately. "They wear their ideals boldly on their sleeve," she said; "but it is no embarrassment for them to show kindness. They will moreover put themselves to considerable inconvenience to do so."

Sigrid Undset put herself immediately at the disposal of the Norwegian information service in America. She thought of herself as mobilised and was proud of it.

American publishers and editors were fully aware of her position in the literary world. To them she was first and foremost the great author, a literary figure of international status. But for us, writes Arne Skouen, it was undeniably an advantage that she also happened to be Norwegian. It meant that the Norwegian information services could command a name which possessed something of the status of an institution. She was a welcome guest on the front page of *The New York Times Book Review*, America's most distinguished literary column, whenever she felt the urge to express her views. It was the same with the *Times'* competitor, *The New York Herald Tribune*. The Norwegian service for cultural propaganda had, with her help, broken down such difficult and important barriers that the wealthy information bureaus of the great powers would have paid fantastic sums to obtain the same privileges for one of their representatives, if such had been for sale (Arne Skouen).

Her activity was intense. She spoke in lecture-halls and on the wireless, she contributed to anthologies, she wrote books, and innumerable articles for American and Norwegian newspapers, periodicals and Christmas volumes.

The platform and the microphone were not the means of communication best suited to Sigrid Undset. She was by no means eloquent. Rhetoric was so far from her nature that she seemed almost to shun anything of the kind, for fear that her words might lose credit with her audience.

The activity in which she was essentially engaged was literary. "I write propaganda," she said with emphasis. Norwegian authors worked for the national cause in various ways, and Sigrid Undset was the epic-writer amongst them, the historian and novelist who threw light on the paths which her nation had striven to follow in the past two thousand years. She knew those paths better than all others, and no one could speak of Norway and its culture and of Scandinavia as a whole with greater authority than she, no matter whether she wrote for foreigners or for Norwegians. And with the possible exception of Fredrik Paasche, there was no one with the same sure instinct, accurate knowledge and wide perspective, who could correct the distorted picture of Scandinavia and of the ideals of the northern peoples, which the Nazis and their predecessors had persuaded the Germans and many others to accept as true.

Sigrid Undset Scorns Nordic Myth read the editorial headline over an article of hers in the *Minneapolis Sunday Tribune and Star*, on October 12th 1941. It is an appropriate title for a whole series of her essays from these years. Her castigation of the "Nordic Myth" of the Germans was not simply restricted to ridicule of the heroes of Wagnerian opera, of the banal rhetoric which dealt with the Aryan race and the *Herrenvolk*, or of the fantasies of authors like Alfred Rosenberg in *Der Mythus des 20. Jahrhunderts* and Hans F. K. Günther in *Herkunft und Rassengeschichte der Germanen*. Against their extravagant hypotheses, she sets factual information about the Scandinavian peoples, and shows that, from the racial point of view, the Germans have very little in common

228

with them, even though the attempt was being made to include them, ethnologically and spiritually, in the German neo-pagan *Lebensraum*.

The most important of these polemic historical essays are *The Real Religion of the Nordic People*, *The Mind of the Nordic People*, *Saint Olav*, *A Book that was a Turning-Point in my Life*, and two small talks in Norwegian, *The Heritage from Sola* (*Arven fra Sola*) and *Justice* (*Rettferdighet*).

Her attack on the romantic idealisation of the Vikings is characteristic of her approach. In this, she does not hesitate to condemn the tendency of her countrymen to glorify the piratical expeditions of their ancestors. She recalls how her history-teacher, a man who was a pacifist and a progressive, had told them with evident satisfaction that the English and French used to pray in their churches: "Spare us, O God, from the fury of the Northmen." She suspects however that this glorification was not merely the result of nationalism, but that it was also part of the necessary intellectual equipment of the loyal progressive if he was to regard the Church and Christianity as reactionary forces, which, for preference, should be strangled at birth. "Die-hard romantics are still to be found, who enthuse over the Viking Age as a period of proud individualism, unaffected by the unhealthy soul-searching of Christianity and by the law of Saint Olav in general" (*Saint Olav*). It was certainly also possible that admiration for the Viking raids could have its origin in "evolutionary optimism". People were so confident that the world had grown out of the mentality of brute force and the madness of war that there could be no harm in a little boasting of a nation's "vigorous youth". But, for the most part, Norwegians have ceased to be so very proud of their ancestors' exploits as pirates and men of violence.

Sigrid Undset wished to reveal, and succeeded in revealing, another Scandinavia—the Scandinavia of justice and peace and a society based on law; and she showed how deeply these ideals have been rooted in the Scandinavian peoples from Arild's time to the present day.

She certainly wishes us to admire the Vikings' lust for adventure and their skill as seafarers. One must remember that not all the voyages of the Northmen were plundering expeditions—they aimed also at trade and discovery. "The discovery of Iceland, Greenland and Vinland were carefully planned voyages of exploration, conscious efforts to find new land and to colonise foreign shores never before settled by man."

Imaginatively and with reference to the results achieved by modern historians—amongst them, Magnus Olsen in the field of place-name research—she can, in a few lines, throw light on the work which must have gone on in the Viking Age, to clear the ground for new settlements along the fjords and valleys and beside the lakes and rivers.

As we have said, however, she wishes chiefly to draw the attention of her readers and audiences to the growth of a society based upon law and justice. She speaks of "our Norwegian passion for justice". "Passion for justice and delight in the creation of law and order in the conduct of human affairs within society"—these can be traced back to pre-Christian times. Christianity hastens the development. In *The Heritage from Sola*, where she tells of the arrangements made by Erling Skjalgsson for the freeing of his thralls, she says, "When Norway was converted, human sacrifice on certain ceremonial occasions was replaced by the liberation of a slave, to whose purchase all the farmers contributed, 'as a good deed acceptable to Christ'." She points to the considerable body of evidence which shows that, in the course of two centuries, not a long period in the history of a country, the Norwegian people became a comparatively highly civilised Christian society. "If there is anything," she writes, "of which we Norwegians may be justly proud, it is not that our forefathers were Vikings, but that these same men grew so rapidly out of their Viking mentality that less than two hundred years after the battle of Stiklestad they were in advance of other nations on the road to our ideas of humanity, justice, and respect for the rights of the individual, whether he be poor or rich,—the road to personal freedom and just dealing."

She re-tells in masterly fashion one of the sagas—called *Flóamanna Saga* in some manuscripts—giving it the title of *Thorgils Arrbeinsstjup*. She introduces the story with some remarks which show why she should choose this particular saga. "As for the religious element in it, it seems to me to give a credible picture of a man who has become Christian at a time when the claims of paganism and Christianity were at odds one with another, not only amongst the Scandinavian peoples as a whole, but in the soul of every Northman. We are doubtless given a good picture of the spiritual life in many a Christian Icelander and Norwegian of that age in Thorgils' unshakable loyalty to Christ, the lord he has chosen after his break with the gods of his ancestors, and in his revolt when he is afflicted with the bitterest of sorrows, one which he could not tolerate in resignation to God's will. For that matter, we who call ourselves Christians today, are not perhaps so very different."

She has extracted the essence of the saga and given it to us in her version. There are animated descriptions of the dangers and difficulties which the first Icelandic voyagers to Greenland had to overcome amid the ice of that icy land, and of men's relations with supernatural powers. But what especially makes her version of the saga so valuable is her understanding of the love for children with which the saga-writer must have been imbued. She comments on this characteristic. "A unique feature of saga-literature is the interest in children which the saga-authors reveal. There are, it is true, other stories about children in the literature of medieval Europe—boys whose mission from birth is to avenge their fathers, and girls destined from the beginning to some unhappy or remarkable fate. But they are never

introduced at play or in misery like real living youngsters;—
outside of Iceland, Shakespeare was the first to take
pleasure in sketching children who talk and behave like
children. The saga-authors must have been fond of little
ones."

Her story of Thorgils and his son, after the baby's mother
has died in the Greenland ice, is alive and graphic. "The
baby cried and cried,—and towards morning, Thorgils
stood up and drew his knife. 'I can't listen to this any
longer, I can't hear the boy cry himself to death. First I'd
rather try to feed him with my blood.' He slashed his
nipples and, says the saga, first blood ran out, then a fluid
clear as water, and finally milk." Thorgils' grief when his
son dies is described in these words: "For three days and
three nights he lay there, without touching food or drink,
without sleeping, without speaking. Only once he did say
that he could feel for all women, because they love the child
they have fed at the breast more than the whole world.
The word used in the saga, *varkunna*, implies both sympathy
and understanding—it is the word used in the old texts for
Christ's love and Mary's tender care for the sinful and
sorrowful. And I have always thought that the words which
the old saga-man put into the mouth of Thorgils Arrbeinsstjup are the most chivalrous words a man has ever uttered
about women."

She now publishes in English, with the title *Sigurd and his
Brave Companions*, a little children's story of her own, set in
the late Middle Ages in Norway, the reign of Haakon V.
It had appeared in German as early as 1931 as *Die Saga
von Vilmund Vidutan und seiner Gefährten*. It is of children
she writes, of their play and the way in which the stories
they hear can influence this and their imaginative life. It
also throws light on the way in which we may conceive the
process by which the Christian ideas of life find their way
into the minds of children and provide controlling and
guiding impulses.

Other of her articles and speeches were more direct contributions to the contemporary ideological conflict. In the company of Thomas Mann, Jacques Maritain and others, she writes an essay for the volume called *The People's Century: The States of the Western Hemisphere*, which appeared at the end of 1942. Her essay is on Scandinavia and the New World. She wrote on the Christian conception of brotherhood in the essay called *Brotherhood*; she wrote on antisemitism in the *Amsterdam News*; she contributed several articles on the totalitarian state to the weekly paper *America*, and others; and in *The Thomist* she published her tribute to Jacques Maritain, the essay on the Christian renaissance in French intellectual life, which we have already discussed. The article *War and Literature*, also belongs to this group.

The subject to which she continually returns to discuss and illuminate is modern paganism's attack on Christianity, and its rejection of the idea that man's purpose in the world is determined by a supernatural power. "In whatever form it may be revealed—Fascism, Nazism or Communism,—it means a break with every religion hitherto known." But, she maintains, the western democracies have themselves helped to pave the way for the paganism of the twentieth century. The materialist philosophy, "man's revolt against every form of transcendental responsibility towards a supernatural order," has undermined the foundations of civilisation and reduced the ideals of brotherhood and liberty to sentimental day-dreams. She repeats: we believed we could pluck the fruits of Christianity, even though we had pulled up the roots of the Christian tree. "Do you remember the old familiar charges against Christianity, especially against the way in which the Church preaches the teaching of Christ? How it was blamed for twisting man's nature, his love for truth and beauty?"

She develops the Christian idea of brotherhood in the article of that name. Brotherhood of the purely natural kind is no guarantee for peace amongst men. The biological

233

interdependence of parents and children, brothers and sisters, and people of the same race, is certainly the source of the strongest and most dependable love we know of between human beings. "But, however dependable it may be, it has its limits." The fact is that with Christianity a brotherhood of another kind enters the world, with its source in the faith that we all have one Father in Heaven. It is the Christian conception of brotherhood which is truly universal and international.

Christianity binds together all men of good will, Christians and non-Christians. As we have seen, Sigrid Undset never ignores the general religious sentiment in mankind. Scattered remarks on the religious experience of the great mystics are characteristic of her attitude. Thus, in a review of H. A. Reinhold's book, *The Soul Afire! Revelations of the Mystics*, she says of Plato and Plotinus that they remind us that the heart's desire for God is fundamental in all humanity and not confined to Christians (*The New York Times Book Review*, March 4th 1945).

On the same occasion, she writes of the importance of understanding the message transmitted to us by the mystics. "Up from our evil and chaotic age, voices are raised calling for a return to religion. There is a feeling, sometimes clearly expressed, more often dimly realised, that when man tries to wrench himself away from his origin, he loses contact with the source which supplies even his temporal life. The call for a religion which can save our world is all too often obsessed by consideration of the service which such a religious regeneration can be expected to render to society. Amongst other things, the message of the great mystics reminds us that the end of society is to serve religion. We are born with the desire to return to the God in whom we have had our being before all worlds and by whose act of creation we have become living individuals. Before everything else, mundane institutions and human society should bear the imprint which God has set on each one of us."

Works of propaganda on a grand scale are *The Ten Commandments: Ten Short Novels*, and *Hitler's War Against the Moral Code* (1944). Ten of the most famous authors of our time—Thomas Mann, Rebecca West, Franz Werfel, John Erskine, Bruno Frank, Jules Romain, André Maurois, Sigrid Undset, Hendrik Willem van Loon and Louis Bromfield—give in this volume examples, half in short-story form, half in the form of journalistic reports, of Hitler's violation of the moral code formulated with such monumental simplicity in the Ten Commandments.

The collection is introduced by Hermann Rauschning, who quotes at one point the following declaration by Hitler: "I am the Lord thy God! Who? The Asiatic tyrant? No, the day shall come when, against these commandments, I shall set up the tables of a new law. All history shall come to acknowledge that our movement is a fight for the liberation of mankind,—liberation from the curse pronounced on Mount Sinai, the damnation brought to us by these nomadic sons of darkness, who did not dare rely on their own healthy instincts, who could only understand the divine in the shape of a tyrant who commands us to do exactly what we do not wish to do. We fight against the masochistic spirit of self-torture, the so-called moral damnation, which has been made into a divine law to protect the weak against the strong, against the eternal laws of war and the mighty precepts of divine Nature. It is against the so-called Ten Commandments that we fight." And Goebbels seconds his master: "Youth is on our side. The youth of the world has done with these old ideologies."

Thomas Mann tells the story of Moses. Naturally, it is no easy matter to compete with the biblical narrative. His historical sketch of the intellectual and spiritual background of the Ten Commandments and their formulation of the distinction between good and evil as the absolute Either-Or, and his interpretation of the commandment *Thou shalt have no gods before me*, are however more than brilliant reflections.

With a simplicity of language unusual for him, he explains the universal religious idea which lies behind the moral alphabet, the covenant between the invisible God and the human individual. From Sinai sounds the voice which cries, "Woe to the man who rises up, saying, 'These commandments are valid no longer'."

These studies on the theme of the Ten Commandments begin thus with an ancient mystery-play in Heaven. The other writers bring us down to earth. Each of them, from his own country or experience, has a report to give of Christian Europe in the twentieth century. The main argument is clear and simple. There has always been violation of the moral code contained in the Commandments, but now that violation is set up as a principle. The old law shall bind us no longer! But has it therefore lost its validity? Must not men become conscious of it just at this time?

Sigrid Undset writes on the Seventh Commandment and the behaviour of the Germans in Norway. The short-story treatment of the subject is not particularly successful, but she describes effectively the reaction of the ordinary Norwegian man and woman, when they come into contact with manifestations of the new morality. Something in them whispers that this is arrogance, violation of the laws laid down for human conduct, which will reap its reward. Their belief is in a *Nemesis Divina*.

On a different level from these direct contributions to the ideological conflict are her essays intended to spread knowledge of Scandinavian literature amongst the American people.

In the essay called *Scandinavian Literature*, originally given in July 1943 as a lecture to the Polish Academy of Arts and Sciences in America, she surveys the whole field, covering not only Norwegian, Danish and Swedish writing, but also Icelandic and Finno-Swedish. The Poles, she says, were most anxious that she should use the term "Scandinavian", because in their ears "Nordic" was an ugly reminder of the racial myth of the Germans, according to which the Germans were also supposed to be of Nordic stock. The task she had undertaken was, by its very nature, impossible in the narrow limits of a single lecture. But without having recourse to facile generalisation, she brings out the significant dissimilarities in the Scandinavian literatures, while noting at the same time what they have in common—realism and a feeling for the individual and peculiar. She expresses it in this way: "The temper of mind peculiar to the Scandinavians as a whole is always in evidence. Their preference for the realities of life, their interest in the different ways in which men and women behave when touched by passion,—by love or hate, by ambition or feelings of honour and glory—their interest in the innate disparities which condition our development and make different people act each in his or her own way in similar situations—it is this, I believe, which is the most deeply-rooted characteristic of Scandinavian literature." The most interesting single passage in this essay is that where she gives examples of the life-like child descriptions in the Icelandic family-sagas, amongst them the charming picture in *Viga-Glúms Saga* of the two small cousins on a visit to their grandmother.

The world-famous figures in Scandinavian literature—Hans Andersen, Søren Kierkegaard, Henrik Ibsen, August Strindberg—receive little more than a mention—and she writes on them nowhere else. She finds it more needful to speak of other writers, the great unknown names. Thus, it was she who took the initiative in bringing out a translation of some of Steen Steensen Blicher's short stories, *Twelve Stories by Steen Steensen Blicher* (New York, 1945), and she wrote an introduction for it, which appeared separately later as a small book. "He is to my mind one of the great story-tellers of world-literature," are words she wrote in an article on Denmark, published in *The American-Scandinavian Review* in 1944. Her essay on Blicher is illuminating and delightful, not least because it tells us something of Sigrid Undset's youthful and intense discovery of this great author, who knew so many secrets of the heart and wrote so truthfully about them—evidence of "the deep undercurrent of realism in Danish Romanticism".

A characteristic counterpart to her essay on Blicher is the introduction she wrote for a selection of Asbjørnsen and Moe's folk-tales, *True and Untrue and other Norse Tales* (edited and compiled by Sigrid Undset, 1945). Her folk-lore study is popular in style but scholarly in substance, solidly based on her familiar knowledge of the migration and inter-relation of such stories—she seems to have as much control over her material as any specialist in the field. The essay is not, however, so compact as her other writing of the same kind often is. It is full of both the poetry and the humour of the Norwegian folk-tales. The motives which are found in them spring from common human nature, but

"they had to make themselves at home in every country they came to. So although the Norwegian folk-tales have wandered far and wide through space and time, to us Norwegians they seem to be blood of our own blood, and bone, as homely as our mountains and forests and fjords. It is our way of looking at life and judging people, they express. We never liked glamour, we always thought it rather vulgar—real life with its troubles and jokes and sorrows and joys was good enough for us, and even when we daydreamed, we dreamed of a world not too unlike the one we knew and loved. Fairy tales like the Irish and the French, we never had. The creation of our fancy that came nearest to a fairy tale was the 'Hulder' and she is a buxom girl, heir to a large farm in the underworld, boy-crazy but handsome—only, she has a tail like a cow. The king of the folk tales does not live in a moated and turreted castle but in a 'kongsgaard',—literally the 'king's farm', even if it is a glorified manor farm like the ones where the old and wealthy rural families have lived for centuries and ruled the countryside as arrogantly and arbitrarily as any lord or baron abroad. The king's daughter is just the spoiled heiress, or the dignified or refined young girl of this rural aristocracy, and it does not make much difference, whether her father is king above or beneath the green fields. The moral of the folk-tales—for the Norwegian folk tales are usually very moral—is the moral our country people believed in: the kind and the generous, the brave and the sincere, will get their rewards in the end. The good step-daughter who steps gingerly over even the brushwood fence, careful not to hurt a twig, is given beauty and riches, but the bad girl who handles dead and living things equally brutally, will get a box full of snakes that kill her. When True overhears the palaver of the animals beneath the lime tree where he has found refuge for the night, they lead him to restored sight and a princess for his bride; to Untrue they bring death. But the favourite hero of the Norwegian folk-tales is Espen Ashlad, the youth who seems too indolent and lazy to do anything but sit in the ingle nook the livelong day. He embodies a wishful dream of the Norwegians, hard-working on their stony soil and along the storm-swept coast. Wouldn't it be a fine thing, if a man could take life easy most of the time and yet come out on top, when he was faced with a difficult or dangerous task, doing ever so much better than all the self-important and careworn drudges who always want the young people to work like slaves? No, Espen Ashlad is a deep one, sly and canny, but he is also courageous and resourceful in a difficult situation. He may be ruthless when he has to deal with a cussed king or dumb trolls, but he is kind to the poor and the old, ever willing to help those who seemingly would never be able to do anything for him in return. So he shall have his reward. The story may waive this strictly moral attitude when the hero is a master thief, or a poor lad who has to use his wits to get along in the world in spite of severe handicaps, but then their victims are always people who did not deserve better.

Though the storytellers never go in for word-painting of the scenery, the whole nature of Norway is in the folk-tales. Storms rage in the North Sea and the breakers thunder along the shores, leaving the shipwrecked sailor marooned on the island where the Big Bird Dam has his home. High above the timber line are the upland fells where Dapplegrim was reared. Through the endless forests the wanderer has to travel, down into one valley and uphill and down again, until he has lost his bearings, but at last he will see the faraway pale blue ridge, where lies his goal. The old crone who lives in the midst of the woods in her tiny hut is more used to talking to the wild animals and the birds and the Moon and the Winds than to seeing human visitors. On the crest of the slope is the stately manor farm, surrounded by fields and pastures where sleek fat cattle and fine horses graze, and the weary wanderer jogs on, hopeful that here he will be given a full meal at nightfall and a soft bed to sleep in. The people go about their business, tilling the soil, caring for their cattle, felling timber or looking after their nets and their boats—and then they sail or walk or tumble down a hole in a field, right into the realm of the supernatural, where after a while they will feel very much at home. It is rather like the world they have come from."

Novel-writing had to take second place. There could be no question of continuing *Madame Dorothea*: "Madame Dorothea," she said, "has become a figure so far away in the remote past that it seems impossible to return to her." But with that power of vivid and animating description which only an artist possesses, she told of her experiences in Norway during the war, and of her impressions from the journey over Russia and Japan to America, in *Return to the Future* (1942). Parts of it have been mentioned and quoted in the preceding pages. And even if *Madame Dorothea* had to remain only the beginning of a novel (and we might have hoped that it was only temporarily put aside), there were memories of past life and of Norway which came to the surface and were given artistic shape in the book, *Happy Times in Norway* (1942), published in Norway as *Lykkelige dager* (1947).

The external occasion for its production was an idea of Mrs Elinor Roosevelt's. She thought that authors from the occupied countries, who were now American allies, might write on the life of children in their homeland before the Germans marched in.

The book is written then with an eye to the young American reader, but this particular purpose does not lessen its value. The accounts of Norwegian history and of everyday life in Norway which find a place in the book, have a fresh and novel effect on grown-ups and children alike, both Norwegian and American. They are introduced naturally and as a matter of course in the picture of the Norwegian home which is presented in the book.

The book has a certain monumental character. It is, after all, a kind of memorial raised to the home Sigrid Undset had created in Lillehammer, the home which she would never see again as it had been, now that one of her sons was dead.

There is not the slightest trace of sentimentality in her description. A clear, peaceful sky arches wide over the whole—its quality is that of *serenitas*. Natural objects, people and events are brought before us in classically moulded descriptive forms. We follow the life of a single family through one year, beginning and ending with the potato-lifting holiday of autumn. Within this frame of the annual cycle, with Christmas, May 17th and the summer holidays as the chief events, she shows how life is shaped for the child, in a happy home, surrounded by Norwegian nature and marked by Norwegian customs and traditions.

In *Happy Times in Norway*, Sigrid Undset gives full-toned expression to her love for the home, which plays such an essential part in all her writing, and it joins with her abundant and all-embracing charity, inspired here not by the bitter grief of an exiled and sorrowful mother, but by deep gratitude and joy.

We find the same feeling, or something very similar, in the delightful sketch of Norway's mountain countryside, *At Home in Værskjei*, which appeared in *Lille Norge Avisen* on June 23rd 1944. Even if she had not written this, Sigrid Undset would still have had a place amongst the greatest of the Norwegian authors who have described the mountains. But this is her finest composition of this kind. "There can be few of us who do not remember one beacon which was our own personal property. There we lay, basking in the sunshine, and gazed out over the scene before us, taking in only half of what we saw—the great waste of woodland below, where we knew every track and path, the deep valley-clefts with their streams, the eternal ring of grey and blue mountains, purple summit beyond purple summit round the whole horizon."

The picture of Norway presented by Sigrid Undset during her stay in America is supplemented by small autobiographical fragments, some in Norwegian and some in English. They are, for the most part, lively, intimate and humorous sketches, like *Florida Water*, recollections from summer holidays spent at Hvitsten, *My Favourite Aunt*, a childhood memory from Kalundborg, *They were Friends of my Parents*, about the Rink family in Lyder Sagen's Street, *The Yule-tide Sheaf (Juleneket)*, an impressionist sketch from the world of folk-lore, and *It's Haunted (Det spøker)*, where she tells of goblins, the old miller, ghosts, the "hidden folk", and strange things she herself had "seen" at Mosetrene in Gudbrandsdal.

Besides this extensive literary production and public activity, Sigrid Undset also performed a task which the

American Department of Defence had assigned to her:
a survey of Norwegian relics of cultural value—monuments
of various kinds, every type of museum, churches, old
buildings and farms, and similar objects,—which would
all have to be safeguarded, should Norway become the
scene of an invasion. The printed sources on which she
could draw consisted only of what was available in the New
York Public Library. What she could not glean there, she
dug for in the solid and capacious store-chest of her own
brain. Luckily there was no need for the catalogue she made;
but it is as good as complete, and so neat and well arranged
that it too tells its story, not only of her indefatigable energy
and powers of memory, but also of her patriotism. Her own
activity proved the truth of what she had said in one of her
speeches, given in the P.E.N. Club in New York: "It takes
more than a little while to part a nation from its history,
and silence all the voices from a people's past."

In August 1945 Sigrid Undset returned to Norway, and
after five years' absence was able to settle down once more
in Lillehammer. The Germans had upset things sadly in
Bjerkebæk—they had chopped up the old desk which she
had inherited from her father and at which she had written
her world-famous novels, and all the silver and linen had
disappeared. Friends had taken care of the most valuable
articles, and in consequence her old home still stood in
something of its old shape to receive her. On her sixty-
fifth birthday, King Haakon awarded her the highest
distinction, the Grand Cross of the Order of Saint Olav,
"for eminent services to literature and to the nation".
No one can accuse Sigrid Undset of a weakness for outward
honour and glory. But she was not *so* great that she could
accept without deep feelings of gratitude this recognition
from her King, the man she had most admired in the
Norwegian struggle for freedom.

The war, the terrific pressure of work, grief for her son
who had fallen before the Nazi onslaught—all this had told

on her strength. She made no new beginnings on creative work, but she was engaged on a biography of the great fourteenth-century Church reformer, Catherine of Siena. In her contributions to newspapers and periodicals, she is as bold and uncompromising as ever. Nazism has been knocked out in the first bout—but it can get on its feet again. And Europe is still threatened by "attitudes to life which to us are just as foreign". *This Is no Time For Pollyannas* (*Dette er ikke noen tid for Polyannaer*) is the headline of an article by her in *Verdens Gang* (November 23rd 1946), aimed at the muddle-heads who, faced with new dangers, want to follow the same course that allowed Hitler to march unopposed for so long. Sigrid Undset is an apostle of peace. In her life and her writing she served the cause of peace as only few people have had the courage and ability to do. But she is not a pacifist. Her unshakable conviction is that of Fridtjof Nansen: those who believe that peace is better than war must be prepared to defend it.

Her religious message has the same character as before. "We find the way forward to our goal only by our own efforts, our unwearying, patient and courageous efforts," she wrote in *Samtiden* in 1946. It is to the intellect and will that she directs her appeal, whether indirectly as in the learned and profound article, *On Abraham's Sacrifice* (*Omkring Abrahams offer*), or directly, as in the inspired Christmas meditations she wrote for *Verdens Gang* and the Christmas volume, *The Bells Are Ringing* (*Det kimer i klokker*). Amongst other things, the former article deals with the way in which the Old Testament should properly be read. Worship of the printed word of God as the only valid source of faith has led to slavery to the letter. The Old Testament is inspired history precisely because it is something more than a bare record of facts, it interprets a series of events, —it is "a history of ideas, open to symbolic interpretation". The story of Abraham's sacrifice stands illumined by a light which can never be quenched. It shows that the duty imposed on Abraham and his seed—i.e. all those who fear and love God above all else—"demanded loyalty and a readiness for self-sacrifice no *less* than the heathen gods demanded of their worshippers". Further, the thought runs like a scarlet thread through the whole of the Old Testament that human beings are always architects of their own misfortune, and that they always forget, with equal rapidity, every instance of God's mercy. "And I must confess that I can discover nothing in the history of the world, from the legendary past to the present day, which is capable of disproving this conviction. So that 'naïve' is the last adjective I should apply to the stories in the book of Moses which tell of the world's first age."

CHAPTER X

Return to the Future

WE HAVE surveyed Sigrid Undset's literary activity in its entirety, the main body of her work and all its parts and varied forms, the mighty medieval epic, short stories and novels of modern life, essays, scholarly treatises, articles, pamphlets, secular and saintly biographies, edifying reflections, speeches, memoirs, even verse and, on one occasion, a dramatic sketch.

What must first cause astonishment is the organic unity of this vast and varied production, the unfailing and inevitable assurance with which the central theme is retained in view—a concentration which bears the stamp of genius. From first to last, her writing is inspired by a living creative ideal, a vision which is continually extending over fresh landscapes and embracing new horizons.

If we try to define this fundamental conception which has inspired her work, we run the risk of oversimplifying in the way we are warned against by the old Norwegian proverb, "Never take hold of the truth with mittens on." For the conception is always developing. It is one with her own mind; it grows deeper and wider with the expansion of her own conscious life. It is not something ready-made, something fixed and finished, which can be served up on a plate and done with. It evolves gradually, and takes artistic shape by virtue of its inherent power of survival. But we are not far from the truth if we say that what is at issue in her imaginative writing, or for that matter in all her work, is the question of *loyalty*. Her novels do not put problems to debate—there is no over-riding bias; they are not doctrinaire in that way. But they answer the question: What is loyalty? In what does the essence of loyalty consist? Can human beings be loyal to each other? Is it in fact possible? Horror at treachery seems to have been the central experience, the first shock and agitation, which, in a literary sense, gave her "vision". Her first book begins: "I have been unfaithful to my husband." In *The Faithful Wife*, her last novel of contemporary life, Nathalie knows of nothing more precious than the possession of something to which she can give her utter and absolute loyalty. It is the same with a whole series of her characters. It is the capacity for loyalty in men and women which is put to the test. The conflict of conscience which results from disloyalty—the conscience tormented and the conscience saved—is the theme which constantly recurs. For this reason, her writing revolves round the central relationships in life in which loyalty is demanded, wherever a pact must be kept or service rendered—between husband and wife, parents and children, the individual and his home, family and country. Most of all it is concerned with man's loyalty and disloyalty towards the Creator, for without loyalty towards Him, no other loyalty is possible. With Christianity, the relationships which depend on loyalty are lifted up into a higher sphere. Only in relation to God and in the light of a theocentric philosophy of life can such human relationships be assigned their proper status and given a place in the hierarchy of values. Religious life is a personal relationship of faith; the history of Christianity—i.e. the history of the Church—gives evidence of the many traitors and the few faithful hearts. As she wrote: "The history of the Church is like a paradigm which illustrates the fate of the divine when it comes into human hands." All her writing deals with the individual's desire to break, and his struggle to keep, the covenant set between God and man; and this is nowhere presented with greater imaginative force and power of artistic realisation than in her profoundest psychological study, *Olav Audunsson*.

That Sigrid Undset wrote so profoundly and vitally on this theme and never allowed it to recede from her view, is due above all to her intense awareness of her own times. As far as that goes, the contemporary world is mirrored in her writing, but in quite another way than in the work of Thomas Mann and André Gide, for example, with whom, in this respect, it seems most natural to compare her. They also express the age, but each is an exponent or medium different in character from Sigrid Undset; they are for this age what August Strindberg and Arne Garborg were for the period at the end of the last century. Sigrid Undset is also the child of her own time, but she never let herself be swept away by its powerful currents. From the beginning, her stay rested in something timeless, eternal and changeless. This is the mystical element in her work.

In consequence, she sees even the great crisis of the age —the crisis of civilisation—with clearer eyes than almost all her contemporaries. She sees isolated man's need for fellowship and his desperate attempts to find the communal solidarity, without which he cannot live. As no other contemporary writer, she has laid bare, in all its crying nakedness, the pseudo-liberalism of the nineteenth century and every form of irresponsible individualism. But she has been equally caustic and merciless in unmasking and branding the collective movements into which rootless modern man has flung himself in order to escape from his isolation. For this very reason, she is in a position to present the fellowship which does not engulf the individual but liberates him—Christian universalism.

Some call her reactionary. Sigrid Undset accepted the title willingly. If a man has taken the wrong road, the only sensible thing to do is to go back to the sign-post which gave the direction. Others called her an escapist, but not even this deterred her. We can let Sigrid Undset answer this criticism herself. In the article, *War and Literature*, she speaks of what she calls the vulgar literature of escape, the easy flight from the world's misery into the irresponsible world of day-dreams—into romantic optimism. The day-dream literature of past times only interests later generations as documentation representative of a certain historical phase. But there is another literature which can, in a certain sense, also be called escapist. To this type, some of the finest literature in the world belongs. Generally, it turns to history for its subjects, to the duties which have been involved in the struggles of the past. It lingers over defeat more often than over victory—indeed, defeat gives particular inspiration, for it urges us to continue the fight. She says that in our time it may seem as if the modern paganism—a paganism completely new in character—is proving triumphant. "The old pagan religions were, or are, much more closely allied to Christianity than is the paganism of our own time." The old heathens believed in powers that ruled men's lives, powers they could approach through prayer and sacrifice, or perhaps only through witchcraft and magic or by the purchase of their favour. But the sacred was not absent from their lives. Christianity could come to them with the highest answer to the riddles of which men have always been conscious: our dependence as created beings on the Creator. It is the aim of the new paganism to root out all religions, from the most primitive up to Christianity, which teach men "how they are truly to worship God". If the new paganism succeeds, it will create a world so different from anything humanity has hitherto known that it is fruitless to speculate on the consequences. Sigrid Undset does not believe that it will succeed. "The springs which have refreshed man's soul on earth may become muddy and turbid—God knows for how long a time—but I do not believe that they can be dried up for ever." Memory of resistance against the oppressors, even if not crowned with physical victory, will be resurrected, she says, in the creative writer's imagination. He will show the people who sit confined in the prison of paganism how they can escape and find their way "back to the future".

In this sense, then, Sigrid Undset is an escapist. She knows of "a door which leads to freedom for the soul of every human being". But the way which she indicated leads in an opposite direction to that taken by one fleeing from reality. She has won her victory, simply because she has "fearlessly seen life as it is". In an age which was moving generally towards an anthropocentric philosophy of life, an age in which men were adopting the cult of self-worship, she declared the eternal message of religion—*Soli Deo Gloria*—and created one of the great monuments of our literature to stand high over the spiritual pilgrim-path of man.

Appendix

. The original title is given, with the title used in this book in parentheses, followed by particulars of the English translation.

1. *Jenny (Jenny)*: *Jenny*, trans. W. Emmé, London 1920.
2. *Olav Audunssøn i Hestviken (Olav Audunsson in Hestviken)*; *Olav Audunssøn og hans børn (Olav Audunsson and his Children)* (both parts referred to in general as *Olav Audunsson*): *The Master of Hestviken* (in four volumes: I. *The Axe*; II. *The Snake-Pit*; I. *In the Wilderness*; II. *The Avenger's Son*), trans. A. G. Chater, London 1928–30.
3. *Kristin Lavransdatter (Kristin Lavransdatter)*: *Kristin Lavransdatter* (in three volumes: I. *The Garland*; II. *The Mistress of Husaby*; III. *The Cross*), trans. Charles Archer and J. S. Scott, London 1930.
4. *Gymnadenia (The Wild Orchid)*: *The Wild Orchid*, trans. A. G. Chater, London 1931.
5. *Den brændende busk (The Burning Bush)*: *The Burning Bush*, trans. A. G. Chater, London 1932.
6. *Ida Elisabeth (Ida Elisabeth)*: *Ida Elisabeth*, trans. A. G. Chater, London 1933.
7. *Norske Helgener (Saga of Saints)* : *Saga of Saints*, trans. S. C. Ramsden, London 1934.
8. *Elleve Aar (Eleven Years)*: *The Longest Years*, trans. A. G. Chater, London 1935.

9. *Fortællingen om Viga-Ljot og Vigdis* (*The Story of Viga-Ljot and Vigdis*): *Gunnar's Daughter*, trans. A. G. Chater, London 1936.

10. *Den trofaste hustru* (*The Faithful Wife*): *The Faithful Wife*, trans. A. G. Chater, London 1937.

11. *Fru Hjelde*, in *Splinten av troldspeilet* (*Mrs Hjelde*, in *The Splinter of the Magic Mirror*): *Images in a Mirror*, trans. A. G. Chater, London 1938.

12. *Madame Dorthea* (*Madame Dorothea*): *Madame Dorothea*, trans. A. G. Chater, London 1941.

The above list contains the most important of Sigrid Undset's works which have been translated into English; it is not intended as a complete bibliography.

Index

Index

Aalheim, Trygve, 34
Aasen, Ivar, 200
Andersen, Hans, 24, 71, 237
Anker, Nini Roll, 2, 48, 51, 52, 57, 58, 59, 60, 61, 76, 84
Archer, Charles, 251
Asbjørnsen, P. Chr., 22, 24, 238
Augustine, Saint, 4, 8, 95, 112
Aukrust, Olav, 7, 155, 172

Balzac, 2
Bang, Bishop A. Chr., 98
Berdiaev, Nicholas, 8, 218
Bergson, Henri, 4, 170n., 205
Bernanos, Georges, 8, 175
Bismarck, 85
Bjørnson, Bjørnstjerne, 21, 27, 33, 200
Blicher, Steen Steensen, 2, 237, 238
Bloy, Léon, 7
Blundell, William, 168
Brandes, Georg, 33
Brøgger, A. W., 97
Bromfield, Louis, 235
Brontë, Anne, 86
Brontë, Charlotte, 86
Brontë, Emily, 86, 149
Brun, Johan Nordahl, 96
Bugge, Sophus, 21, 97
Bull, Edvard, 97, 99, 103, 136
Bull, Olaf, 42, 48, 205

Cather, Willa, 224, 225
Catherine of Siena, Saint, 244
Chambers, R. W., 167
Chater, A. G., 251, 252
Chaucer, 8, 9, 34, 86
Chesterton, G. K., 7, 48, 78, 79

Christiansen, Sigurd, 5, 155, 193
Claudel, Paul, 7, 48, 78, 156, 194
Collett, Camilla, 2
Croce, Benedetto, 4
Cromwell, Oliver, 168

Daae, Ludwig, 21
Dante, 109
Dass, Petter, 10
Dentzmann, Casparus, 209
Dickens, Charles, 2, 8, 33, 68, 86
Dostoievsky, 110, 142
Duun, Olav, 48, 150, 155, 195

Egge, Anna, 51
Egge, Peter, 51
Ek, Sverker, 103
Eliot, T. S., 7, 154, 194
Ellefsen, Johan, 61
Elster, Kristian (the elder), 2
Elster, Kristian (the younger), 48, 51, 52
Elster, Ragnhild, 51
Emmé, W., 251
Erskine, John, 235
Eskeland, Lars, 160

Fagstad, Helene (later Mrs. Frøysland), 49
Falkberget, Johan, 10, 48, 155
Falkland, Lucius Cary, 168
Fangen, Ronald, 88, 155, 159, 194
Fett, Harry, 97, 99, 172
Fisher, John, Cardinal and Saint, 168
Forsberg, Dea, 29
Francis of Assisi, Saint, 66
Frank, Bruno, 235
Freud, Sigmund, 4

Index

Frimann, Claus, 96
Frost, Robert, 225

Garborg, Arne, 7, 142, 248
Gide, André, 6, 248
Gilman, Mrs. Charlotte Perkins, 58
Gilson, Étienne, 4, 8, 176
Gleditsch, Bishop Jens, 159, 160
Goebbels, 235
Goethe, 195
Greene, Graham, 8, 175
Grønbech, Vilhelm, 79
Grundtvig, 161n.
Günther, Hans F. K., 228
Gyth, Anders Broch, 13
Gyth, Charlotte, 13, 14, 15, 18, 20, 22, 23, 29

Haakon, King, 223, 243
Hagberg, Knut, 173
Hamsun, Knut, 36, 67
Hassel, Mathilde, 14, 15
Hegel, 85
Heiberg, Gunnar, 1, 35, 38, 55
Hemmer, Jarl, 94, 193
Herder, 95
Hitler, Adolf, 154, 218, 226, 244
Hoel, Sigurd, 142, 143
Høffding, 78
Holberg, Ludvig, 208
Holst, Carl Vigo, 156
Holst, Elling, 22
Homer, 150
Huxley, Aldous, 5, 194

Ibsen, Henrik, 33, 38, 143, 144

Jefferson, Thomas, 226
Jónsson, Finnur, 100, 101
Jørgensen, A. D., 98
Jørgensen, Johannes, 7, 86
Joyce, James, 2, 5

Kafka, Franz, 5, 194
Kamstrup, Kitty, 49
Keats, 33
Kent, Charles, 139

Keyser, Rudolf, 97, 98, 106
Kielland, Alexander, 2
Kielland, Eugenia, vii, 113n.
Kierkegaard, Søren, 206, 237
Kinck, Hans E., 36, 98, 99, 143, 153
Kittelsen, Theodor, 26
Kjelstrup, Fr. Karl, 89
Klaveness, Mathilde, 14, 15
Koht, Halvdan, 97
Kolsrud, Oluf, 97, 108
Krogh-Tonning, 161n.
Krohg, Chr., 26
Krokann, Inge, 155

Laache, S., 21
Lagerquist, Pär, 194
Landstad, M. B., 97
Lange, Chr. A., 97, 106
Langland, 86
Lawrence, D. H., 164–5
Lie, Bernt, 22
Lie, Jonas, 2, 33
Liestøl, Knut, 97, 151
Linné, Carl (Linnaeus), 222
Loon, Hendrik Willem van, 235
Luther, 160, 161, 162, 163
Lutz, Fr. A. J., O.P., 156

Macaulay, Rose, 167
Malory, Sir Thomas, 85–6
Mann, Thomas, 233, 235, 248
Maritain, Jacques, 4, 8, 156, 157, 158, 233
Marlowe, 58
Martinson, Harry, 5
Marx, 4, 85
Massinger, 58
Mathiesen, Henrik, 11
Maurer, Konrad, 98
Mauriac, François, 8, 175, 194
Maurois, André, 235
Moe, Jørgen, 22, 238
Møller, Ingeborg, 155
Møller, Kitti Anker, 81, 82
Montesquieu, 96
More, Thomas, Saint, 168
Munch, P. A., 11, 33, 97, 106

Münster, Emma, 27

Nacrup, Carl, 192
Nansen, Fridtjof, 244
Nansen, Peter, 34
Newman, Francis, 78
Nielsen, Ragna, 26, 29
Nietzsche, 3, 85, 143
Nissen, Fernanda, 57
Nordal, Sigurður, 97, 101
Normann, Pastor Sigurd, 159
Normann, Regine, 51, 52, 57, 77
Novalis, 95
Noyes, Alfred, 6n.

Olav, Saint, 92, 104, 105, 107, 115, 118, 122, 123, 126, 131, 145, 172, 173, 217, 229
Olsen, Magnus, 97, 101, 230
Otto, Rudolf, 79
Øverland, Arnulf, 48, 155, 194

Paasche, Fredrik, 97, 99, 100, 101, 108, 120, 172, 221, 228
Paasche, Stina, 221
Pascal, 78, 189
Péguy, Charles, 8, 48, 100, 156
Plato, 234
Plotinus, 234
Proust, Marcel, 5, 205

Ramsden, S. C., 251
Rauschning, Hermann, 235
Rawlings, Marjorie Kinnan, 225
Reinhold, H. A., 234
Rilke, Rainer Maria, 5
Røddinge, Pastor, 32
Rokseth, Peter, 156
Romain, Jules, 235
Roosevelt, Elinor, 241
Rosenberg, Alfred, 228
Runeberg, 151

Sandemose, Aksel, 5
Sandvig, Anders, 93
Sars, Ernst, 21, 200
Scheler, Max, 8
Schilling, Fr. Karl, 172
Schliemann, 13

Scott, J. S., 251
Scott of the Antarctic, 59, 63
Scott, Sir Walter, 110, 151
Shakespeare, 8, 33, 65
Shelley, 33
Shetelig, Haakon, 97
Sick, Ingeborg Maria, 195
Sivle, Per, 200
Skavlan, Einar, 56
Skouen, Arne, 224, 227
Skram, Amalie, 2
Snorri Sturluson, 11, 152
Søderblom, Archbishop Nathan, 159, 162
Sommerfelt, Karl L., 25
Southwell, Bl. Robert, 168
Stalin, Josef, 223
Steen, Johannes, 200
Steenstrup, Japetus, 21
Stjernstedt, Marika, 86
Strindberg, August, 7, 237, 248
Struensee, 14
Svarstad, A. C., 50, 58, 60, 93
Sverdrup, Georg, 110, 169

Thomas Aquinas, Saint, 15, 162
Thomas, Signe Undset, vii, 28, 35
Thompson, Francis, 146n.
Thorvaldsen, Caroline, 22, 23
Tolstoy, 2
Tordenskjold, 10
Toynbee, Arnold, 4, 87

Undset, Halvor, 10, 25
Undset, Ingvald, 10, 11, 12, 13, 16, 17, 18, 21, 22, 25, 28, 204
Unger, C. R., 34, 97, 100

Valéry, Paul, 8
Vaughan, Henry, 47
Vermeil, Edmond, 218n.
Vesaas, Tardjei, 5
Vogt, Nils Collett, 15, 47, 51, 61
Voltaire, 6, 6n.
Vullum, Erik, 87

Washington, George, 226
Waugh, Evelyn, 8, 175

Webster, 58
Werenskiold, 26
Werfel, Franz, 235
Wergeland, Henrik, 143
Wessel, Johan Herman, 10, 23
West, Rebecca, 235
Whitehead, A. N., 4
Wildenvey, Herman, 48
Winter-Hjelm, 22
Winter-Hjelm, Anna, 22, 23

Wisbech, Chr., 30
Wolfe, Thomas, 225
Woolf, Virginia, 2, 5
Worsøe, Dean Adolf, 14, 208
Worsøe, Signe Dorthea, 14, 23n, 24, 208
Wyller, Anders, 221

Zola, Émile, 150, 204
Zwilgmeyer, Dikken, 22